Safe and Healthy Children's Environments

Ingrid Crowther
Athabasca University

PEARSON
Prentice
Hall

Toronto

National Library of Canada Cataloguing in Publication

Crowther, Ingrid, 1944–
   Safe and healthy children's environments/Ingrid Crowther.

Includes index.
ISBN 0-13-177638-X

   1. Day care centers—Safety measures—Textbooks. 2. Day care centers—Health aspects—Textbooks.
3. Child care—Textbooks. 4. Early childhood education—Textbooks. I. Title.

HQ778.5.C76 2005   362.71'2'0289   C2004-905249-7

0-13-177638-X

Vice President, Editorial Director: Michael J. Young
Acquisitions Editor: Dave Ward
Marketing Manager: Toivo Pajo
Developmental Editor: Matthew Christian
Production Editor: Richard di Santo
Copy Editor: Susan Broadhurst
Proofreader: Tara Tovell
Production Manager: Wendy Moran
Page Layout: Laserwords
Art Director: Mary Opper
Cover and Interior Design: Michelle Bellemare
Cover Image: Iconica/Peter Cade

1 2 3 4 5   09 08 07 06 05

Printed and bound in Canada.

Brief Contents

Contents

Preface

The information covered in any text about health, safety, and nutrition is of critical importance. However, most textbooks on this subject are comprised of dense text, burying valuable information so students have to dig deeply to uncover it. In contrast, the information in *Safe and Healthy Children's Environments* is presented in a learner-friendly fashion. Photographs and scenarios of children and families are included throughout the text to reinforce understanding and provide a realistic context. All references to children and families are based on actual examples. In most cases, children's actual first names have been used. However, in some examples, fictitious names have been used in order to protect the privacy of the individuals concerned.

This text has been written to facilitate easy research, using clear and concise language and alternative formats to aid the student in gaining information. The text is intended to:

- be useful as a learning tool, with inclusive coverage of child-related health, nutrition, and safety issues
- be useful as a reference tool, with photographs to explain written scenarios and/or replace written descriptions, and many charts and tables to find information at a glance
- help students gain understanding of a child-centred approach as well as child-related issues in health, nutrition, and safety by focusing on the child as a starting point and weaving information and theory around this focus
- respect student learning styles with clear, concise information presented in a logical sequence; a focus on understanding child health, nutrition, and safety; simple, jargon-free language; key points at end of chapters; the inclusion of charts, forms, and observational tools to facilitate the application of learning; exercises in each chapter; and an interactive CD-ROM
- deliver Canadian content by focusing on the diversity of Canadian children and their families, and by including Canadian medical and legislative requirements and comparative charts of requirements per geographic area on topics such as safety requirements within childcare

Information that is needed to understand children's health, nutrition, and safety is presented in alternative formats to encourage understanding of the content, application of the information, and ease of retrieval of pertinent information. Content such as symptoms of ill health or abuse, immunization requirements, and documentation of children's health is presented in a chart format that identifies each category and provides information in bulleted entries. Checklists, such as safety checks in the environment, and record-keeping forms, such as child-related background information or records of daily activities of various age-groups, are included to provide opportunities for application exercises.

Interactive CD-ROM

The CD-ROM included with this book contains additional exercises in an interactive format. It includes:

1. presentations of scenarios with photographic support, which will lead to a number of responses about the photograph/scenario (similar to a multiple choice test). This requires that:

   • the learner picks the response that he or she thinks most appropriate

   • an analysis of the response leads the learner to a dialogue that indicates why the response might be correct or leads the learner to look for additional information that has been missed

2. blank forms, charts and other tools for easy replication

3. resources for teaching, including links to relevant websites

Instructor's Manual (ISBN 0-13-149294-2)

The instructor's manual serves as a guide in helping to create a learning environment that is based on principles of adult learning. Information is presented to help instructors to:

   • build curriculum to engage learners in active participation
   • engage students in exercises that will foster long term retention of what they are learning
   • engage students in practical applications of principles discussed
   • effectively utilize the text and CD-ROM in classroom activities

ACKNOWLEDGEMENTS

I would like to acknowledge the help of the children and families across Canada who are portrayed in this text, especially Lara, Lauren, Rashawn, Aleah, and their families. Additionally, I would like to acknowledge the help of the staff and families of the following childcare settings: Aakuluk Day Care Centre, Iqaluit, Nunavut; Brite Beginnings, Edmonton, AB; Capilano College Childcare, Vancouver, BC; Cedar Road Aboriginal Head Start Program, Prince Rupert, BC; Family Space Ontario Early Years Centre, Belleville, ON; Kitsilano Area Childcare Society, Vancouver, BC; Loyalist College Curriculum Lab Preschool, Belleville, ON; Village Day Care Society, Vancouver BC; Sheridan Child Care Centre, Oakville, ON; and Whispering Hills Child Care Centre, Athabasca, AB.

I would also like to acknowledge the assistance of the following reviewers, whose comments were very helpful to me as I prepared the manuscript:

Pam Belli, *Loyalist College*

Anne Carr, *Capilano College*

Anita Cooper, *Lethbridge Community College*

Mabel Higgins, *Lambton College*

Dale Long, *Seneca College*

1

CHAPTER

Promoting Children's Well-Being

Chapter Outline

"Children are more vulnerable to changes in their physical, emotional and social environments because of their rapid physical and mental health growth and smaller body size. The health and well-being of children depends on the safety and quality of their Physical/Natural Environments, Built Environments and Social Environments—at home, school and in the community." (Health Canada, 2001: 1)

Chapter Outcomes

After reading this chapter, the reader will:

1. Define and describe the concepts of good health and safety and security.

2. Describe a variety of activities that lead to good health.

3. Discuss the interaction of heredity and environment on the developing child.

4. Discuss how each of the following affects physical development:
   • nutrition
   • poverty and neglect
   • physical abuse, substance abuse, and endangerment
   • environmental toxins and pesticides
   • physical exercise
   • access to medical and dental care

5. Describe the influences of nutrition, stimulation stress, and negative experiences on the developing brain.

6. Describe how the learning environment and the interactions of children and adults relate to emotional, language, and cognitive development.

7. Discuss how theoretical viewpoints support healthy growth and development.

8. Identify the importance of prevention practices as linked to health practices and safety practices.

Defining Healthy Families

✳ Health

According to *The Progress of Canada's Children 2002* (Hanvey, 2002: 42), healthy families are those that have a **health** status of "optimal well-being." Optimal well-being for all individuals includes "physical, social and emotional health."

According to the National Children's Agenda of Canada, the following goals describe optimal well-being for young children:

1. "Good Health—Children who are as physically, emotionally and spiritually healthy as they can be, with strong self-esteem, coping skills and enthusiasm."

2. "Safety and Security—Children whose basic needs are met, including food, shelter, clothing and transportation. Children who are protected from victimization, including abuse, neglect, discrimination, exploitation and dangerous environments, and who are given support by caring adults." (Health Canada, 2001: 1)

Good Health, Safety, and Security

Lara and her family enjoy many activities together (photo 1.1). Activities such as swimming develop a variety of "good health"-related habits. Lara builds skills in:

- physical exercise—learning to control her body in the water, learning to swim, transferring skills from one setting to another
- emotional well-being—enjoying the water activity, enjoying her mother's interactions with her, increasing her self-esteem through learning to control her body, increasing her enthusiasm to try new things

Photo 1.1

- coping skills—learning to transfer skills such as crawling to new settings (photo 1.2)

Lara's interaction in the pool, with both the materials in the pool and her mother, builds Lara's confidence and trust in:

Photo 1.2

- her ability to actively and safely explore her environment—The water in the pool was an appropriate temperature, the water level was low enough to encourage crawling, materials in the pool could be picked up and manipulated (they were large enough to prevent choking, had a lip around them to help Lara grasp them, and were colourful to help Lara distinguish them)
- her caregiver to recognize and meet Lara's basic needs—As soon as Lara's activity in the water was over, she was wrapped in a large towel so she would not become cold (photo 1.3). After Lara was dressed, her mother provided a snack and a drink. On the way home Lara was securely fastened into her car seat, where she fell asleep. When Lara arrived home her mother removed her coat and put her into her crib, where she continued to sleep for an hour.

Lara had all her needs met during this activity. She was protected from danger (safe pool, supervision while in the pool, car seat). Her physical needs were met (shelter, appropriate clothing, nourishment, sleep). She was protected from danger by a mother who offered positive supervision of all activities. Lara was never left unsupervised or exposed to dangerous situations. When she was in deeper water, her mother held her. Her mother was in close proximity when Lara played in shallow water.

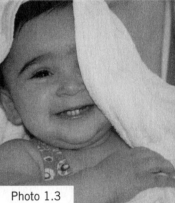

Photo 1.3

By exposing children to joint physical activity with adults they gain lifelong habits that lead to good health and self-confidence in their ability to be safe and secure in many different environments. Health, safety, and security affect all areas of development—physical, social, emotional, language, and cognitive—to varying degrees. The following section will analyze the interrelationship of these factors.

Interrelationship of Health, Safety, and Security and Areas of Development

1. Physical Growth and Development

A) HEREDITY Who and what we are is a combination of **heredity** and **environment** (Figure 1.1). "Heredity sets the limits for growth, development, and health potential." (Marotz, Cross, & Rush, 2001: 6) Look at photo 1.4. Jordan (in the back of the photo), Emily, Ted (in front of Emily), and Jakob (front left) are from different families. These children are all healthy and normal. However, their growth patterns are quite different. Jordan is the same height as Ted, but is a year older. Emily is taller than Jakob, but is the same age. None of these four children have allergies, yet one of their peers within the preschool program is highly allergic to nuts. That child inherited this condition.

 Heredity

 Environment

FIGURE 1.1

Interplay Between Heredity and Environment

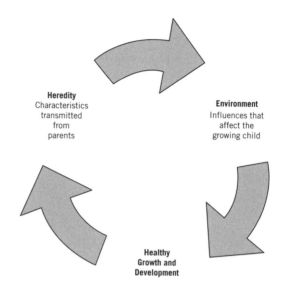

Heredity
Characteristics transmitted from parents

Environment
Influences that affect the growing child

Healthy Growth and Development

B) ENVIRONMENT The environment also plays an important part in shaping individuals' growth and development.

> While heredity provides the basic building materials that determine one's health, the environment plays an equally important role. In a simplified way, the environment is made up of physical, social, economic, and cultural factors. These factors influence the way people perceive and respond to their surroundings. In turn, they affect one's physical, mental, and behavioral pattern, and ultimately influence the way in which an individual's inherited potentials will be realized. (Marotz, Cross, & Rush, 2001: 6–7)

Jessica (photo 1.5) has been involved in many physical activities from an early age. She has developed the strength, skill, balance, and endurance needed to navigate across the swinging rings. She is able to complete this task because she developed these skills over time. Another child, two years older than Jessica, was not able to use the rings. This child had had very little opportunity to engage in such tasks.

C) FACTORS THAT INFLUENCE PHYSICAL DEVELOPMENT A variety of factors have both direct and indirect influences on normal growth and development. An infant who does not get enough nourishment may fail to thrive. This infant may actually lose weight instead of gaining it. War orphans in the former Yugoslavia spent much of their time confined to cribs. As a result, many of these infants learned to walk much later than their peers. Factors that may influence physical development are:

- *Appropriate nutrition.* "Nutrition is a very important factor in determining whether a particular individual will reach his full potential over time. Unlike some other health-related factors, nutrition is something over which people have direct control. Each time people put food in their mouths—or provide food for the children in their care—they make a choice." (Duyff, Giarratano, & Zuzich, 1995: 4)

Photo 1.4

- *Poverty.* The economic status of families directly affects the quality and quantity of food they can afford to buy.
- *Physical abuse.* Lasting damage to bones, vital organs, ears, and eyes can occur due to physical violence.
- *Physical endangerment.* Kevin's family was finishing their dinner in the dining room. Kevin, two-and-a-half years old, had been excused from the table. Suddenly, a little voice was heard saying, "Hot, hot, hot!" When his parents ran to investigate, they found Kevin standing on the stove. He had managed to turn on all the elements and was standing in the centre of the stove-top, lifting his feet and crying, "Hot, hot, hot!" Luckily, Kevin was not hurt. Kevin's parents immediately removed all knobs from the stove to prevent this situation from occurring again. It is very easy, even for the most caring families, to fail to prevent potential accidents. However, if appropriate care is taken, most accidents can be avoided.
- *Accidents.* Car accidents, accidents at birth, or falls can cause lasting damage. Sonia, a bright and healthy two-year-old, was in a car accident. Even though she was safely confined in an appropriate car seat, she received a severe head injury. Sonia's cognitive and physical abilities suffered permanent damage.
- *Substance abuse.* Children exposed to drugs, alcohol, and smoking during the prenatal stage may suffer permanent physical, cognitive, social, and emotional damage. Children who are exposed to second-hand smoke run the risk of increased respiratory problems.
- *Environmental toxins.* Continued exposure to environmental toxins may lead to greater risks of respiratory problems and illnesses. According to *The Progress of Canada's Children 2002* (Hanvey, 2002), children are more vulnerable than adults to pollutants in the air because:
  - they breathe more quickly
  - they inhale more air per breath
  - they are more active outdoors
  - they are closer to the contamination of vehicle fumes
  - their lungs are immature
- *Pesticides.* "Recent studies have linked pesticides to leukemia and brain cancer in children, as well as a host of neurological and developmental disorders." (Hanvey, 2002: 23)
- *Access to dental and medical care.* Many serious problems can be avoided if children receive regular medical attention.
- *Access to regular exercise and rest.* Exercise and rest help grow healthy bodies and healthy minds. Exercise strengthens muscles and provides oxygen to the blood and brain. Rest provides relaxation of muscles and the brain. Both are needed to be healthy mentally and physically.

In summary, physical growth and development of children depends on both environmental factors and heredity. Many factors influence how our children grow and develop physically. Caregivers must ensure that children's environments are safe and healthy places to in which to grow and develop.

Photo 1.5

2. Brain Development

Brain development begins in the fetal stage. When a child is five years old, his or her brain is almost the same weight as an adult's (Schickedanz, Schickedanz, Forsyth, & Forsyth, 2001). The most rapid development of the brain is in the first three years of life. "The effects of early experiences, particularly during the first three years, on the wiring and sculpting of the brain's billions of neurons last a lifetime." (McCain & Mustard, 1999: 7)

Brain development is dependent on all the factors that influence physical development. However, brain development is also particularly susceptible to outside influences. Table 1.1 lists some of the common influences on brain development.

TABLE 1.1   INFLUENCES ON BRAIN DEVELOPMENT

Influence	Explanation
Nutrition	- Good nutrition is critical to brain development. - Malnutrition leads to brain impairment and later negative effects on learning (Schickedanz, Schickedanz, Forsyth, & Forsyth, 2001).
	- Production of the myelin sheath depends on good nutrition (Figure 1.2). The myelin sheath that surrounds the axon leads to increased speed at which impulses are transmitted in the brain.
Stimulation	- "A young child's brain develops through stimulation of the sensing pathways (e.g., seeing, hearing, touching, smelling, tasting) from early experiences. A mother breastfeeding her baby or a father reading to a toddler on his lap are both providing essential experiences for brain development. This early nurturing during critical periods of the brain development not only affects the parts of the brain that control vision and other senses, it influences the neural cross-connections to other parts of the brain that influence arousal, emotional regulation and behaviour." (McCain & Mustard, 1999: 7)
Stress	- Ongoing chronic stress may reduce ability to cope with stress and new sensory stimulation, and may influence mental health.
Lack of stimulation or negative family environments	- Leads to poor development of cognitive, social, and emotional domains, difficulty succeeding during school years, and more anti-social behaviours (McCain & Mustard, 1999)

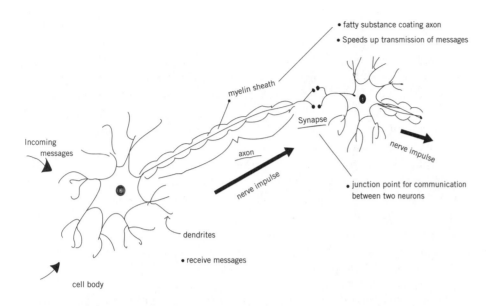

FIGURE 1.2
Neuron

In summary, proper brain development is highly affected by appropriate nutrition and appropriate positive stimulation in the early years. A brain that has grown and developed properly will help the child conquer many of the life skills awaiting him or her. "A baby is born with a head on her shoulders and a mind primed for learning. But it takes years of experience—looking, listening, playing, interacting with parents—to wire the billions of complex neural circuits that govern language, math, music, logic, and emotions." (Begly, 1997: 28)

3. Social Development

Lauren and her mother share many moments of face-to-face interaction (photo 1.6). Lauren initiates a string of "ba, ba, ba!" Louise smiles at Lauren and repeats the string with a different intonation. Lauren laughs. Louise responds, "You think that was funny, do you?"

Photo 1.6

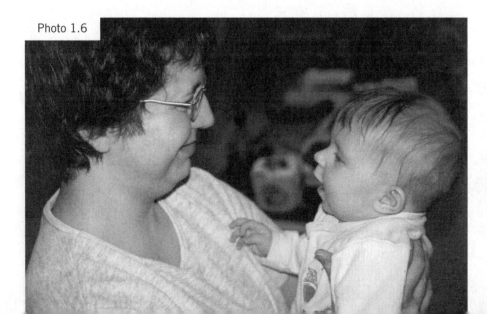

Photo 1.7

During this social interaction several things are happening. Lauren is learning valuable socialization skills, but she is also learning to trust that her actions and vocalizations are listened to and responded to. This type of stimulation continues to build and strengthen connections in the brain. It provides Lauren with a safe, nurturing environment in which her feelings are recognized, responded to appropriately, and enriched. It establishes a close attachment between Lauren and Louise. This will give Lauren the self-confidence to initiate and maintain contacts with others as she develops and grows (photo 1.7).

Jonathan and Adam negotiated their own play (photo 1.8). They listened to each other, shared their materials, and played in an area safe from physical danger. At one point, Adam decided that the play should change. Jonathan did not agree. Adam responded, "Then you can't play. I'll use all the toys." Sandra quickly walked over and asked Adam, "What is the problem?" Adam responded, "I don't want to play with Jonathan any more." Sandra said, "Look at Jonathan. How do you think he feels about this?" Adam looked at Jonathan (photo 1.9) and said, "Sad." "Do you want him to be sad?" Sandra asked. Adam shook his head. "What could you do about this?" asked Sandra. Adam looked at Jonathan and said, "Do you want to play with me?" Jonathan nodded. The boys continued to negotiate their play.

Sandra provided a safe and supportive environment for the children to solve their own problems, recognize their feelings, and express how they felt. Through this process, children continue to reinforce connections in the brain, feel supported to make their own decisions, and learn about their own feelings and the feelings of others.

In summary, children need safe, nurturing environments that include sensitive, caring adults to develop social skills of sharing, negotiating, problem solving, interacting appropriately, listening, and learning about different points of view. During these interactions there is continued brain development through reinforcement of neural connections. "We know that rich and positive experiences stabilize certain connections in the brain." (Shore, 1997: 40)

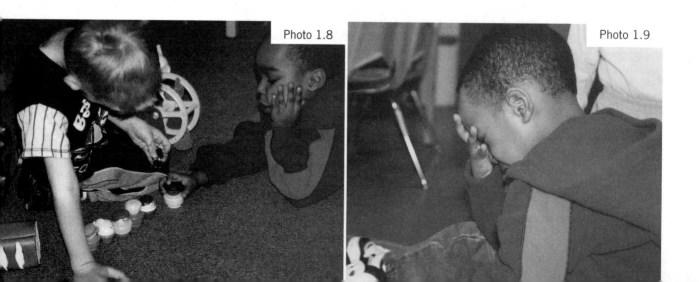

Photo 1.8

Photo 1.9

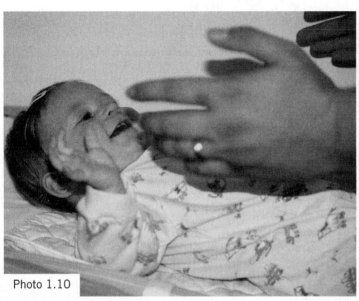

Photo 1.10

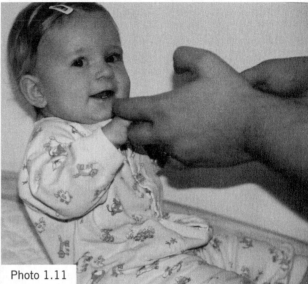

Photo 1.11

4. Emotional Development

Lauren's independence was nurtured by her parents at a very early age. For example, after her diaper was changed, Lauren was given an opportunity to do things for herself. Louise extended her hands to Lauren and said, "Time to get up" (photo 1.10). Lauren grasped her mother's hands and managed to pull herself up (photo 1.11).

Through this experience, Lauren gained:

- self-confidence in her ability to do things for herself
- pride in her accomplishments—Note the expression of pride on her face in photo 1.11.
- trust in her caregivers to support her need for independence
- increased ability—strengthened grasp and arms and increased balance

Lara enjoys exploring by herself. She is given many opportunities to practise her skills in a variety of settings (photo 1.12). This provides her with chances to practise and strengthen emergent motor skills and to transfer these skills to different settings. It also ensures that the appropriate neurological connections are formed. "Early neurological development is shaped not only by the physical conditions, but also by an individual's social environment." (Shore, 1997: 29) Lara will gain confidence in her ability to do things by herself. Her caregivers must ensure that:

- the physical environment is free from harm
- close supervision is provided
- positive recognition is provided
- activities are developmentally appropriate

Photo 1.12

In summary, early emotional development is closely linked to the ability of the child to start to build positive self-esteem through his or her interactions with others, the physical environment, and the materials within that environment. "One source of self-esteem is internal—the young child's own pleasure at having accomplished a task. Another is external, feedback from parents who recognize the child's achievement." (Brazelton, 1997: 77)

5. Language Development

✳ Critical period

There is strong evidence of a critical period for language development (McCain & Mustard, 1999). A **critical period** can be defined as follows: "It refers to a limited time span during which the child is biologically prepared to acquire certain adaptive behaviours but needs the support of an appropriate stimulating environment." (Berk, 2002: 24)

✳ Phoneme

Language development is strongly linked to the number of times children hear sounds and words. "By 12 months, an infant's auditory map is formed. He will be unable to pick out **phonemes** he has not heard thousands of times for the single reason that no cluster of neurons has been assigned the job of responding to that sound." (Begly, 1997: 31)

Lara (photo 1.13) delights in pointing to things she has heard about. She especially likes to point to her own body parts and has learned to transfer that information to other objects—for example, her nose and the toy dog's nose. She is growing up in a bilingual environment and can identify items in Arabic and English. Lauren has progressed to finding specific objects, naming them, and making a related sound—"Moo!" (photo 1.14). Both girls have grown up in an environment rich in language. Their ability to use language will continue to grow and develop.

In summary, the ability to develop language skills is highly dependent on appropriate brain development. With timely stimulation of language, children develop the ability to interact appropriately.

Photo 1.13

Photo 1.14

Photo 1.15

6. Cognitive Development

Emily is actively engaged in building an arena for her horses (photo 1.15). As she plays, she names the items she is using. When she does not know a word for something, she asks what it is. During this activity she is learning about:

- how things fit together—creating a circle out of four semicircles and fitting four curved blocks around the smaller circle
- size—smaller and larger circles
- matching identical shapes—cylinders around the outside of her structure
- memory—She previously had observed horses perform in an arena.

All children's abilities relate to a combination of heredity and environment. Emily's cognitive skills, as well as her fine motor skills and her language skills, were enhanced by her building activity. It does not matter so much what materials children use, but that these types of activities are encouraged. "In the most extensive study yet of what makes a difference, Craig of the University of Alabama found that it was blocks, beads, peek-a-boo and other old-fashioned measures that enhance cognitive, motor and language development—and, absent traumas, enhance them permanently." (Begly, 1997: 30)

Emily was in a learning environment that encouraged her to:

- explore materials that were safe to use
- interact with adults in a positive manner
- sustain her play in an environment free from danger and supportive of her needs

In summary, cognition is a way of knowing built upon internal processes and products of the mind. To establish these internal processes the child needs to experience learning activities within an environment that provides:

- activities related to what the child already knows
- safety from physical danger
- opportunities to explore freely without fear of negativity
- safe and secure interactions with adults and peers
- opportunities to manipulate and experiment with materials that are safe to use

7. Theoretical Viewpoints

Irrespective of what theoretical approach one may use in raising or caring for young children, there are underlying principles that all theories support to varying degrees:

- Development is an interaction between heredity and environment.
- Appropriate nutrition is essential to growth and development.
- Children learn best in a safe, supportive environment that supports active play.
- Children learn best when they are free from disease, abuse, stress, and health problems.
- Children learn best from adults who are nurturing, respectful, and consistent.
- Children grow and flourish when all their needs are consistently met.

Summary of Interrelationship of Health, Safety, and Security and Areas of Development

Children do not grow and develop in isolation. Healthy growth and development is a combination of many factors (Figure 1.3); it is impossible to identify one factor that leads to greater success. As children actively explore the environment, they:

- enhance their motor control
- socialize with the individuals in that environment
- learn the language associated with their exploration
- learn about the people and things within that environment
- develop a good concept about their ability to act and react to the things around them

Additionally, for optimal growth and development children need to experience learning environments that are free from negative influences. The United Nations Convention on the Rights of the Child (Covell & Howe, 2001) promotes the rights of children. Table 1.2 summarizes these rights with respect to health and safety.

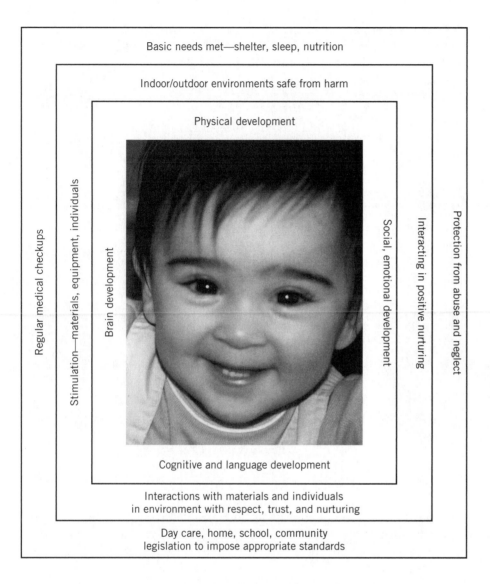

Basic needs met—shelter, sleep, nutrition

Indoor/outdoor environments safe from harm

Physical development

Regular medical checkups

Stimulation—materials, equipment, individuals

Brain development

Social, emotional development

Interacting in positive nurturing

Protection from abuse and neglect

Cognitive and language development

Interactions with materials and individuals
in environment with respect, trust, and nurturing

Day care, home, school, community
legislation to impose appropriate standards

FIGURE 1.3
Building a Healthy Child

Prevention Practices

The purpose of prevention practices is to:

- identify children who might need medical attention
- identify problems early to be able to correct them before more damage occurs. For example, children who have periodic fluid buildup in their ears may not hear as well. As a result, their language development may be delayed.
- identify patterns of behaviour that may signal a medical problem or condition— hard of hearing, visual impairments
- evaluate past treatment practices. Are the ear tubes effective? Is the hearing aid working? Can the child see better with glasses?
- identify children at risk due to environment, economy, or abuse

TABLE 1.2   RIGHTS OF THE CHILD

Rights	Health- and Safety-Related Rights
1. Identity, learning, and self-expression	- Right to free expression - Freedom of thought, conscience, religion, and freedom to interact with whom they wish - Education that includes respect for the child, the family, values, and cultural background
2. Family and community	- Protection from being removed from their homeland
3. Mental and physical well-being	- Protection from abuse, neglect, and sexual exploitation - Right to "highest standards" of health care - Adequate standard of living to meet basic needs—physical, moral, and spiritual - Protection from armed conflict - Appropriate treatment for injuries, torture, neglect, abuse, and exploitation resulting from armed conflict
4. Protection	- Same rights as adults to be protected by state - Protection against any threats to health, education, or development - Protection against substance abuse - Protection against abduction, sale, and trafficking - Protection against all forms of abuse

Source: Adapted from Covell and Howe (2001).

- ensure that intervention strategies such as immunization are regularly checked and updated
- protect the child from potential harm from the environment or materials in that environment
- protect the child from negative interactions

1. Health Practices

"Many positive changes have taken place over the last several years in attitudes and practices relative to personal health. The concept of preventative health care has emerged in response to costly medical care and realization that the medical profession alone cannot cure every health problem." (Marotz, Cross, & Rush, 2001: 2) Some **preventive** health practices can occur at a personal level, by personal choice. These include:

 Preventive

- avoiding smoking and smoke-filled environments
- avoiding substance abuse—alcohol and drugs

- eating nutritious foods
- exercising regularly
- practising sanitary habits such as washing hands and brushing teeth
- scheduling regular appointments with doctors and dentists

Other preventive health practices must be promoted. Children must learn about healthy living so they can make choices about their well-being when they grow up. "Research has shown that the health of children during their first years has an impact on how they function later in life." (Government of Canada, 2002: 2)

A) MEDICAL INFORMATION Child-care providers are often in a position to notice initial signs of illness or physical injury. The information a child-care provider gathers about a child is part of a three-way communication cycle (Figure 1.4). The information about the child needs to be shared with the child's family and the child's physician or dentist. However, information usually cannot be shared directly with the child's physician or dentist. This can be done only if the parents give written permission to do so. It is therefore critical that child-care providers keep accurate records that can be accessed by all individuals concerned about the child's health. Typical information that should be shared is included in Figure 1.5.

B) IMMUNIZATION "Immunization offers permanent protection against all preventable childhood diseases including diphtheria, tetanus, whooping cough, polio, measles,

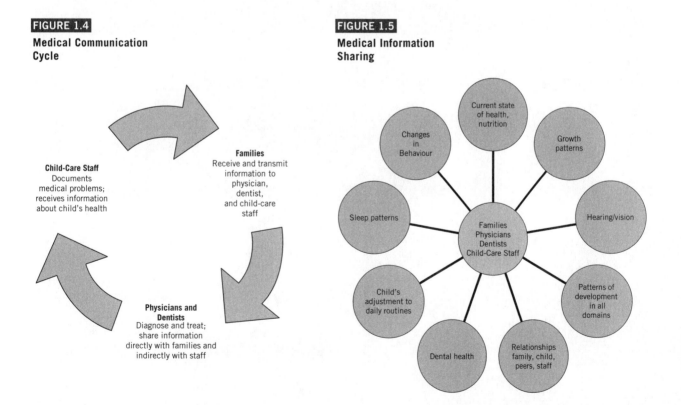

FIGURE 1.4
Medical Communication Cycle

Families
Receive and transmit information to physician, dentist, and child-care staff

Child-Care Staff
Documents medical problems; receives information about child's health

Physicians and Dentists
Diagnose and treat; share information directly with families and indirectly with staff

FIGURE 1.5
Medical Information Sharing

Families Physicians Dentists Child-Care Staff

- Current state of health, nutrition
- Growth patterns
- Hearing/vision
- Patterns of development in all domains
- Relationships family, child, peers, staff
- Dental health
- Child's adjustment to daily routines
- Sleep patterns
- Changes in Behaviour

mumps and chicken pox." (Marotz, Cross, & Rush, 2001: 118) Immunization is nationally and publicly funded through the Canadian health care system. However, approximately 15 percent of Canadian children under two years of age have not been immunized, and this percentage is even higher for Aboriginal children (Berk, 2002: 33). It is important to ensure that children have been immunized, not only to protect each individual child against disease, but also to protect other children from being exposed to disease. "Few measures in preventive medicine are of such proven value and as easy to implement as routine immunization against infectious diseases." (Population and Public Health Branch, 2002: 1)

Children who enter a daycare system or the public school system in Canada must have completed the immunization schedule required in their particular jurisdiction. Each area has a standard schedule for immunization that starts in infancy and continues throughout the life of an individual. Immunization schedules vary considerably from jurisdiction to jurisdiction. Therefore, it is important to check with local pediatricians, family doctors, pharmacists, health units, or the public health nurse about the schedule for a particular jurisdiction.

C) HEALTH APPRAISALS The early childhood educator plays a key role in providing for children's well-being. Daily observations and health checks help monitor the child's general health. An alert early childhood educator not only will be able to identify problems quickly, but also will be able to provide valuable help to families of the children and other professionals. Information that might be gathered is presented in Figure 1.6.

FIGURE 1.6
Information Gathering

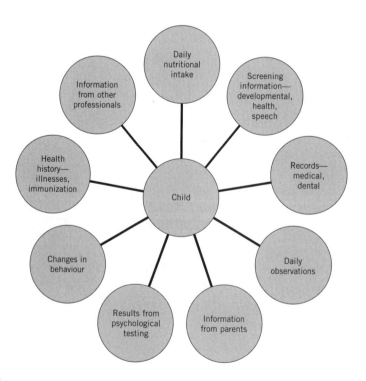

Health appraisal forms can be developed in a variety of ways. An overview of the most common tools is presented in Table 1.3. All information gathered should be kept in a child's file, dated, signed, and locked to ensure privacy.

All observations need to be reviewed and interpreted. Often the health appraisal process will include other staff members, other professionals, and family members. The intent is to make sense of what has been observed and to decide what should be done with the information collected.

D) SANITATION ROUTINES One of the easiest and most effective ways to prevent the spread of communicable disease is to keep all areas clean and sanitized. To disinfect surfaces, use a solution of *one tablespoon of bleach per litre of water*. Areas that should be disinfected include furniture, toys, railings, cribs, cots, sinks, taps, toilets, toilet flushers, and door handles.

TABLE 1.3 **OVERVIEW OF COMMON HEALTH APPRAISAL TOOLS**

Tool	Description and Use
Observation checklists	- Common symptoms are listed—flushed, hot. - Applicable symptoms are checked off.
Daily/weekly charts	- Chart is developed with spaces for major activities during day/week—eating, napping, indoor activity, outdoor activity, transitions, interactions with adults. - Information is filled in anecdotally—two-hour nap, hard to wake up, missed snack.
Family chart	- Families fill in daily to provide information about the child's activity at home.
Charts for ill health	- Record specific signs of ill health, what was done, and who was contacted.
Serious occurrence forms	- Used in case of accident—broken arm, head injury, wound requiring stitches. - Detailed information about what happened, when, where, who observed it, what was done, and who was contacted.
Routines charts	- Identify major routines—bathroom, meals, sleeping. - Used to indicate unusual behaviour.
Medical information	- Medical permission forms that include information about types of medication to be given and descriptions of circumstances.

E) CLEANING ROUTINES Due to the high volume of traffic within a child-care centre, floors, carpets, and bathrooms may need to be cleaned more than once a day. Garbage should be placed in containers with tight lids and taken out daily. This ensures that:

- the spread of communicable disease is decreased
- the surfaces children walk on are clear, to prevent slipping
- appropriate cleaning routines are modelled

F) BATHROOM ROUTINES Several areas in a bathroom are prone to contamination—taps, doorknobs, and toilet flushers. These areas need to be disinfected often. Appropriate handwashing needs to be reinforced (Figure 1.7).

Bathrooms can quickly become messy and slippery. The floor needs to be monitored to ensure it is dry. Children need to be reminded to flush toilets and throw dirty towels in the garbage. Personal grooming items such as facecloths, toothbrushes, and combs must be stored in personal storage containers to prevent other children from using them. Care must be taken to ensure these personal items are also kept clean routinely.

2. Safety Practices

A) ACCIDENT PREVENTION "Children are too often injured and sometimes die as a result of hazards in their environment. Unintentional injury continues to be the greatest cause of mortality, morbidity and disability for children and youth in Canada." (Health Canada, 2001)

Many accidents can be prevented. Child-care providers must schedule routine evaluations of the environment to ensure that children are safe from physical harm (Table 1.4). "Protection from physical injuries is a key aspect of a healthy physical environment." (Health Canada, 2001)

B) STORAGE Appropriate storage of children's toys and materials should emphasize accessibility and ease of finding what a child may wish to retrieve. When what one

FIGURE 1.7
Appropriate Handwashing

- Turn on tap and wet hands
- Wash hands with soap
- Rub hands to clean thoroughly
- Wash off soap
- Dry hands with paper towel
- Use paper towel to turn off tap
- Use paper towel to open door
- Put paper towel in garbage

TABLE 1.4   **SAFETY CHECKS**

Type of Safety Check	Description
Emergency numbers	- Up-to-date numbers for police, fire, doctor, poison control, and emergency contact posted near phone
Controlled entry	- Doorways/playground gates protected from intruders - Children protected from wandering away
Running water	- Temperature of tap water not too hot
Choking	- Removal of small toys, small parts, and food that can cause choking (see Figure 2.1 on page 35) - Removal of loose, dangling strings and cords
Poisonous plants/products	- Dangerous products locked away - Elimination of poisonous plants indoors and outdoors
Fire and danger from burns	- Have an emergency plan. - Conduct regular fire drills. - Have protected entrance to kitchen/laundry room.
Emergency preparation	- Have emergency kit. - Have emergency location. - Have first aid kit.
Furniture and equipment	- Sturdy and in good repair - No loose parts
Toys	- No sharp corners or broken parts
Soft areas	- Areas under climbing or sliding equipment are raked and are the required thickness.
Sand	- Raked, covered if outside, and replaced as needed
Water centre	- Water is cleared out at the end of the day, and container is disinfected.

is looking for cannot be found, it is easier to dump out all the materials to find the desired piece. This becomes not only messy and hard to clean up, but also dangerous. The dumped materials obstruct the playing surface, spill onto the floor, may be stepped on and broken, or may cause a child to trip and fall (photo 1.16). Toys scattered in a large sandbox are quickly buried, can very easily break, and are hard to find (photo 1.17). This is dangerous for small fingers that could inadvertently land on sharp edges.

Photo 1.16

Photo 1.17

Photo 1.18

Appropriate storage should conform to the following criteria:

- Storage equipment should be sturdy.
- Containers should be clear, so it is easy to see what is inside.
- Storage equipment should be clearly labelled with pictures and words on both the container and the shelf, so that materials are easy to find and return.
- Materials should be organized by type—one container for all the dogs, one for all the cats, etc.
- Containers should be easily accessible, on low, sturdy shelves.
- Cleanup needs to be modelled. When a child finishes with an activity, that activity needs to be cleaned up and materials put away. Children love to help with cleanup if it is fun and becomes part of a routine (photo 1.18). Children who become involved in the process learn to take responsibility for themselves and to help create a safer and healthier environment for everyone.

C) HEALTHY ENVIRONMENTS Healthy environments model cleanliness through various routines for both children and adults. Regular routines that should be in place include:

- regular handwashing—after painting or other types of messy play, before preparing food, before and after eating, and after toileting
- cleaning up messy surfaces—tabletops after eating, surfaces that have become messy after play (cutting and pasting, painting, creating mixtures)
- cleaning the floor—mopping up spills, sweeping debris, cleaning up scraps and toys
- wiping down toys if they have been put into someone's mouth or sneezed on

Rooms with many children and adults in them tend to have poor air quality. Opening windows and doors to clear out stuffiness often helps. "Circulation of fresh air helps to reduce the concentration of infectious organisms within a given space." (Marotz, Cross, & Rush, 2001: 123) In larger centres that use mechanical air circulation systems, it is important to ensure that the system is regularly cleaned and checked.

Another important factor is the humidity level in rooms. If spaces are too dry, children may have cracked lips and noses. Air that is too dry can also lead to increased chances of respiratory infections. If humidity is too low, moisturizers can be added to the heating system, or cool air vaporizers can be placed in each room. These units need to be cleaned and disinfected regularly. Plants not only add aesthetic value to learning spaces but also help clear the air and add humidity to rooms.

The lighting in a daycare centre needs to be a combination of natural light and, if possible, **full spectrum fluorescent lighting**—light fixtures that include the full spectrum of wavelengths of natural light. Full spectrum fluorescent lighting most closely matches sunlight. With some learning activities, such as reading and writing, it is more important to be near natural light. No matter how appropriate the lighting is inside any room, children must spend time outside. Children gain by being outside in fresh air and by getting the natural light they need (Crowther, 2003).

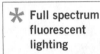
Full spectrum fluorescent lighting

Children are active learners. They will explore their environment with boundless energy. The room temperature in a child-care centre should reflect this active participation. Temperatures of 20 and 21 degrees Celsius are most appropriate. At these temperatures, spread of infectious disease is less favourable and comfort level is high.

Children still in diapers need to have a separate change area. Adults changing diapers should wear disposable gloves, disinfect the diapering area, and wash their hands immediately after every diaper change. Dirty diapers should be stored in a diaper pail with a tight lid. The smell of dirty diapers may permeate the facility. Sprays used to control odour may cause allergic reactions in some children and staff. Baking soda left in an open container may relieve some odour. Periodic airing out of the change room will also help.

Accidents may occur if a child is left unattended on a diapering table. Adults need to be careful to always keep at least one hand on a child to prevent a fall from the table.

Sleep time needs to be carefully orchestrated. The spread of infectious disease is more likely when individuals are in close proximity. Cots and cribs need to be placed at least one metre apart. If possible, windows should be opened slightly to allow fresh air to circulate. Lights should be dimmed and soothing music played. Children should use individual cots and bedding. Both should be cleaned and cots disinfected regularly. Children who do not sleep should have a comfortable area with adequate lighting and quiet activity materials to encourage relaxation.

SUMMARY

Children flourish in environments that encourage safety, healthy habits, and protection from harm.

Children are shaped by the world around them, and many environments affect their development. It is generally accepted that "healthy children emerge most often from healthy families, and healthy families are in turn promoted by healthy communities." Understanding the key factors that influence child development can help society make choices that build supportive environments for children. (Government of Canada, 2002: 6)

KEY POINTS

Good health
- Physically, emotionally, and spiritually healthy
- Strong self-esteem, good coping skills, and enthusiasm

Safety and security
- Basic needs met—food, shelter, clothing, transportation
- Protected from victimization—abuse, neglect, discrimination, exploitation, dangerous environment
- Supported by caring adults

Activities for health, safety, and security
- Physical exercise
- Exploring in safe environment
- Meeting basic needs

Heredity
- Sets limits for growth, development, and health potential.

Environment
- The physical, social, economic, and cultural factors that influence perception and interaction

Factors influencing physical development
- Nutrition
- Poverty
- Abuse—physical abuse, substance abuse, neglect
- Endangerment and accidents

- Environmental toxins, pesticides
- Access to medical and dental care
- Regular exercise and rest

Influence on brain development
- Nutrition—production of myelin sheath
- Myelin sheath increases speed at which impulses are transmitted.
- Malnutrition has lasting effects
- Stimulation—leads to stronger connections, influences emotional regulation and arousal.
- Stress—reduced capacity to cope, may influence mental health
- Negative experiences—poor cognitive development, possible anti-social behaviour

Social development
- Dependent on nurturing, safe environment
- Need close attachment to caregiver
- Need sensitive, caring adults
- Appropriate positive interactions lead to stronger neural connections.

Emotional development
- Need positive interactions with caregivers to build self-confidence and self-esteem
- Need safe environments in which to explore to gain trust in own abilities

Language development

- Critical periods—time in which children hear sounds and words repeatedly to learn to speak
- Dependent on brain development

Cognitive development

- Need to explore safe environments and materials actively
- Need to build on what they already know
- Need to be protected from physical danger
- Need to engage in safe and secure interactions with adults and peers

Theoretical viewpoints

- Development is an interaction between heredity and environment.
- Appropriate nutrition is essential.
- Children learn best when free from disease, abuse, stress, and health problems.
- Children grow and flourish with adults who nurture, are respectful and consistent, and meet children's needs.

Rights of children

Children have the right to:

- personal identity
- learning
- self-expression
- mental and physical well-being
- protection from being removed from their homeland
- protection from threats to health, abuse, abduction, sale, and trafficking

Purposes of prevention practices

Identify:

- need for medical attention
- problems at an early stage
- patterns of behaviour that may signal other problems
- children at risk

Protect:

- from negative interactions
- from potential harm from environmental hazards

Evaluate:

- effectiveness of past treatment and intervention strategies

Health practices

- Avoid smoking and smoke-filled environment.
- Avoid substance abuse.
- Provide adequate nutrition.
- Provide opportunities for regular exercise.
- Practise sanitary habits.
- Schedule regular appointments with doctors and dentists.

Medical information

- Gather regular information from medical and dental sources.
- Gather and share information about behaviour, health status, growth patterns, hearing/vision, developmental patterns, relationships, dental health, child's adjustment to daily routines, and sleep patterns.

Immunization

- Gather record of immunization.

Health appraisals

- Dated, individual, confidential charts containing information about child's health
- Checklists—listing and checking off symptoms
- Daily/weekly charts—information about daily or weekly routines filled in anecdotally
- Family charts—families record pertinent daily information about child's activity at home
- Charts for ill health—record symptoms and activity around suspected illness
- Serious occurrence forms—record accidents, including detailed information

- Routine charts—record child's routines, such as bathroom, meals, sleeping, and unusual behaviour
- Medical information—permission to take medicine, when, and how often

Sanitation
- Disinfect surfaces and toys with one tablespoon of bleach per litre of water.
- Cleaning routines—Clean high-volume areas daily; disinfect taps, doorknobs, and toilet flushers; dry slippery floors

Safety checks
- Emergency numbers posted—police, fire, doctor, poison control, emergency contact
- Controlled entry
- Check water temperature
- Protect children from choking—small parts, loose dangling strings or cords
- Lock away poisonous products, avoid poisonous plants indoors and outdoors
- Conduct regular fire drill and establish emergency plan.
- Identify emergency location; provide emergency kit and first aid kit.

- Check furniture, equipment, and toys for loose parts and disrepair.
- Maintain soft areas under climbing/sliding equipment.
- Rake sand and keep covered outside.
- Replace water in water play areas daily.

Storage
- Provide adequate labelled storage to avoid accidents due to areas cluttered with toys.

Healthy environments
- Regular routines for handwashing, cleaning messy surfaces, cleaning floors, wiping/disinfecting toys.
- Provide adequate ventilation.
- Check and adjust humidity levels.
- Provide adequate lighting—combination of natural and, if possible, full spectrum fluorescent lighting.
- Adequate room temperatures—20 or 21 degrees Celsius
- Sanitary diapering facilities
- Adequate sleeping/rest spaces

EXERCISES

1. In small groups discuss what is meant by:
   a) good health
   b) safety and security
   Compare your answers to the information in the text. How were your answers the same or different?

2. Reflect on the activities you engage in that lead to good health. Form a small group and discuss your activities.
   a) What activities are similar or different?
   b) Are there any activities you have missed?
   c) Which of these activities should young children engage in?
   d) What additional activities would be advisable for young children to engage in?

3. Define heredity and environment. How does heredity affect the developing child? What impact does the environment have? Reflect on the impact the environment has had on you. List three major environmental impacts on your life. How have they affected you? Share one of these impacts with the class.

4. In small groups discuss how each of the following items affects physical development. Use the charts on the next page. Check your answers against the information provided in this chapter.

CHART 1	NUTRITION
	Effect
Physical development	
Brain development	

CHART 2	ABUSE
Type of Abuse	**Effect on Physical Development**
Physical abuse	
Mental abuse	
Neglect	
Substance abuse	

CHART 3	STIMULATION AND EXERCISE
	Effect
Physical development	
Brain development	

5. Observe a learning environment for preschoolers.

   a) What positive interactions do you observe? How do these activities enhance positive emotional development?

   b) What different opportunities for language development do you see?

   c) How do the observed interactions create opportunities for language development?

   d) What different types of activities do you observe that encourage cognitive development? How is cognitive development enhanced?

6. Interview an early childhood educator to find out what types of health and safety practices are used within his or her centre. For each practice, describe the strategies used to ensure implementation of that practice. What other practices might you suggest be added?

7. Reflect on health and safety practices your family insisted on when you were growing up. How are these similar to or different than the health and safety practices you read about in this chapter? Why might you see differences?

*Glossary

Critical period (page 12) "It refers to a limited time span during which the child is biologically prepared to acquire certain adaptive behaviours but needs the support of an appropriate stimulating environment." (Berk, 2002: 24)

Environment (page 5) Includes the factors that influence growth and development—physical, social, economic, cultural.

Full spectrum fluorescent lighting (page 23) Light fixtures that include the full spectrum of wavelengths of natural light. Full spectrum fluorescent lighting most closely matches sunlight.

Health (page 4) Well-being of an individual; combination of wellness in all domains—social, emotional, physical, cognitive.

Heredity (page 5) Characteristics transmitted from parents to a child at conception.

Phoneme (page 12) A unit of sound that distinguishes one word from another—i.e., both *cat* and *phone* have three phonemes.

Preventive (page 16) Actions put in place to stop the possibility of accidents and illnesses occurring.

REFERENCES

Begly, S. (1997). How to build a baby's brain. *Newsweek, 28,* 28–32.

Berk, L. (2002). *Child development.* Toronto: Pearson Education Canada, Inc.

Brazelton, T. (1997). Building a better self-image. *Newsweek, Spring/Summer,* 76–77.

Covell, K., & Howe, B. (2001). *The challenge of children's rights for Canada.* Waterloo, ON: Wilfrid Laurier University Press.

Crowther, I. (2003). *Creating effective learning environments.* Scarborough, ON: Thomson Nelson.

Duyff, R., Giarratano, S., & Zuzich, M. (1995). *Nutrition, health and safety for preschool children.* Westerville, OH: Glencoe/McGraw-Hill.

Government of Canada. (2002). *Early childhood development agreement.* Ottawa: Government of Canada.

Hanvey, L. (2002). *The progress of Canada's children 2002* (Rep. No. 2002). Canadian Council on Social Development. Ottawa: Renouf Publishing.

Health Canada. (2001). *Safe & supportive environments.* http://www.hc-sc.gc.ca, accessed 3 May 2003.

Marotz, L., Cross, M., & Rush, J. (2001). *Health, safety and nutrition for the young child.* Albany, NY: Delmar.

McCain, M., & Mustard, F. (1999). *Early years study, final report.* Toronto: Publications Ontario.

Population and Public Health Branch. (2002). *Immunization schedule: A. Immunization schedules for infants and children.* Health Canada. http://www.hc-sc.gc.ca, accessed 23 April 2003.

Schickedanz, J., Schickedanz, D., Forsyth, P., & Forsyth, G. (2001). *Understanding children and adolescents.* Toronto: Allyn and Bacon.

Shore, R. (1997). *Rethinking the brain: New insights into early development.* New York: Families and Work Institute.

2

CHAPTER

Creating Safe Environments

Chapter Outline

"Experts don't talk about 'childhood accidents' any more; they talk about 'preventable child injuries.' That's because studies have shown that the majority of injuries, which are the leading cause of death for children under age nineteen, are preventable." (Langlois, 1998: 120)

Chapter Outcomes

After reading this chapter, the reader will:

1. Identify and describe common safety issues as related to the various stages of development during:
   • infancy
   • the toddler years
   • the preschool years
   • the school-age years.

2. Identify and describe safety issues common to all age groups—infant, toddler, preschool, and school age.

3. Identify and describe the elements that must be considered for playground safety.

4. Explain the interrelationship of development and safety.

Safe Environments for Infants

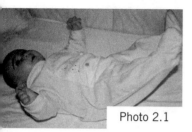

Photo 2.1

Photo 2.2

As a young infant, Lara spent much of her time dependent on her family to provide her with a safe and secure environment. Much of Lara's time was spent lying on the floor or in her crib (photo 2.1), sitting in her chair or stroller, or being carried. Her parents ensured Lara's safety by:

- protecting her from bumps and bruises—bumper pads in her crib; when on the floor, placing her on a mat, away from sharp objects and any obstructions
- supporting her back when lifting her or carrying her around (photo 2.2)
- making sure she is securely fastened—in her stroller, in her car seat
- protecting her from choking—dressing her in appropriate clothes (no drawstrings, buttons, or decorative items such as pompoms), clear spaces to sleep or lie on (photo 2.1)

As Lara became more agile, her parents continually adapted the environment and their actions to ensure her safety. When Lara began to push herself up from the floor (photo 2.3) and roll over, it became critical that:

- there were no sharp or hard objects she could roll onto
- she was not near any furniture she could roll into
- there were no dangling cords near enough for her to grab
- she was not left unsupervised near any stairs or on a changing table
- she wore a safety harness when in a stroller, chair, or car seat

Photo 2.3

When Lara first started to sit up by herself, she often fell over, especially when distracted. Lara's mother sat her on a large pillow, which gave her support but also protected her when she fell (photo 2.4). Soon after Lara learned to sit up by herself, she started to crawl. This gave her much greater independence, as the world becomes a wonderful place to explore. As a result of Lara's increased mobility and independence, her parents needed to take even more precautions to prevent injury. Lara could now go where she wanted, and nothing in her visual range escaped her notice (photo 2.5). Her parents quickly learned to:

- avoid leaving anything on the floor that might be dangerous to Lara
- close doors or prop them open with a wedge to avoid pinching fingers
- put safety locks on cupboard doors and drawers to prevent Lara from opening them
- move dangerous products to high or locked shelves
- remove any dangling cords—electrical, curtain, and blind cords
- move furniture likely to tip or fall
- erect safety gates in dangerous areas such as at the stairs or in workrooms

Photo 2.4

Lara's next developmental milestone was to pull herself up into a standing position (photo 2.6). She quickly learned that she could walk while holding on to a surface (**cruising**). Additional safety precautions needed to be considered at this stage:

- Provide sturdy furniture that will not tip as Lara pulls herself up and walks while holding on to its surface.

✳ Cruising

- Ensure that the crib mattress is in the lowest position and that the crib sides are always in a locked position.
- Provide toys that are sturdy and that can be pushed without tipping as Lara walks and holds on to them.
- Move objects off tables—tablecloth, breakable objects, small objects that can be swallowed.
- Remove furniture with sharp edges or pad corners.
- Remove or stabilize swinging parts—doors, rocking chairs, gliders.

Photo 2.5

Not long after learning to stand by herself, Lara learned to walk. As infants learn to walk, their environment becomes much more accessible. They can find their own things to play with (photo 2.7). The increased standing height provides opportunities not only to see things from a different perspective, but also to retrieve things from higher storage areas such as cupboards, shelves, and tabletops. The increased mobility of the infant makes providing a safe environment a challenging process. Caregivers should:

- provide large open spaces both indoors and outdoors to encourage walking and running freely
- ensure that open spaces have surfaces that are smooth and free from obstruction—furniture, toys, books, etc.
- keep bathroom doors closed
- place latches out of reach on all doors and gateways (indoors and outdoors)

Along with her gross motor skills, Lara's fine motor skills develop very rapidly during this period. Her increased gross motor ability empowers her to actively explore her environment. If things are out of reach, she will climb to get them. Lara loves to pick up objects and put them into containers. She especially likes to **manipulate** (touch, feel, look at closely, and put in her mouth) small objects (photo 2.8). Lara needs

✳ Manipulate

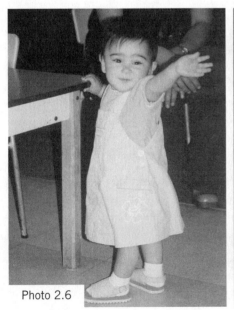

Photo 2.6

Photo 2.7

Photo 2.8

to develop her manipulative skills to handle objects of varying sizes. As well, she needs to learn that some objects should not be put in her mouth. Additional safety precautions at this time include the following:

- If Lara is given objects that may cause problems when put in her mouth, careful supervision at all times is required. These toys should be available only when the caregiver is interacting directly with the child and should be placed out of reach at other times.
- Sturdy furniture to climb and sit on should be provided, and all furniture that could fall when climbed on should be eliminated.
- For independent play, caregivers should provide objects that are easy to grasp and large enough to be mouthed (Figure 2.1).
- Lara must be kept safe from sharp corners, broken parts, slivers, and pinching.

In summary, Lara's skills evolve quickly over a very short period of time. Caregivers must carefully observe a child's changing skills to provide an environment that meets the evolving safety needs of the developing infant (Table 2.1). Infants who are empowered to actively explore a safe environment develop lifelong skills of trust in their abilities to interact with the world around them.

Safe Environments for Toddlers

1. Independence and Safety

Rashawne is a typically active toddler, curious about the world around him (photo 2.10). He is able to remember past experiences he has had himself or has seen modelled. He is very independent and wants to do things by himself. Many of the safety considerations for infants discussed in Table 2.1 still apply to toddlers, but some additional safety issues need to be addressed. Rashawne needs to be able to do things by himself without frustrations. To assist in this, caregivers should provide:

- safe equipment that toddlers can use, such as a child's CD player or nonbreakable dinnerware to encourage self-help, and adaptive low switches that encourage a child to turn things on and off
- alternative materials such as toy telephones or telephones that no longer work with cords removed
- child-sized materials to encourage helping—brooms, dustpans, mops, snow shovels, gardening tools
- opportunities to help with household tasks to increase awareness and skill

2. Play and Safety

One of Rashawne's favourite activities is filling and dumping. He loves to take objects out of one container and place them in another. Often, in the process, he leaves his toys scattered throughout the room as he becomes distracted by other items (photo 2.11).

Use a film container as a guide. The diameter of a film container is 3.18 cm.

Testing Toys for Size

Objects larger than this diameter are safe. They are too big to swallow.

Objects that fit into the container are too small. The closer the fit, the greater the danger of choking.

TABLE 2.1 **SAFETY CONSIDERATIONS FOR INFANTS**

Safety Category	Considerations
Choking	- Avoid any ties around the infant's neck—pacifier, necklace - Be careful when using clothing with drawstrings—e.g., hoods, tops. - Check size of small toys (see Figure 2.1).
Diapering	- Arrange space so that all materials are readily accessible (photo 2.9). - Ensure a washable surface and disinfect after every use. - Keep safety pins out of reach. - Ensure that there is a lip on the diapering area to prevent infant from falling off. - Keep one hand on infant to prevent infant from falling off table.
Feeding	- Hold infant; never leave infant alone with bottle propped up. - Never drink hot liquids while feeding an infant. - Place high chairs away from dangling cords, source of heat, countertops, plants, table, and traffic patterns. - Strap child into high chair. - Never leave child unsupervised. - Be careful not to trap fingers when removing or inserting tray.
Play	- Avoid shaking, throwing, or dropping infant on a bed. - Ensure that environment is safe for crawling—no sharp edges, small pieces, broken pieces, slivers. - Place toys within easy reach of infant.
Safety straps	- Always strap infant into strollers, car seats, shopping carts, and high chairs.
Sleeping	- Check label on crib to ensure it was made after September 1986; cribs made in Canada before this date do not meet government standards. - Keep sides of crib in locked, upright position. - Ensure that mattress is tight against all four sides of crib. - Ensure that mattress is firm. - Move mattress down to lowest setting as soon as infant is able to sit up by himself/herself. - Place crib away from windows, curtains, cords (blinds, curtains, light switches, lamps, fans), electrical outlets, extension cords, and heat outlets.

TABLE 2.1   CONTINUED

Safety Category	Considerations
Sleeping	- Check often to ensure that frame is solid and screws are tight. - Avoid using pillows in crib (they are a choking hazard since an infant cannot move his or her face off a pillow). - Avoid use of waterbeds—the surface is too soft and prevents infant from raising head to breathe. - Add securely fastened bumper pads around sides of crib, but remove once the child can stand by himself/herself. - Remove large toys when infant is able to sit up by himself/herself. - Check sleepwear to ensure that it is flame retardant. - Use only cool air vaporizers. - Ensure that room is well ventilated.
Supervision	- Supervise older children around infants. - Never leave infant unattended on the floor, in the car, in the high chair, in the stroller, alone in the house, or out of visual or auditory range.
Walking	- Provide cushioned, non-slippery area for walking. - Avoid cluttered floor areas. - Secure doors—latches out of reach, freezer locked. - Avoid hanging cords, long tablecloths, and handles that protrude. - Avoid leaving small electrical appliances near the sink (danger of electrocution). - Use elasticized pads to cover sharp corners (some corner guards may not adhere well). - Use safety gates—avoid gates with toeholds that encourage climbing. - Teach child to walk down stairs. - Secure windows—don't rely on window screens. - Protect railings with webbing to prevent head from becoming stuck. - Place secure lid on garbage cans. - Always use safety harness with strollers; reinforce sitting; do not overload handlebars (may tip stroller).
Washing	- Never leave infant unattended near water. - Check temperature of water—should be comfortable; turn down hot water heater to 48 degrees Celsius; check temperature with elbow.

Photo 2.9

Photo 2.10

He notices that the sound, shape, and texture of the box is quite different from the bowls he had been using. He turns the box around over and over again as he touches and looks at all parts of it. Rashawne continues to look at the box for several minutes. He then turns the box upside down on the floor. He decides that this is a good platform on which to balance. He climbs on the box (photo 2.12) and eventually manages to stand on it.

Caregivers need to encourage these types of activities. To prevent accidents such as tripping over small toys, the following safeguards should be considered:

- Confine this type of activity to a smaller area that is enclosed by low shelves to prevent spill of materials all over the room.
- Provide toys that are sturdy and will not break even if stepped on.
- Provide storage that is easy and logical to use—containers of toys sorted by shape, size, or colour; shelves labelled with pictures and words; low, accessible shelves.
- Provide continual supervision to monitor unexpected behaviour, and step in only if the behaviour becomes dangerous to the child or to other children.
- Engage the child in a cleanup activity that is fun once he or she has finished playing. For example, pretend to use your hand as a digger to return toys to their containers, talk about what you are doing, model enjoyment, and praise any helping efforts.

3. Gross Motor Activities and Safety

✳ Dexterity

Rashawne's increased **dexterity** (ability to use his fingers nimbly and efficiently) and increased motor abilities are starting to give him the coordination to do more than one thing at a time. He can perform motor skills with greater speed and accuracy—squatting with balance to pick up items from the floor and running and kicking a ball (photo 2.13). He has mastered the skill of pushing himself along on a riding toy (photo 2.14).

Toddlers need opportunities to practise these **emergent skills** (skills that are starting to develop but need practice in a variety of settings before the child becomes more proficient at them). Safe environments for practising these skills have the following characteristics:

- large open spaces to practise running, playing with balls, and riding a variety of toys
- soft, cushioned floors (toddlers tend to fall a lot as they practise these new skills), rugs in playrooms, and sand or other absorbent surfaces under climbers and slides (see Table 2.4 on page 48)
- a variety of toys and equipment
- close supervision—caregivers need to find a balance between encouraging toddlers to take safe risks and knowing when to step in to prevent potential accidents

4. Sharing and Safety

Lauren is playing with a dinosaur toy. Rashawne watches her play. Finally he runs over and roughly grabs the dinosaur out of her hands and shouts, "Mine!" (photo 2.15). Lauren tries in vain to get the dinosaur back. Jennifer, an early childhood educator, quickly walks over, bringing Lauren an identical dinosaur. Both children continue to play with their dinosaurs.

Photo 2.11

Photo 2.12

Photo 2.13

Photo 2.14

Photo 2.15

Photo 2.16

A little later, Lauren picks up a book about dinosaurs. Rashawne runs over to look at the book, which is on the floor in front of Lauren. Lauren points out a picture of a dinosaur and growls. Rashawne laughs and also growls. Jennifer notices the interaction and promptly praises the two children.

Toddlers have not yet mastered the concept of sharing. Toddlers are focused on themselves; they see the world from their own perspective. If they want something they may take it forcefully, not yet realizing that someone else may be hurt in the process. Toddlers think: If it does not hurt me, it will not hurt someone else. An aware caregiver will try to prevent altercations by:

- providing several identical or similar toys—Toddlers will want the same toy they see another child using.
- carefully observing children to know when to step in—Jennifer stepped in to give Lauren another dinosaur before anyone got hurt
- talking about sharing and praising it when it does happen—"Lauren, you are telling Rashawne about the pictures in the book. You are both sharing the book. Good job!"
- modelling sharing with children

5. Creative Art and Safety

Lauren loves to paint and colour (photo 2.16). She also likes to squeeze and shape dough. As toddlers start to create using paint, crayons, playdough, and other creative media, certain precautions must be taken:

- All materials must be non-toxic—toddlers still like to put things in their mouths.
- Supervise toddlers using wax crayons, as they may bite off the tips and swallow them.
- Avoid any substances such as dyes or inks that stain the hands, as these may be absorbed through the skin.
- Model and provide opportunities to wash hands after creative experiences.
- Discourage eating of any materials by reinforcing the proper use of those materials—"Crayons are used to draw on the paper."
- Ensure that toddlers wear protective smocks when painting as the paint may end up everywhere (photo 2.17).

A philosophical question arises when infants and toddlers use creative art materials. Some individuals argue that using food products with these age groups is more appropriate because these products are safer for children. For example, these individuals would recommend using edible products such as pudding to paint with.

Another group argues that it is inappropriate to use food products. These individuals point out that children in these age groups need to learn what items are and are not appropriate to eat. By using food products in creative play the children are given a conflicting message—food is to play with. Additionally, this practice might encourage eating since the food provided to play with also tastes good.

A third group argues that no food products should ever be used for play. There is too much hunger in the world to use food in a frivolous manner. Children need to learn to respect materials for what they are and for the purpose they serve.

As an early childhood educator, you need to find that balance yourself. You need to decide what is most appropriate for you, your children, and their families. Certainly, if the families that bring their children to your child-care centre are economically stressed, using food for any purpose other than eating would be highly inappropriate.

6. Additional Safety Concerns

Toddlers are much more aware of their environment and are eager to explore. This is a good time to model, teach, and reinforce safety rules. These rules should be simple, talked about, and reinforced every time a toddler is in a position to use them. For example:

- Cross the street only if an adult is with you. Hold the adult's hand.
- Don't talk to strangers.
- If you get lost, talk to a police officer or, if you cannot find one, a clerk in a store.

In summary, toddlers still need many of the safety precautions outlined in Table 2.1. It is particularly important to ensure that a toddler's environment is safe, since toddlers are at the **egocentric stage of development.** This means they see the world from their own viewpoint and do not think about the consequences of their actions; rather, they act impulsively. They learn through their interactions with their environment and continually strive toward independence; they want to do things by themselves. This combination very easily can lead to a number of potentially dangerous situations. Additional safety considerations for toddlers are listed in Table 2.2.

Safe Environments for Preschool Children

1. Blocks and Safety

The children in the preschool had spent a lot of time creating a large enclosure. They had used the hollow blocks to create a platform and a collection of painted cardboard boxes, covered shoeboxes, and cardboard bricks to complete the walls of their structure. They asked the adults to help create a roof using materials that would hang from the ceiling and a curtain for a doorway (photo 2.18). Several stages of block play had preceded this effort. Children had learned a variety of safety features before building this large structure:

1. They had learned the difference between types of blocks—some were hard and some were soft. Benjamin had tried to climb on the painted cardboard boxes (photo 2.19). Jennifer, an early childhood educator, noticed what he was trying to do. She quickly went over and explained to him that this type of box was not

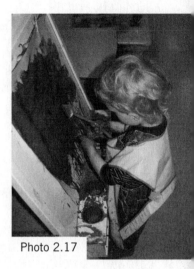

Photo 2.17

* Egocentric stage of development

Photo 2.18

TABLE 2.2 ADDITIONAL SAFETY CONSIDERATIONS FOR TODDLERS

Safety Category	Description
Choices	- Toddlers are easily distracted; therefore, their choices should be limited to encourage safe and appropriate use of materials and equipment. - More than one item of each type needs to be available, since toddlers do not share. This will prevent potential arguments and possible injury. - Encourage toddlers to use tools—scissors, plastic knives—safely.
Cleanliness/tidiness	- Cleanup should be encouraged so that toddlers learn and understand sanitary and safe practices—tidy up toys on the floor, clean tabletops after messy play. - Regular handwashing needs to be modelled and encouraged—after toileting, messy play, eating. - Clean up spills to prevent slipping. - Ensure that rugs and floors are clean, since toddlers still spend much time on the floor.
Choking	- Check size of small toys (see Figure 2.1 on page 35). - Cut up grapes and other small fruit and vegetables.
Independence	- Ensure that there is a child-sized sink within an easily observed area. - Provide child-sized cleaning tools to encourage children to help in cleanup.
Mealtime	- Arrange space so that toddler can serve himself/herself and learn to use utensils safely. - Wash hands before and after meals. - Clean table surface after meals.
Play	- Ensure that environment is free from clutter. - Provide large open spaces for play indoors and outdoors. - Provide cushioned floor surfaces—carpets and/or other materials under climbers (see Table 2.4 on page 48). - Provide paved areas for riding toys.
Safety straps	- Ensure that they are present and used on car seats and strollers.
Sleeping	- Mattress on floor or cot - Well-ventilated sleeping area - Away from heat source - Away from dangling cords

TABLE 2.2 CONTINUED

Safety Category	Description
Safety rules	- Engage children in road safety activities—walks, stories, dramatic play, riding toys. - Engage children in safety rules on playground equipment—only go down the slide, wait until child ahead is up the ladder before starting up, watch other riders so you won't bump into them. - Teach children not to talk to strangers. - Reinforce role of community helpers—police officers, ambulance drivers, firefighters. - Talk about preventing injury to self—danger of hot stoves, electrical outlets.
Set-up of learning areas	- Clear supervision of whole room - Stable furniture - Non-slip floor surface - Stable, accessible storage labelled with pictures and words
Supervision	- Carefully monitor all activities to prevent possible injury while toddlers are engaged in active play. - Always face children's activities. - Never leave toddlers unattended.
Security	- Ensure that door handles are placed where children can't reach them, or that door handles have child-proof covers to prevent children from leaving. - Lock gate outside to prevent wandering. - Ensure that there are accessible telephones both inside and outside for emergency calls. - Lock away cleaning products in original containers to retain details of ingredients and antidote information, if available. - Tie knots in plastic bags before throwing them away or saving them—children could choke if bags placed over their heads. - Secure bookshelves to wall.
Water	- Never leave toddlers unattended anywhere near water—bathroom, wading pools.

sturdy enough to climb on. Benjamin was not convinced and wanted to try it himself. Jennifer held his hand and he stood on the box. He said it felt "wiggly" as the box started to sag in the middle. When Benjamin got off the box, he noticed it was "dented." Next, he stood on one of the hollow blocks, which neither wiggled nor sagged. Benjamin proudly told his peers what he had learned.

Photo 2.19

Photo 2.20

2. Rebecca and Danika had built a tower with cardboard bricks, and hollow wooden blocks as a base. However, they could not make the tower as tall as they wanted, as it kept falling over (photo 2.20). Finally they decided to increase the size of the tower's base and were successful in building a taller tower. When other children had a similar problem, Rebecca and Danika were quick to help solve the problem. These children learned to create a stable structure.

3. Josh had carried over a large hollow block to use in the dramatic area. It slipped out of his hands and landed on his foot. He became upset because it hurt. Jennifer used the opportunity to talk about the different blocks in the room and what happens when they drop. Children learned that the heavier blocks hurt if they fall on you and that the lighter blocks were safer. The children later went to visit a construction site, where they noticed that the workers wore hard hats. The children decided it was a good idea to use hard hats in the classroom.

When you look more carefully at the structure the children built, you will notice that they applied what they had learned:

- building using a stable base with sturdy blocks
- using lighter blocks as walls
- using light materials to cover the structure

The adult caregivers ensured that the material hung from the ceiling was protected with a fire-retardant spray. They carefully monitored the building process and offered advice and suggestions when asked or when the situation was deemed potentially dangerous. As a result, the children built a very stable structure that lasted for many days.

Not all aspects of safety can be as easily experienced and learned. Many aspects within the preschool environment need careful attention from adults. The preschool years involve active exploration in the environment, and children need to learn to take safe risks. It is up to caregivers to provide a safe environment that encourages safe risk taking. It is also up to caregivers to discuss, model, and reinforce safety habits. Common safety procedures are listed in Table 2.6 on page 52.

2. Carpentry and Safety

The carpentry area is one learning area not often seen in early childhood settings because many practitioners worry about children's safety. If set up appropriately, children gain many skills from carpentry, such as measurement (finding the correct nail for the wood), eye–hand coordination (hitting the head of a nail with a hammer), problem solving (how to attach pieces of wood), and pride in accomplishment. Miranda loved to hammer nails into wood (photo 2.21); she was very excited when she was able to pound her nail all the way into the wood.

Several safety rules need to be discussed, modelled, and reinforced with all children prior to engaging in carpentry tasks. These include the following:

- All items must be clamped down before hammering begins—it is difficult to hammer into wood and easy to hit a finger when the wood moves.

- All tools and equipment must be returned to the properly labelled storage area—tools and nails bounce around when the wood is hit and may drop to the floor or on someone's hand or foot; nails on the floor are easy to step on.
- The size of the nail should match the thickness of the wood—otherwise, the wood will be nailed to the table.
- Soft wood should be used. Hard wood is too hard to saw or hammer into.
- Safety glasses must be worn when sawing.

3. Creative Arts and Safety

Children like Anna (photo 2.22) enjoy the variety of activities and choices—painting, drawing, moulding, sewing, sculpting, or cutting and pasting—provided in the creative area. Anna was especially proud to be able to cut her own paper to the desired size. The creative area is often overlooked when looking at safety issues. However, there are many things to consider when setting up learning experiences in the creative area that are safe and challenging.

Photo 2.21

a) Examples of Safe Products
- Wet clay and water-based paints, markers, and glues
- Food colouring or natural vegetable colouring
- Papier mâché made of flour or white paste, water, and newspaper
- Playdough made of salt, flour, and water
- Crayons or oil pastels
- Chalk on wet surfaces
- Blueprint paper

b) Use of Tools
- Scissors—blunt ends, sharp enough to cut, checked often to ensure they cut (if not sharp enough, scissors are more dangerous since inappropriate use may occur)
- Needles—blunt ends, sturdy (if too flimsy, they may break when pushed through fabric and puncture hands), large eyes, checked to ensure they will go through material easily to prevent the child from using force
- Knives—sturdy plastic to cut playdough or clay (flimsy knives break when pressure is put on them and sharp breaks may cut hands)
- Brushes—blunt ends to prevent accidental poking
- Cookie cutters—checked to ensure edges are not too sharp to cut child's hands
- Rolling pins—checked for appropriate weight (if too heavy, they are easy to drop and may land on toes)
- Paint and markers—non-toxic
- Other sharp objects—blunt ends of any objects, such as toothpicks, that can hurt little fingers

Photo 2.22

c) Safe Storage
- Scissors and knives—Store in a rack with points downward to prevent incorrect handling.

- Rolling pins, markers, crayons, and pencils—Store in containers to prevent items from rolling and falling off tables and onto toes or where they can cause someone to slip and fall.

d) Supervision
- Redirect "eating" of materials to actions—Roll the playdough out, stick something on your paper with the glue.
- Monitor children at all times to help prevent potential accidents.

e) Cleanup
- Wipe up spills to prevent slipping.
- Clean messy surfaces and tools—tabletops, brushes, etc.
- Pick up items dropped on floor to prevent slipping.
- Wash hands.

Playground Safety

Photo 2.23

Preschool children, in comparison to toddlers, have a much greater ability to engage in gross motor tasks. As preschoolers practise their new-found skills, they become involved in a number of risk-taking situations (photo 2.23). Preschoolers have no awareness of the risks they take. They are not aware that their actions may cause injury. "A child can receive a fatal head injury from falling just 30 cm onto concrete." (Pimento & Kernested, 1996: 212) Caregivers can protect children from injury by carefully setting up outdoor play areas to minimize dangerous risks. The Canadian Playground Safety Institution (CPSI) has issued standards for safety requirements (Table 2.3).

In summary, preschool children need to learn to take safe risks. Caregivers must carefully check the environment daily to ensure that potential hazards are eliminated. Planning of children's learning spaces both indoors and outdoors must take safety factors into account. Table 2.5 lists additional safety factors for preschool children.

Safe Environments for School-Age Children

Safety for school-age children focuses much more on children understanding and following safety rules and expectations. Children in this age group are encouraged to be much more independent. Developing safety rules and procedures together leads not only to better understanding of safety, but also to greater acceptance of rules and procedures. Safety rules and procedures tend to revolve around road safety, personal safety, learning to use tools safely and effectively, and developing skills to increase coordination of a variety of skills.

1. Road Safety

- When walking alongside a road, stay on the sidewalk; if there are no sidewalks, walk facing traffic. Obey traffic lights, look both ways before crossing any street, and cross at crosswalks. Do not run out between parked cars.

TABLE 2.3 **PLAYGROUND SAFETY**

Safety Consideration	Description
Protection from heat	- Metal slides on hot days - Lack of shaded areas in which to play
Protection from falls	- Cushioned surfaces under slides, swings, and climbers (see Table 2.4 on page 48) - Height of equipment for preschoolers should not exceed 1.8 metres. - Height of platforms should be between 1.2 and 1.8 metres for school-age children. - Railings on all platforms, ramps, stairs. - Wear CPSI-approved helmet while using riding toys. - Loosen and check cushioned areas to provide maximum safety against falls and protection from foreign objects.
Protection from tripping	- Keep all areas free from small debris. - If mats are used, check for curled edges. - Ensure that treads on stairs, climbers, and ramps are securely fastened. - Check for protruding parts.
Protection from being hit	- The distance in front and behind swings must be four times the height of the swing to prevent injury. - Wear CPSI-approved helmets. - Ball area should be away from traffic areas. - Equipment should be 2.74 metres away from other equipment or paved areas, and 4.6 metres away if using equipment with moving parts.
Stability of equipment	- Equipment should be anchored at least 30.5 to 45.7 cm into the ground or 15.2 cm into concrete. - Ensure that equipment is sturdy; check for rot in wooden structures. - Check stability of ladders, ramps, poles, platforms, and moving parts.
Protection from entrapment	- All openings, rungs, and space between railings should be closer than 8.9 cm or more than 22.9 cm apart. - Check for "S" hooks or protruding parts (bolts and nuts) that could catch fingers or clothing.
Accessible	- Paved pathways should be 8.9 cm apart for wheelchair accessibility.
Protection from splinters	- Protect wood from deterioration and metal from rusting. - Check frequently for slivers, rust, and bumpiness.

TABLE 2.3 CONTINUED

Safety Consideration	Description
Supervision	- All areas should be able to be visually monitored. - At all times adults supervise while facing group of children. - Telephone accessible outside.
Protection from weather	- Dress appropriately for all weather conditions. - Avoid dangling scarves or hats. - Provide wind and sun shelter.
Poisonous materials	- Cover sand to prevent animal excreta. - Check plants for safety. - Use organic pesticides on lawn areas. - Playground area should be away from traffic and protected from loud noises.
Protection from glare	- Avoid bright primary colours and silver material (high glare for eyes). - Wear UV-protected sunglasses.

Source: Adapted from the Canadian Playground Safety Institution.

TABLE 2.4 ABSORBENT MATERIALS

Type of Material	Description
Bark mulch—granulated pine bark, wood chips Install 30 cm deep (photo 2.24)	- Easily obtained, cheap, and easy to install - Offers good cushioning and has good drainage - Must be replaced periodically as it decomposes quickly - Must be raked regularly to prevent compacting, find hidden materials potentially dangerous to children, and redistribute after heavy rainfalls - May need to be replaced if it becomes infested with insects or microbes
Pea gravel Install 20 cm deep (photo 2.25)	- Easily obtained, cheap, and easy to install - Long-lasting material with excellent water drainage - Advantage over mulch and sand: It does not attract animals, does not usually become infested with microbes or insects, and does not decompose. - Compacts when wet or frozen, so care must be taken under these conditions - Should be contained by a barrier as it scatters easily and may cause tripping or falling - Must be raked because small, potentially dangerous objects are easily hidden - Younger children must be supervised carefully as some may stuff gravel into their mouths, ears, or noses.

Photo 2.24

Photo 2.25

TABLE 2.4 **CONTINUED**

Type of Material	Description
Sand Install 25 cm deep (photo 2.26)	- Commonly available, easy to install, and cheap - Popular because it does not deteriorate or decompose and it is not prone to infestations of microbes or insects - Must be raked to avoid compacting and remove small hidden objects including animal excreta - Must be replenished periodically as it is easily blown or washed away - May become dangerous if tracked to other areas since it can cause slipping.
Shredded tires Install 1.75 to 2.5 cm deep	- Cheap, offer good drainage, do not decompose or compact, and provide an excellent cushion - Harder to obtain since not all areas have tire shredding facilities - Must be treated to prevent staining - Not recommended in some areas since they are highly flammable - Difficult to rake and therefore it is hard to find hidden objects
Rubber mats or tiled system Install according to manufacturer's recommendation (photo 2.27)	- Ideal surface that provides a uniform cushion, is easy to clean and maintain, and allows small objects to be seen easily; in comparison to other surfaces, it is the most accessible as it provides easy access for wheelchairs - Expensive to purchase and must be installed professionally; edges must be firmly attached to prevent curling; some surfaces may be affected by cold weather conditions

Source: Standards Council of Canada

Photo 2.26

Photo 2.27

- When riding bicycles, use hand signals. Obey traffic lights, ride on correct side of the road, and wear CPSI-approved safety helmets and enclosed shoes. Adults should help children learn about bike safety, help inspect bicycles regularly—tires, brakes, handlebars, rear deflectors, bell—and provide bikes of the appropriate size (child's feet should be flat on the ground when sitting on the bike).

TABLE 2.5 **ADDITIONAL SAFETY CONSIDERATIONS FOR PRESCHOOLERS**

Safety Category	Description
Carpentry area	- Use only soft wood, such as pine—it is easier to drive nails into. - Confine area with shelves or in a corner to prevent traffic behind working children. - Supervise closely at all times. - Organize clearly—tools hung on pegboard with labels, nails sorted by size in individual containers. - Always return tools and materials after use to prevent accidents—falling tools, picking up tools the wrong way. - Make sure tools stay in the carpentry area. - Wood must always be clamped when cutting or hammering to prevent injuring fingers.
Creative area Avoid products listed on area right as they may: - be easily inhaled and damage lungs - cause allergic reactions - contain toxic or poisonous materials	- Avoid mixing dry clay or tempera paint—if necessary, mix only when children are not present in a well-ventilated while wearing a dust mask. - Check glazes before using—may contain lead. - Avoid solvents such as benzene, turpentine, toluene, thinners, rubber cement, epoxy, printing ink, or photographic chemicals. - Avoid cold water dyes or permanent dyes. - Avoid instant papier mâchés—may contain asbestos fibres or lead. - Avoid aerosol paints and lacquers and dust from chalk or pastels.

Source: Portions adapted from Marotz, Cross, and Rush (2001: 208).

2. Personal Safety

- Do not touch any stray animals or animals that are unknown, including pets. Report strange behaviour of animals. Adults should help children learn about common diseases in animals.
- Do not talk to, accept food or gifts from, open the door to, or get into a car with strangers.
- Learn emergency numbers such as 911, and post other emergency numbers by phones—fire department, police department, poison control, family contacts, ambulance, hospital.

- Adults always need to know where children are.
- Play in safe places such as parks, playgrounds, and backyards.

3. Using Tools

- Use the correct tool for a job. Learn correct handling, maintenance, and storage of tools.
- Machinery such as lawn mowers, electrical power tools, and saws may only be used with adult supervision.

4. Increased Coordination

- Learn rules of water safety—do not swim alone or in supervised areas, do not jump into unknown waters.
- Wear life jackets while boating and ensure that there is proper adult supervision.
- Follow the rules of the sport being played.

In summary, school-age children are more independent and have more freedom to act on their own. They need to be taught safety rules to increase their awareness and demonstrate safety procedures at home and in their neighbourhoods. School-age children are particular vulnerable because:

- modelling of adults is not always consistent—for example, adults often cross the street against the lights, which may cause children to think this is appropriate behaviour for them as well
- when a child becomes involved in an activity it is easy to forget other things— for example, while a group of children are playing floor hockey the puck is flipped onto the street; the child chases after the puck without looking both ways
- they have increased ability to understand safety concepts but often still need concrete examples. However, some of the concepts are more abstract—for example, if a child has been able to jump safely off a dock at a cottage, he or she may not realize that it is not safe to jump off a dock elsewhere. Further, the child might not understand that currents and water levels change, making jumping off even a familiar dock dangerous.
- they need reminders about safety practices, good modelling from adults, and supervised practice to ensure that they can act independently

Many of the issues involved in creating safe environments for children have been covered for particular age groups. Many of the skills listed are cumulative. Safety issues remain static; it is the ability of different age groups to act on their environment that changes. Some safety issues remain constant across all age groups (Table 2.6).

TABLE 2.6 **SAFETY CONSIDERATIONS COMMON TO ALL AGE GROUPS**

Safety Category	Description
Car seats	- "Motor vehicle collisions are the Number One cause of death and injury for young children, according to the Infant & Toddler Safety Association." (Langlois, 1998: 121) - All children should sit in the back since, once inflated, an air bag is potentially lethal to a young child. - Check label for Canadian Motor Vehicle Safety Standards (CMVSS). Infants up to 9.1 kg: - Safest location is middle of back seat facing backwards - Never in seat on passenger side equipped with air bag (impact of air bag potentially lethal) - Infant-only car seat converts into carrier, rocker, baby feeding chair - Five-point harness required Children 9.1 to 18.2 kg and able to sit up by themselves: - May be seated in the back facing the front of the car. Children who have outgrown a car seat and are less than 63 cm tall: - Combination of booster seat and seat belt—lap belt and shoulder belt Children at least 63 cm tall: - May use regular seat belt
Electrical outlets	- Cover each outlet to prevent child from poking items into small holes—childproof receptacles are the best method. - Place a shelf or other piece of furniture in front of an outlet; place an electrical appliance such as a CD player on top of furniture with cord running behind furniture.
Emergency contacts	- Keep emergency numbers beside the phone—hospital, ambulance, poison control, doctor, fire department. - Keep individual emergency information on child—family numbers and alternative number to reach in case of an emergency.
Field trips	- Transporting children in personal cars requires that caregivers ensure that all safety regulations and insurance requirements in their jurisdiction have been met; child-care centres are vulnerable to lawsuits and charges of negligence.

TABLE 2.6 **CONTINUED**

Safety Category	Description
Field trips	- Plan trips ahead of time—route, names of adults, number of children per adult, strategies for unplanned emergencies (ill child, flat tire), emergency cards, designated meeting place, information sheets for adults containing names of children travelling with them, purpose of trip, route, and safety reminders. - Look over the area prior to the field trip to identify potential dangers. - Take supplies of items such as tissues and sunscreen.
Fire safety	- Post an emergency plan in every room—exits, meeting point, and procedure (Figure 2.2). - Practise fire drills—announced and unannounced—and fill in report of drill (Figure 2.3); report should include details of what was done (feeling doors for heat; staying close to ground to avoid heat and smoke; stop, drop, and roll techniques). - Create portable emergency cards (Figure 2.4)—file cards, single paper copies. - Assign duties—calling fire department (from outside, if possible), collecting attendance and emergency files, assembling children and leading them outside, ensuring everyone is out of building, turning off lights and closing doors and windows, taking attendance. - Keep a fire extinguisher mounted on the wall out of reach of children. - Use fire-retardant materials for draperies and floor coverings. - Protect materials with fire-retardant spray.
Medical	- Read labels on all medication carefully. - Give medication only with signed consent of parents. - Avoid taking pills in front of children—may model that pill-taking is appropriate. - Avoid leaving pills in purses or cases unless these are locked away. - Ensure that medicine containers have child-resistant caps, but do not rely on these since child may still be able to open them.
Pets	- Consider allergies before adopting or bringing in pets for visits. - Avoid animals that carry disease (turtles, birds). - Ensure that animals are immunized as appropriate. - Protect pets from rough handling to prevent scratching or biting.

TABLE 2.6   CONTINUED

Safety Category	Description
Pesticides	- Avoid the use of pesticides on lawns around child-care facilities; use organic products instead.
Poisonous substances	- Lock away all cleaning products in original containers to retain information on ingredients and antidotes. - Post phone number of local poison control centre. - Keep ipecac syrup on hand—use only on advice of poison control centre or medical authority. - Be aware of poisonous plants (Table 2.7) and their symptoms—burning sensation in mouth, nausea, vomiting, dizziness, convulsions, diarrhea, confusion, irregular pulse, coma, paralysis, slow pulse, shortness of breath, rashes, fatality.
Room temperature	- Maintain between 20 and 25 degrees Celsius year-round.
Fencing	- Fence at least 1.8 metres around playgrounds and pools—check local requirements for fence height. - Locked gate for entry.
Weather and sun protection	- Wear appropriate clothing. - Provide daily opportunities for outdoor activity. - Children should wear wide-brimmed hats and wear sunscreen of SPF 30. - Sunglasses with UV protection can be worn by one year of age (child may not leave them on). - Provide shaded areas outside.

FIGURE 2.2   Emergency Plan

Fire department number.................... Posted by telephone.

Exit to leave by ....

Alternate exit...

Designated meeting place...

Emergency shelter location ....

Persons responsible (if absent, another designate to be appointed):

1. Telephone fire department ....
2. Take children out of building ....
3. Bring flashlight and emergency cards or files ....
4. Ensure that no one is left in rooms...
5. Turn off lights and close doors and windows..
6. Take attendance at designated meeting place...

FIGURE 2.3   **Fire Drill Report**

Date of drill.....................................Time to clear building...........................

Summary of practice drill..

....

....

Signature of supervisor..

FIGURE 2.4   **Emergency Cards**

Child's name...Date of birth...........................

Address.. Home phone...........................

Family members' names:

1. Name ....

   Relationship ....

   Contact phone number ....

   Alternate phone number ....

2. Name...

   Relationship ....

   Contact phone number ....

   Alternate phone number ....

Emergency contact name ....Phone number ....

Alternate emergency contact name ....Phone number ....

Allergies ....

Physician's name ....Phone number...........................

I, ..., authorize the staff of .... to take

whatever emergency medical measures needed for my child, ..., for his

or her care or protection.

Signature of guardian...

Signature of witness ....

Date...

TABLE 2.7   POISONOUS PLANTS

Poisonous Plants*

Amaryllis	Crown of thorns	Philodendron family
Arrowhead	Dieffenbachia	Poison oak/ivy/sumac
Azalea	English ivy	**Poinsettia—leaves**
Barberry	Euonymous privet	Pokeweed
Berries of bittersweet, mistletoe	Four o'clock	Rhododendron
	Fruit pits or seeds	**Rhubarb—raw leaves**
Black lotus tree—bark, leaves, pods, and seeds	Gladiola	Water hemlock
	Golden chain tree—acorns, leaves	Wisteria—seed pods
Boxwood		**Yew—berries, foliage**
Bulbs of daffodil, hyacinth, narcissus, jonquil	Holly	
	Hydrangea	
	Iris underground roots	
Buttercup	Jerusalem	
Caladium	Jimsonweed	
Castor bean	Lily-of-the-valley—leaves, flowers	
Cherry tree—leaves, twigs	Mountain laurel	
Chinaberry	Nightshade family	
Chinese evergreen	Oak acorns	
Chrysanthemum	Peony	

* Plants highlighted in bold may cause fatality if ingested.

SUMMARY

For children to be encouraged to actively explore their indoor and outdoor learning spaces, these environments must be safe from physical and emotional harm. Caregivers must be able to identify safety issues for various age groups. Many safety issues are common to all age groups, but each group also requires specific safety concerns. Careful monitoring of the learning environments allows caregivers to:

- predict potential safety problems
- ensure the safety of all children
- adapt or change potentially dangerous situations
- provide an environment that is safe to explore actively
- provide materials and equipment that are safe and developmentally appropriate for all age groups

KEY POINTS

Safe environments for infants

- Knowledge of developmental stage and abilities of the infant
- Preventing possibilities of choking
- Ensuring safety while diapering the infant
- Aspects of safety while feeding the child
- Safety at play
- Use of safety straps
- Creating a safe sleeping environment
- Providing supervision
- Creating a safe environment for crawling and walking
- Water safety

Safe environments for toddlers

- Providing appropriate choices
- Encouraging cleanliness and tidiness
- Preventing choking
- Encouraging independence in a safe environment
- Safety at meal times
- Use of safety straps
- Creating a safe sleeping environment
- Developing safety rules
- Providing supervision
- Setting up safe learning areas
- Providing security
- Water safety

Safe environments for preschool children

- Learning to use materials and equipment safely
- Creating safe block play, carpentry play, and creative art areas
- Safe storage of materials
- Providing supervision
- Encouraging cleanup

- Use of safe products and materials
- Identification of poisonous products

Playground safety

Includes protection from:

- heat
- falls
- tripping
- being hit
- entrapment
- splinters
- the weather
- poisonous materials
- glare

Also includes:

- providing stable equipment
- access to equipment
- providing close supervision
- providing cushioned materials to break landing or falls from equipment

Safety for school-age children

1. Developing rules and procedures for:
   - road safety
   - personal safety
   - using tools
   - increasing coordination
2. Adult help and modelling:
   - safety procedures
   - choosing safe equipment and toys—bikes, sports equipment
   - developing safe habits

Common safety considerations for all age groups

- Car safety
- Safety in the environment—electrical, medical, room temperature, pets, fences
- Posting emergency contacts
- Planning safe field trips

- Fire safety
- Use of pesticides
- Poisonous substances
- Sun protection
- Protection from weather

EXERCISES

1. Visit an infant centre. List all the safety precautions you see within that environment.

2. Visit a centre that cares for both infants and toddlers. Explain how the safety precautions differ in the two locations you have visited.

3. Visit a toy store. Pick out a toy suitable for a preschool child. What potential dangers may arise from improper use of that toy?

4. Develop a safety checklist for use in a preschool setting. Now, use that list within a preschool. How effective was your list? Do you need to make any adjustments?

5. Develop a safety checklist for use in an outdoor playground. Now, use that list within an outdoor playground. How effective was your list? Do you need to make any adjustments?

6. Visit an outdoor playground in your community and observe the activity there for 20 minutes. List any unsafe practices or potentially dangerous situations you observe. How could you correct these potentially dangerous situations?

7. How would you deal with an eight-year-old who has just crossed the street in the middle of the block? When you asked why she crossed the street in this manner, she responded that her parents always do this.

8. Develop a plan you might use to develop greater awareness of road safety among:
   a) preschoolers
   b) school-age children

*Glossary

Cruising (page 32) Infant pulls herself or himself to standing and moves around furniture while holding onto surface.

Dexterity (page 38) Ability to use fingers nimbly and efficiently.

Egocentric stage of development (page 41) Child sees world from his or her perspective and cannot understand someone else's viewpoint.

Emergent skills (page 39) Skills that are starting to develop but need practice in a variety of settings before a child becomes more proficient at them.

Manipulate (page 33) Explore objects by touching them, moving them, looking at them, and for young children, putting them in the mouth.

REFERENCES

Canadian Standards Association and Standards Council of Canada. (2003) *Children's Playspaces and Equipment*. Mississauga, ON: Canadian Standards Association.

Langlois, C. E. (1998). *Growing with your child*. Mississauga, ON: Ballantine Books.

Marotz, L., Cross, M., & Rush, J. (2001). *Health, safety and nutrition for the young child*. Albany, NY: Delmar.

Pimento, B., & Kernested, D. (1996). *Healthy foundations in child care*. Scarborough, ON: Nelson Thomson Learning.

3

CHAPTER

Illness and the Child

"It has become increasingly apparent that culture is a dominant factor in determining views on health, beliefs about health, and health-related behaviours. To optimize health for everyone in Canada, including children who are new to the country, health care must be delivered in a manner that is culturally sensitive and respectful, while keeping in mind that general-izations that are based solely upon ethnic background are detrimental to good health care decision making." (Canadian Paediatric Society, 1999: 1)

Chapter Outcomes

After reading this chapter, the reader will:

1. Identify how contagious disease is spread.

2. Identify and describe the symptoms and management of infectious diseases.

3. Identify the importance of universal pre-cautions.

4. Demonstrate the steps of universal pre-cautions.

5. List and discuss the importance of rec-ognizing the general symptoms of ill health.

6. Identify and discuss the importance of relevant health care documentation techniques.

7. Describe the symptoms, causes, and treatment of allergies and asthma.

8. Identify the importance of prevention practices.

9. Discuss why immunization is critical.

10. Discuss the role of the child-care provider in immunization practices.

11. Identify and discuss the importance of san-itary practices in child-care environments.

Transmission of Contagious Disease

For any illness to be transmitted, a pathogen, a susceptible host, and a method of transmission must be present (Marotz, Cross, & Rush, 2001). A **pathogen** is the virus, bacteria, or parasite (fleas, lice, ticks) that causes a particular disease such as measles or meningitis. The pathogen is most commonly found in live hosts in:

* discharges from the nose, throat, or lungs
* the intestinal tract
* discharges from the eyes or skin
* blood, stool, or urine

A **susceptible host** is an individual (human or animal) that becomes infected by a pathogen. After infection, the individual will exhibit the symptoms of a particular illness.

For an individual to become infected, the pathogen must be transmitted from the source to the susceptible host (Figure 3.1). Table 3.1 describes the most common methods of transmission of a pathogen.

"The absence of any one of these factors (pathogen, host or method of transmission) will prevent the spread of communicable illness. This is an important concept for teachers to remember when trying to control outbreaks of communicable illness in group settings. It also lessens the risk of teachers carrying illnesses home to their families." (Marotz, Cross, & Rush, 2001: 112)

✳ Pathogen

✳ Susceptible host

FIGURE 3.1

The Spread of Disease

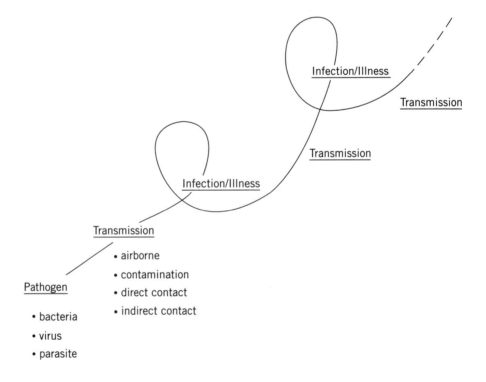

TABLE 3.1	TRANSMISSION OF A PATHOGEN	
Method of Transmission	**Description**	**Types of Diseases**
Airborne	- Pathogen carried in moisture droplets - Droplets dispelled by sneezing, coughing, laughing, or talking	colds, chicken pox, fifth disease, influenza, measles, meningitis, mononucleosis, mumps, rubella, streptococcal, tuberculosis
Contamination	- Lack of handwashing, lack of disinfection areas, toilet areas too close to food preparation	AIDS, hepatitis A, giardiasis pinworm, salmonella, strepto-coccal, hepatitis B
Direct contact	- Touching an infected area such as table that has been sneezed on - Pathogen is transferred directly from source to new host	AIDS; athlete's foot; conjunctivitis; cytomegalovirus (CMV); hepatitis B; hand, foot, and mouth disease; head lice; herpes; impetigo; ringworm; roseola infantum; scabies; herpes simplex (cold sores)
Indirect contact	- Transfer from an infected host to an intermediate object - Examples of intermediate objects—animals, dust, eating utensils, food, insects, milk, toys, towels, water - Transferred to susceptible host by touching nose or eyes or by being bitten	colds, dysentery, E. coli, encephalitis, head lice, impetigo, influenza, malaria, rabies, ringworm, Rocky Mountain Spotted Fever, tetanus, West Nile Virus, Severe Acute Respiratory Syndrome (SARS)

Source: Marotz, Cross, and Rush (2001).

Symptoms and Management of Contagious Disease

"Getting sick is an occupational hazard in early childhood settings. Young children get colds, with runny noses and crusty eyes. They get gastrointestinal viruses and may vomit or have diarrhea. Early childhood practitioners who are exposed to these germs, and other common childhood diseases, risk becoming sick. Personal health care and preventive measures, as well as excellent hygiene practices in the early childhood setting help to reduce the likelihood of illness. But, compared to most work environments, there is increased exposure to infectious disease in work with young children." (Gestwicki & Bertrant, 2003: 151)

To reduce the risk of the spread of communicable disease, child-care providers should:

- learn to recognize symptoms of various diseases (post Table 3.2 in a central location for quick reference)
- post Table 3.2 in the parents' corner and include a copy in the family handbook to inform families about diseases and control measures
- invite a public health nurse to conduct a workshop for staff and family members to gain more understanding of appropriate preventative measures and to understand required actions in the event of illness
- check the Health Canada and Canadian Paediatric Society Web sites for up-to-date information on current health care issues
- post and send home periodic reminders and bulletins about appropriate preventative practices and measures

> ✳ Universal
> precautions

Some diseases are so dangerous that **universal precautions** must be taken for the protection of all individuals. These are the blood-borne transmitted diseases: Acquired Immunodeficiency Syndrome (AIDS) and hepatitis B. These diseases may be contracted through contact with contaminated blood and body fluids. An individual may contract these diseases through:

- contact with contaminated surfaces
- contact with contaminated items such as needles
- cleaning bloody diarrhea
- cleaning open wounds
- stopping nosebleeds

Individuals who have open nicks and cuts on their hands while dealing with the above health emergencies are particularly at risk. Additionally, caregivers may not know that the child they are dealing with has a contagious disease. It is therefore critical to follow these universal precautions:

- Always wash hands prior to dealing with a health emergency (if handwashing is not possible, carry and use disinfectant liquid soap).
- Wear disposable latex or rubber gloves when dealing with vomit, urine, feces, or saliva.
- Dispose of contaminated materials by sealing clothing in plastic bags or pulling one end of a diaper over the soiled part and placing it in a sealed garbage bag.
- Remove gloves by grasping a glove's outer edge and peeling it away from hand to avoid touching the outer surface of the glove with your bare hand.
- Wash hands (see Figure 3.8 on page 85) or use disinfectant soap again after dealing with a health emergency.

TABLE 3.2 **SYMPTOMS AND MANAGEMENT OF COMMUNICABLE DISEASES**

Illness	Symptoms	Incubation and Length of Communicability	Control
Chicken pox	May have: - low-grade fever - irritable behaviour - itchy red rash—looks like insect bites, changes to blisters, scabs over at later stage - rash on chest, neck, mouth, forearm, back	- 2 to 3 weeks incubation - Infectious 2 to 3 days prior to onset of symptoms until 5 to 6 days after eruptions; scabs non-infectious	- Isolate from other children until child is picked up. - Call family to pick up child. - Careful handwashing. - Post alert to families. - Child returns only when all blisters have formed dry scabs.
Common cold	May have: - low-grade fever - dry cough - bouts of sneezing - watery eyes - runny nose - chills - muscle aches - headaches - fatigue	- 12 to 72 hours incubation - Infectious 1 day before onset and for up to 2 to 3 days during acute stage	- Good hygiene, especially handwashing. - Discard tissues in closed garbage container. - Wipe noses. - Stay home for first 2 days. - Watch for other symptoms—earaches, croup, chest pains. - Disinfect items used.
Conjunctivitis/pinkeye	May have: - yellow drainage from eyes - red swollen eyelids - itching, watery eyes - bloodshot eyes - burning sensation - eyes "glued" shut in the morning - swollen eyelids	- 1 to 3 days incubation - Contagious during active stage and from several days to 2 to 3 weeks	- Call parents to pick up child. - Stay home for 24 hours after starting medication. - Handwashing - Disinfect toys and surfaces.
Cytomegalovirus (CMV)	May have: - no symptoms under two years of age - sore throat - fever - fatigue - high risk of fetal damage if exposed during pregnancy	- Incubation may be 4 to 8 weeks - Contagious during active stage up to 2 to 3 weeks	- May stay in care. - Handwashing, especially after diaper change or contact with saliva - Avoid kissing and sharing utensils. - Wash and disinfect toys and surfaces.

TABLE 3.2 CONTINUED

Illness	Symptoms	Incubation and Length of Communicability	Control
E. coli	May have: - diarrhea - blood in diarrhea	- 3 to 4 days (may be up to 10 days) incubation - Infectious for duration of diarrhea	- Isolate child until picked up. - Call parents to pick up child. - Stay at home until diarrhea has cleared— several days. - Handwashing - Disinfect diapering and toilet areas - Post alert to families.
Encephalitis	May have: - sudden headaches - high fever - convulsions - stiffness in back and neck - tremors - lapse into coma	- 5 to 15 days incubation - Not infectious	- With severe symptoms, take directly to hospital - Call parents to pick up child. - Use mosquito repellent when outside. - Post alert to families.
Giardiasis	May have: - no symptoms - chronic diarrhea - abdominal cramps - bloating - pale, smelly stools - weight loss - fatigue	- 7 to 10 days (may be up to 25 days) incubation - Infectious as long as parasite is in stool	- Call parents to pick up child. - Stay at home until diarrhea has cleared. - Handwashing - Disinfect diapering and toilet areas. - Post alert to families.
Hepatitis A	May have: - fever - fatigue - loss of appetite - nausea - pain in area of liver (right side of abdomen) - yellow skin and whites of eyes	- 10 to 50 days incubation - Infectious 7 to 10 days before onset of symptoms	- Isolate child until picked up. - Call parents to pick up child. - Return with physician's approval (minimum one week). - Handwashing - Alert public health authority. - Post alert to families.

TABLE 3.2 CONTINUED

Illness	Symptoms	Incubation and Length of Communicability	Control
Fifth disease	May have: - bright red rash - rash on face and cheeks	- 4 to 14 days incubation - Infectious prior to development of rash	- Once rash appears child is not infectious - Frequent handwashing - Post alert to families. - Disinfect toys and surfaces.
Hand, foot, and mouth disease Children under 10	May have: - fever - ulcerated sores in mouth—tongue, gums, and inside of cheeks - poor appetite - feelings of sickness - sore throat - flat or raised red spots and blisters - rash on palms, soles of feet, and buttocks	- 3 to 7 days incubation - Infectious 7 to 10 days from onset of symptoms	- Isolate child until picked up. - Call family to pick up child. - Careful diaper changing - Handwashing - Disinfect surfaces - Post alert to families.
Haemophilus influenza Type b	May have: - fever - loss of appetite - vomiting - lethargic behaviour - stiff neck and back - bulging soft spot (infants) - high-pitched crying	- 2 to 4 day incubation - Not infectious after 24 to 48 hours of starting antibiotics	- Isolate child until picked up. - Contact family to pick up child. - With severe symptoms, take to hospital - Return with physician's approval - Disinfect items touched. - Careful handwashing - Post alert to families.
Head lice	May have: - itching of scalp, area behind ears, and back of neck - white cigar-shaped nits (eggs) attached to base of hair shafts	- 2 to 5 days incubation - Infectious until nits and adult lice have been destroyed	- Stay home until infestation is over. - Careful cleaning—wash rugs and soft furniture - Wash dress-up clothes, pillows, stuffed toys, dramatic clothes, hats.

TABLE 3.2 CONTINUED

Illness	Symptoms	Incubation and Length of Communicability	Control
Herpes simplex (cold sores)	May have: - blisters on tongue, lips, face, gums, and around mouth that crust over - low-grade fever swollen, red, bleeding gums - irritable behaviour	- Up to 2 weeks incubation - Virus remains in saliva for up to 7 weeks after start of symptoms	- May stay in care - Frequent handwashing - Eat soft foods and drink non-carbonated, non-acidic fluids.
Impetigo	May have: - crusty, moist lesions on skin - lesions on face, ears, and around nose - itching of scalp, area behind ears, and back of neck	- 2 to 5 days (may be up to 10 days) incubation - Contagious until lesions are healed	- Stay home until lesions have been treated for 24 to 48 hours. - Cover lesions with bandages.
Influenza	May have: - fever - headache - fatigue - dry cough - sore throat - nasal congestion - body aches	- 1 to 4 days incubation - Infectious 3 to 7 days from onset of symptoms	- Isolate child until picked up. - Call family to pick up child. - Stay home for at least 7 days. - Handwashing - Disinfect items used by child.
Measles	May have: - fever - runny nose - eyes sensitive to light - dark red, blotchy rash - rash beginning on face and neck - rash spreading over whole body	- 8 to 13 days incubation - Infectious from start of symptoms to 4 days after rash appears	- Isolate child until picked up. - Call family to pick up child. - Stay home for at least 4 days after appearance of rash. - Handwashing - Disinfect items used by child. - Post alert to families.

TABLE 3.2   CONTINUED

Illness	Symptoms	Incubation and Length of Communicability	Control
Meningitis	May have: - sudden high fever above 39.4 degrees Celsius - vomiting - drowsiness - headache - irritable behaviour - stiff neck - stiffening of legs when raised - bulging soft spot in infants - pale face - seizures	- Varies—2 to 4 days average incubation	- Take child to hospital immediately. - Contact family. - Stay home until medical treatment is completed. - Use universal precautions. - Frequent handwashing - Disinfect all items used by child. - Post alert to families.
Mononucleosis	May have: - sore throat - intermittent fever - fatigue - enlarged lymph nodes - headache	- 2 to 4 weeks incubation - Length of infectious state unknown	- Stay home during acute stage. - Handwashing - Discard tissues in containers with lids after use. - Post alert to families.
Mumps	May have: - decreased appetite - low-grade fever or sudden onset of fever - swollen glands - swollen cheeks - pain when opening mouth - headache	- 12 to 26 days incubation - Infectious 6 to 7 days from onset of swelling until swelling disappears (7 to 9 days)	- Isolate child until picked up. - Call family to pick up child. - Stay home until all symptoms are gone. - Post alert to families.
Pinworm	May have: - intense itching of anal area - small, 0.85 cm long, white, threadlike worms in stool - restlessness - bedwetting problems	- After ingestion of eggs, 2 to 4 weeks incubation - Cure within a few days of one dose of treatment	- Inform and ask family to take child to doctor. - Handwashing - Disinfect diaper table and washroom facilities. - Post alert to families.

TABLE 3.2 CONTINUED

Illness	Symptoms	Incubation and Length of Communicability	Control
Ringworm (athlete's foot)	May have: - flat, spreading, oval-shaped lesions - dry or scaly lesions - moist and crusted lesions - nails that become discoloured, brittle, chalky - nails that disintegrate	- 4 to 6 days incubation - Infectious until all lesions disappear	- Ask family to take child to physician. - Exclude child from pools, gym, water activities. - Disinfect these areas with fungicide, - Stay home until treated by physician. - Post alert to families.
Roseola infantum Children 6 to 24 months	May have: - rise in fever—39.4 degrees Celsius or higher - loss of appetite - listlessness - runny nose - rash on trunk, arms, and legs	- 10 to 15 days incubation - Infectious 1 to 2 days before onset of rash to several days after rash appears	- Isolate child until picked up. - Call family to pick up child. - Stay home until all symptoms are gone. - Post alert to families.
Rocky Mountain Spotted Fever	May have: - abrupt onset of fever—38.3 to 40 degrees Celsius - joint and muscle pain - intense nausea - white coating on tongue - rash on forehead, wrists, and ankles - rash spread over whole body	- 2 to 14 days incubation - Not infectious person to person	- Call family to pick up child. - Call professionals to check for ticks in outdoor play areas. - Wear insect repellent on clothes while outside. - Post alert to families.
Rubella/German measles	May have: - mild fever - pinkish-red, spotted rash on face - rash spread over rest of body - swollen glands - slight redness of throat and whites of eyes	- 4 to 21 days incubation - Infectious 1 week before onset of rash to 5 days after rash appears	- Isolate child until picked up. - Call family to pick up child. - Stay home for at least 7 days from appearance of rash. - Post alert to families.

TABLE 3.2   CONTINUED

Illness	Symptoms	Incubation and Length of Communicability	Control
Scabies	May have: - intense itching - bumpy rash, burrows, or - linear tunnels - rash most frequently between fingers and around wrists, elbows, waist, thighs, and buttocks	- 2 to 4 weeks incubation - Infectious until all mites and eggs are destroyed	- Isolate child until picked up. - Call family to pick up child. - Stay at home until treated. - Launder all dress-up clothes and bedding. - Post alert to families.
Shingellosis (dysentery)	May have: - sudden onset of vomiting - diarrhea - high fever - headache - abdominal pains - blood in stool	- 1 to 7 days incubation - Variable infectious period—up to 4 weeks	- Isolate child until picked up. - Call family to pick up child. - Stay home for acute stage of illness. - Return with physician's approval - Handwashing - Disinfect diapering and toilet areas - Extreme care in food handling - Post alert to families.
Salmonella	May have: - abdominal pain - cramps - sudden fever - severe diarrhea - diarrhea containing blood - nausea - vomiting	- 12 to 36 hours incubation - Infectious throughout acute illness May be carrier for months	- Isolate child until picked up. - Call family to pick up child. - Return with physician's approval - Handwashing Disinfect diapering and toilet areas. - Avoid individual contact in food handling. - Post alert to families.

TABLE 3.2   **CONTINUED**

Illness	Symptoms	Incubation and Length of Communicability	Control
Streptococcal infections (strep throat, scarlatina, rheumatic fever)	May have: - sudden high fever of 39.4 degrees Celsius or higher - sore, red throat - nausea - vomiting - white patches on tonsils - swollen glands - rash	- 1 to 4 days incubation - Infectious state eliminated within 36 hours hours of start of treatment	- Isolate child until picked up. - Call family to pick up child. - Return with physician's approval - Handwashing - Care in food handling - Post alert to families.
Tetanus	May have: - convulsions - muscle spasms and stiffness, especially around neck and mouth - inability to breathe	- 2 to 4 week incubation - Not infectious	- With severe symptoms, take child straight to hospital. - Recommend that family takes child to physician.
Tuberculosis	May have: - no symptoms - cough - weight loss - fatigue - loss of appetite - chills - bouts of sweating	- 2 to 3 months incubation - Contagious until 2 to 3 weeks after medication	- Contact family and physician. - Stay home until physician approves return. - Handwashing - Test children and staff in program for tuberculosis. - Post alert to families.

Sources: Marotz, Cross, and Rush (2001); Shore & Sears (2002); Canadian Paediatric Society (1999).

- Clean all surfaces with disinfectant (see Figure 3.9 on page 88).
- Encourage all staff members to be immunized for hepatitis B.

A good example of the transmission and control of a communicable disease is the outbreak of Severe Acute Respiratory Syndrome (SARS) in Canada. SARS was spread from Hong Kong to Canada through infectious individuals travelling to Toronto by airplane. As individuals became ill and sought medical help, the disease spread to medical facilities. In response to this outbreak:

- individuals who had come into contact with the disease were quarantined (voluntary)

- hospitals that had treated SARS patients established isolation wards or were closed to the public
- airports carried SARS notification notices
- the world health authority issued a traveller's advisory identifying areas of the world travellers should avoid
- travellers from countries that had experienced an outbreak of SARS were screened before leaving airports
- medical staff used universal precautions and wore face masks
- facilities catering to the elderly, such as nursing homes, severely limited public access (the elderly are more susceptible to SARS and more likely to become seriously ill)

The measures taken quickly brought SARS under control before it could escalate to epidemic proportions.

General Symptoms of Ill Health

"Children, especially those under three years of age, have an increased susceptibility to illness and infection. Group settings such as preschools, childcare centres, and daycare homes encourage rapid transfer of illness among children and adults. Therefore, every effort must be made to establish policies and practices that protect young children from unnecessary exposure." (Canadian Paediatric Society, 1999: 129)

In many areas across Canada, individuals require little or no training to work with children. In Alberta, legislation requires that only one in four individuals working in a daycare must have a full two years of training. The other individuals may work with children with minimal training requirements. An individual may be hired without training or experience in child care. Within three months of hiring, the individual must take one course: Introduction to Early Childhood Development. These individuals will have very little knowledge about the health and safety needs of children. Additionally, these individuals may bring their personal habits and biases to the workplace. These could include lack of knowledge of appropriate sanitary procedures and possible inappropriate treatment of children's illnesses due to lack of experience. For example, Cindy has three children of her own. She finds that giving her children an Aspirin when they have a fever is an effective method of lowering their temperature. When Jason, a three-year-old, develops a temperature, Cindy immediately gives him a children's Aspirin. Jason later develops symptoms of chicken pox. By giving Jason an Aspirin at that time, she increased his risk of developing **Reye's syndrome.** Reye's syndrome symptoms are flu-like or exhibit as upper respiratory problems. In severe cases, Reye's syndrome can lead to death. Jason did develop a mild form of Reye's syndrome, but he luckily was cleared of infection within a few days.

 Reye's syndrome

Health departments, physicians, and pediatricians recommend many of the control measures listed in Table 3.2. However, not all child-care centres in all jurisdictions follow these guidelines. For example, children with a common cold are seldom required to stay at home. Many centres do not exclude children with head lice. Children with chicken pox may return to daycare at the family's discretion as long as they are being treated, even though these children may still be infectious.

These practices acknowledge the parents' need to return to work. There is little alternative care for children who are sick when parents must return to work. Consequences of a sick child returning to daycare too early include:

- increased chance of infection of staff and other children
- increased chance of infection of family members of staff and other children
- increased risk of exposure during critical periods for pregnant women, increasing chances of abnormal fetal development
- a hard-to-manage child—a child not well enough to participate in regular routines and limited opportunity to provide the one-on-one care or restful environment needed for that child
- risk of secondary infection—the child is more likely to contract other illnesses since he or she has weaker defences against infection
- increased stress to the child
- increased stress to the daycare staff
- increased absenteeism of staff and other children

Many of the symptoms of ill health, infectious disease, general malaise, and infections are very similar. Therefore, it is easy to miss symptoms, with potentially serious results. The child may become more seriously ill, other children and staff in the child-care centre may become infected and in turn infect family members, and in rare cases death may occur (meningitis, Rocky Mountain Spotty Fever, tetanus, dysentery, encephalitis). Children may exhibit signs of illness in their behaviour or physical appearance.

1. Behavioural Signs

General symptoms may include:

- general fussiness or irritability
- difficult to soothe
- easily upset
- listlessness
- fatigue and sleepiness
- lack of interest in what is going on around them
- increased activity level
- lack of appetite
- behaviour different from normal

2. Physical Signs

General symptoms may include:

- hot or cold, clammy skin
- flushed appearance

- dry, hot or cold skin
- loose bowels
- smelly bowel movements
- distended abdomen
- rubbing or scratching of body parts
- complaints of nausea, stomach pain, or muscle aches
- complaints of headache

3. Management of Ill Health

The following steps should be taken if a child is showing any of the above behavioural or physical symptoms:

- Soothe the child.
- Check the child for any sign of injury or infection.
- Take the child's temperature.
- Check to see if any of the child's symptoms match the symptoms outlined in Table 3.2 on page 65. If so, follow the control procedures outlined; if not, observe the child carefully. Note child's symptoms on a Record of Ill Health (Figure 3.3 on page 77) to share with parents and medical officials.
- If the child is vomiting, has a temperature, or has diarrhea, isolate him or her and call the family immediately for a pickup.
- If the symptoms are severe (seizure, convulsions, sudden high temperature, or unconsciousness), take the child to a hospital immediately. Another staff member should contact and inform the family to meet the child at the hospital.

4. Procedures

The following procedures should be taken to safeguard all those within the child-care setting:

- Establish written policies and procedures about managing illness and sanitary practices and share these with all staff and families.
- Provide annual training on policies and procedures. Staff then sign a statement that they understand and will follow these procedures.
- Reinforce up-to-date immunization of staff—hepatitis B, tetanus, diphtheria.
- Require regular medical checkups, including chest X-rays and tuberculosis tests.
- Set up an isolation area within the centre. This area should be as far away from children as possible, include a comfortable resting place, have lights that dim, be free from interruptions, and be monitored by an adult. The isolation area could be an office space, a staff room, or if these are not available, a corner of the playroom.
- Establish a routine emergency procedure and have forms signed by parents or guardians giving permission to take the child directly to hospital (see Figure 2.4 on page 55).
- Obtain written consent to share medical observations (Figure 3.2).

FIGURE 3.2

Permission to Share Information

I, ..., give permission to the staff

of .... to talk to and provide the written medical

records of my child, ..., to Dr. ....

and the emergency department of .... hospital.

Signed..

Dated...

- Review regularly with staff and families and post sanitary procedures to encourage greater awareness and adherence to these procedures.
- Post handwashing routines at all sinks.
- Use checklists to monitor health and sanitation within the centre and to establish routines and designate responsibilities. Ask individuals to date and check off as their assignments are completed (Table 3.7 on page 89).
- Engage in advocacy activities to encourage better health care policies within local jurisdictions and help establish centres for sick children whose parents must return to work.

5. Record Keeping

It is critical to keep an accurate record of a child's ill health. This information will help a physician make an accurate diagnosis of the child's health problems. Reports that need to be kept include a record of the child's illness (Figure 3.3), a record of the treatment given (Figure 3.4), and a record of any medication administered (Figure 3.5).

Allergies and Asthma

"An allergy refers to a misguided reaction by our immune system in response to bodily contact with certain foreign substances. It is misguided because these foreign substances are usually harmless and remain so to non-allergic people. Allergy-producing substances are called **allergens**. When an allergen comes in contact with the body, it causes the immune system to develop an allergic reaction in persons who are allergic to it." (Shiel et al., 1995: 2)

Allergens

"Allergies and asthma can be everything from annoying to life-threatening. Among the most misunderstood chronic health conditions, they are a part of the lives of millions of Canadians." (Health Canada, 2003: 1)

Allergies can cause reactions that range from relatively mild to deadly. Symptoms can occur immediately or sometime later. A severe reaction may lead to **anaphylactic shock** (a response that involves more than one organ and may be life threatening). Table 3.3 describes common substances that may lead to allergic reactions, the various types of reactions, and possible treatment.

Anaphylactic shock

FIGURE 3.3

Record of Ill Health

Name .... Date.............................

When started.................   Length of time continued.................

Symptoms observed..

....

....

....

....

Temperature.......................   How taken............................

Additional problems observed:

    1. Change in behaviour...

    2. Change in habits:

          - eating..

          - drinking..

          - toileting..

Additional information—List exposure to new food, situations, animals, medication,

insects, experiences, other illnesses......................................

....

....

Steps taken to help child..

....

Signature of caregiver..

Child-care facility...

Telephone number...

FIGURE 3.4

Record of Treatment Given

Child's name...

Health Problem	Date	Action Taken
....	....	....
....	....	....
....	....	....
....	....	....
....	....	....
....	....	....
....	....	....

FIGURE 3.5

Administration of Medication Form

Child's name..

Family Permission

I, ..., give permission to the staff of ....

to administer the medication identified below to my child, ...

The staff will not be held responsible for any adverse reactions or other complications

arising from administering this medication to my child.

Signed... Dated.....................................

NOTE: MEDICATION MUST BE IN ORIGINAL CONTAINER WITH ORIGINAL LABEL

Prescription number........................ Date of prescription........................

Physician's name............................. Medication given for......................

Last dosage received......................... Given by......................................

Staff Record

Name of staff member giving the medication...

Signature of staff member ....

Record of Administration

Date	Time	Dosage	Staff Name	Signature

One needs to be aware of the dangers of insect repellent for various ages. N-diethylmeta-toluamide, or DEET, can be toxic in concentrations above 30 percent and has been known to cause cephalopathy (brain disease) in young children. For safe use of insect repellent, see Figure 3.6. Products containing citronella work to repel insects but need constant reapplication. Avon's Skin-So-Soft is not effective. Mechanical traps are expensive and of debatable effectiveness (*Maclean's*, 2003).

In 1997, 12.2 percent of Canadian children had been diagnosed with asthma; 43 000 Canadian children and adults are hospitalized with asthma every year (Health Canada, 2003). Its exact cause is not known. According to Health Canada, asthma is

TABLE 3.3   COMMON ALLERGIES

Allergy	Symptoms	Causing Agents	Treatment
Respiratory allergies	- Runny nose - Stuffy nose - Itchy nose - Sneezing - Nasal itching - Itchy ears and throat - Post-nasal drip - Clearing of throat - Red, watery eyes - Persistent cough - Wheezing - Recurrent colds - Recurrent ear infections - Shortness of breath	- Pollen - Dust mites - Moulds - Cigarette smoke - Types of grass - Trees - Pet dander (tiny flakes of skin that are shed with pet hair) - Feathers - Cosmetics, perfumes, hairspray, powders, deodorants	- Stay indoors on windy days or when pollen count is high. - Keep windows closed during allergy season. - Install or use portable air filters in furnace or cooling system. - Remove dust-catching items—curtains, rugs. - Wash bedding and clothing frequently. - Damp-mop. - Avoid pets. - Clean dark, cool areas frequently to avoid mould buildup—cubbies, garbage cans, bathrooms, water play. - Consult physician about allergy shots.
Skin allergies	- Eczema—itching; redness; dry skin; rashes on face, around eyes, in elbow creases, and behind knees - Hives—raised red welts, itching - Inflammation of skin—rash	- Eczema is usually not caused by contact with an allergen, but can be an allergic reaction - Food - Medication - Latex - Plants (see Table 2.7 on page 56) - Dyes, chemicals - Metals - Cosmetics	- Consult physician. - Avoid contact with materials causing allergy.
Bites	- Localized swelling - Wheezing - Swelling of upper airway, making breathing difficult - Swelling of face - Anaphylactic shock	- Bees, wasps - Mosquitoes - Black flies	- Avoid walking in areas where, and at times when, insects are most active. - Use insect repellent. - Wear light-coloured and insect-repellent clothes. - Eliminate standing water. - Avoid eating sweet-smelling food outdoors.

TABLE 3.3   CONTINUED

Allergy	Symptoms	Causing Agents	Treatment
Food allergies	- Vomiting - Diarrhea - Bloody stools - Symptoms similar to bites - Anaphylactic shock	- Eggs - Peanuts, nuts - Shellfish - Dairy products and lactose - Wheat	- Avoid foods causing allergic reaction. - Contact a physician. - For severe reactions, carry adrenalin injection kit, administer immediately, and call an ambulance.
Chemical/ medication allergies	- Similar symptoms as with other categories	- Substances such as chlorine and asbestos - Fabric softener - Antibiotics such as penicillin	- Similar treatments as with other categories

FIGURE 3.6

Insect Repellent and Safety

Age of Child	Concentration of N-diethylmeta-toluamide (DEET)
Less than 6 months	Do not use products containing DEET
6 months to 2 years	10 percent concentration of DEET or less. Use sparingly.
2 to 12 years	10 percent concentration of DEET or less. Apply no more than three times a day and avoid face and hands.
12 years and older	Up to 30 percent concentration of DEET

the result of an interaction of three factors:

1. *Predisposition factor.* An individual has a tendency to have allergic reactions to certain foreign substances.

2. *Causal factor.* The causing agent of the allergic reaction can be identified—cats, dogs, other animal dander, dust mites, cockroaches, workplace contaminants.

3. *Contributing factor.* These factors may lead an individual to develop asthma—exposure to cigarette smoke during prenatal stage and childhood, respiratory infections, air pollution.

A report by Health Canada (2003) recommends the following strategies to help reduce the risk of asthma:

- Avoid smoking while pregnant or in the presence of young children.
- Breast-feed infants and delay introduction of solid foods.
- Keep homes and daycare settings clean and ventilated to decrease exposure to dust mites, cockroaches, and moulds.
- Minimize exposure of children to known triggers of asthma attacks.
- Reduce airborne contaminants in child-care settings.

Prevention of Illness

1. Immunization

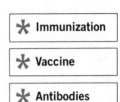

Immunization is a process that helps build defences against infectious disease caused by viruses and bacteria. When an individual is given a vaccination (an injection or shot), the **vaccine** injected into the body contains tiny amounts of the disease-causing virus or bacteria. The body's response is to produce **antibodies**, which attack and destroy the disease-causing virus or bacteria. The body's immune system then stores this information. Later, if the body again comes into contact with this virus or bacteria, antibodies are produced to fight the disease.

"Few measures in preventive medicine are of such proven value and as easy to implement as routine immunization against infectious diseases."(Health Canada, 2002b: 1). Immunization practices start at two months of age and continue into the teen years. Since 1998, all provinces and territories have had routine immunization schedules in place. Immunizations are given to protect children from nine serious, infectious diseases—diphtheria, pertussis (whooping cough), tetanus, polio, measles, mumps, rubella, influenza type b, and hepatitis B. The cost of routine immunization is covered by medicare. Table 3.4 identifies recommended immunization schedules for children in Canada.

However, not all Canadian children are immunized, nor are they necessarily immunized according to the schedule in Table 3.4. Some explanations for this lack of immunization include:

1. Not all individuals in Canadian society believe that children should be immunized. The Canadian Immunization Awareness Program (2003) lists the following reasons why parents may not wish their children to be immunized:
- religious or philosophical reasons
- fear that the immunization may not be safe or effective
- fear of adverse side effects or allergic reactions due to immunization
- belief that mandatory immunization interferes with personal choice
- belief that vaccine-preventable diseases are not a serious health risk
- belief that immunization is not natural

2. Child-care regulations for immunization vary across Canada.

3. Children from immigrant families may come from countries that have different immunization schedules. Families from these countries often do not understand

TABLE 3.4 **IMMUNIZATION SCHEDULE FOR INFANTS AND CHILDREN**

Age of Vaccination	Required Vaccination								
	dTaP 1	IPV	Hib 2	MMR	Td^3 or dTap^{10}	Hep B^4 3 doses	V	PC	MC
Birth									
2 months	X	X	x			Infancy		x^8	x^9
4 months	X	X	x			or		x	X
6 months	X	(x)^5	x			pre-		x	X
12 months				x		adole-	x^7	x	
18 months	X	X	x	(x)^6 or		scence			Or
4 to 6 years	X	X		(x)^6		(9 to 13			
14 to 16 years					(x)^{10}	years)			x

Vaccine	Immunization Against
dTap	Diphtheria, tetanus, pertussis (acellular)
IPV	Inactivated poliovirus
Hib	Haemophilus influenza type b conjugate
MMR	Measles, mumps, and rubella
Td	Tetanus and diphtheria oxoid, adult type and reduced diphtheria toxoid
dTap^{10}	Tetanus and diphtheria oxoid, acellular pertussis, adolescent/adult type with reduced diphtheria and pertussis component
Hep B	Hepatitis B
V	Varicella
PC	Pneumococcal conjugate
MC	Menincoccal C conjugate

Source: Health Canada (2002a).

either English or the health care system well enough to seek out medical advice about immunization practices within Canada.

4. Immunizations are not up to date. This may be because the pace of family life is too hectic, families have children of various ages that need immunization at different times, and families do not have a regular physician (Pimento & Kernested, 1996: 120).

When children are not immunized, there is a danger that infectious disease will spread to epidemic proportions. Before immunization was used regularly, diseases like polio affected thousands of people. Many individuals who contracted these diseases were left with permanent physical disabilities. With immunization, these types of outbreaks are rare, and many serious illnesses have been virtually eliminated. To protect individuals and prevent the spread of disease, all children and staff who have not been immunized are excluded from any child-care centre by the health department in the event of an outbreak of any of the infectious diseases listed in Table 3.4.

2. What Can Child-Care Providers Do?

- Establish a policy for immunization as a requirement for attendance.
- Collect a copy of the immunization record from the family of each child. The record can be obtained from the doctor or health nurse and is updated when immunization is received.
- Provide immunization information to families. This may be obtained free of charge from any public health office, or you may find information on the World Wide Web (Health Canada, 2002b).
- Children cannot be denied access because of refusal to immunize. Before a child is accepted into a program, parents are required to submit a letter from the child's physician stating that the child is exempted from immunization. This letter should be kept on file.
- Maintain accurate immunization records for each child (Figure 3.7).
- Continue to update children's immunization records as per the immunization schedule.
- Inform new families about the centre's immunization policy. Direct new families to a public health clinic to receive appropriate immunization.
- Advocate for legislative changes to mandate immunization in your area.

3. Sanitary Practices

A) HANDWASHING "Washing your hands and your kid's hands is the best thing that you can do to stop the spread of germs. The moment that you finish washing your hands, you start to collect germs again by opening doors, wiping faces, playing with children's toys, and changing diapers. You cannot avoid collecting germs, but you can reduce the chance of infecting others by knowing when to wash your hands." (Canadian Paediatric Society, 2001)

Hands should be washed before:

FIGURE 3.7   Immunization Record

Name of child.............................   Date of birth............................

Physician's name..........................   Date of enrollment....................

Immunization Against	Dates of Immunization					
	2 months	4 months	6 months	12 months	18 months	4 to 6 years
Diphtheria, tetanus, pertussis Poliomyelitis, haemophilus Influenza type b[3]						
Hepatitis B[3]						
Mumps, measles, rubella						
Chicken pox						
Pneumococcal disease[5]						
Meningococcal disease[5]						

- any food preparation
- setting the table
- eating
- feeding children—including breast-feeding
- giving medication to children
- playing in water

Both adults and children should wash their hands after:

- arrival at the daycare setting
- eating or feeding children
- handling any items containing mucus, urine, feces, vomit, or blood
- cleaning messy areas such as the creative area
- diaper changes
- using the toilet
- helping a child use the toilet
- caring for someone who is ill
- handling animals or pets
- cleaning animal cages or litter
- wiping noses
- sneezing
- sand play

The instructions and images shown in Figure 3.8 should be posted at all sinks. The images are suitable for non-readers to reinforce correct handwashing procedures.

FIGURE 3.8
Handwashing Procedure

Turn on tap.

Wet hands thoroughly up to elbows.

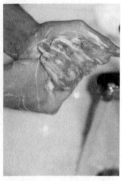

Put soap on hands from liquid soap dispenser and lather vigorously for at least ten seconds.

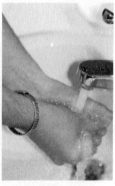

Rinse thoroughly.

Dry hands with paper towel.

Turn off tap with paper towel.

Post procedure over every sink.

B) TOILETING ROUTINES Washrooms tend to become easily contaminated. For example, a child uses the toilet, wipes himself or herself, then flushes. The flusher is the first point of contamination. When the child goes to the sink, the first thing he or she touches is the tap, again a point of contamination. When the tap is turned off after hand-washing, a third point of contamination occurs. The child now enters the playroom or lunchroom, ready to continue the contamination process. Proper bathroom and diapering techniques (Table 3.5) are essential to avoid the spread of germs throughout the environment.

As children learn to use potty chairs and toilets, they should be taught to:

- wipe their bottoms
- flush the toilet
- wash and dry their hands
- throw paper towels in the garbage

TABLE 3.5 **DIAPERING ROUTINES**

Routine	Description
Physical space	- Isolated from any food-handling areas - Used for diapering only - Running water within reach, if possible - Flat surface, appropriate height so caregiver can work without bending back - Surface easy to clean and disinfect—free of cracks, tape, and crevices - Surface covered with cheap butcher paper, shelf paper, disposable squares—avoid paper towels as they are too absorbent - Keep all lotions and cleaning items out of reach.
Steps for diapering	- Ensure all supplies are available and within reach. - Place disposable material on diapering surface. - Wash hands. - Put on disposable gloves, if using. - Place child on surface. - Remove diaper; fold soiled surface inward and place in plastic bag or plastic-lined receptacle; if safety pins are used, close them and put them out of reach. - Check clothing; if soiled, remove and keep in separate plastic bag. - Clean and dry child's bottom using pre-dampened towelette or paper towel.

TABLE 3.5   CONTINUED

Routine	Description
	- Remove and dispose of covering under child. - Remove and dispose of gloves. - Wipe hands with pre-dampened towelette. - Dispose of all items—diapers, towelettes, covering, gloves—in plastic-lined receptacle with close-fitting lid. - Diaper infant. - Wash child's hands. - Return child to supervised area. - Clean and disinfect diapering area (Figure 3.9). - Wash hands. - Record information about diaper change (Table 3.6).
Types of diapers	Irrespective of whether cloth or disposable diapers are used, the following criteria should be met: - Containment of feces and urine to prevent contamination of children, staff, and environment - Inner absorbent liner with outer waterproof covering - Both outer and inner linings must be changed—either disposed of or cleaned and disinfected. - Avoid pull-down diapers—as the diaper is pulled down, the child's legs become contaminated and need to be washed.
Safety	- Provide steps so toddlers can climb up to diapering surface (protects caregiver's back). - Require an extra set of clothing—bag soiled clothing and tie securely to be sent home for cleaning. - Disposable gloves act as a barrier to infection; hands should be washed before and after using gloves; wear gloves when in contact with blood-containing fluids, when caregiver's hands have cuts or open sores, when child has diarrhea or diagnosed gastrointestinal disease, and when cleaning surfaces are contaminated with blood or body fluids. - Do not rinse diaper in toilet as this may contaminate toilet. - Empty cloth diaper in toilet; store in sealed bag to be sent home for cleaning; flush toilet. - Discard soiled diapers daily or as needed.

Sources: Shapiro Kendrick, Kaufman, and Messenger (1995); Pimento and Kernested (1996); Aronson and Spahr (2002); Warrick and Helling (1997).

FIGURE 3.9   Daily Disinfection Solution

Mix:

2.5 ml (1/2 tsp) bleach

250 ml (1 cup) water

Check label of bleach to ensure that percentage of sodium hypochlorite is 5.25.

Mix daily, as solutions deteriorate rapidly.

Keep in labelled bottle out of reach of children.

TABLE 3.6   DIAPERING INFORMATION

Name ....

Date	Time	Dry Diaper	Bowel Movement	Comments (unusual occurrences such as loose movement, rash, diarrhea)

Toddlers will need supervision and help with these steps. Preschoolers will need to be reminded of the steps. Preschoolers will enjoy pictorial reminders that are changed periodically to catch interest and maintain attention. These reminders could be:

- a picture or photograph of a child washing his or her hands
- a funny picture posted on the door, such as one of a favourite doll washing his or her hands
- a stop sign that needs to be turned around to find a surprise picture or photograph

C) SANITIZING THE ENVIRONMENT   All early childhood education programs should have written policies and procedures for maintaining sanitary standards within the environment (Tables 3.7 and 3.8). These procedures not only will help prevent the spread of germs, but also will help create an environment that is clean and aesthetically pleasing. These practices provide opportunities to model and reinforce behaviours that will become entrenched for a lifetime. Some of the routines that should be considered include the following:

- Clean the facility both indoors and outdoors.
  - Floors and walkways should be swept, vacuumed, and/or washed as needed.
  - Wash kitchen and bathroom floors daily.

TABLE 3.7   **SANITIZING CHECKLIST**

Tasks	Dates (daily unless otherwise stated)
ROOMS	
- Tabletops, counters cleaned	
- Food-handling area cleaned—counters, tabletops	
- Easels and other painting surfaces cleaned	
- Floors and walkways swept	
- Floors washed	
- Carpets vacuumed	
- Carpets deep-cleaned once every six months or as needed	
- Walls washed once every six months or as needed	
- Windows and screens washed (inside and outside) as needed	
- Small mats/rugs vacuumed	
- Small mats/rugs laundered weekly	
- Clear storage room of clutter.	
- Clean shelves at least weekly.	
TOYS	
- Sand toys washed and air-dried	
- Rake sand and eliminate small pieces.	
- Replace sand in indoor sandbox regularly.	
- Disinfect toys that have been mouthed.	
- Dramatic clothes, props, and large stuffed toys laundered weekly or as needed	
- Hats cleaned after each use	
- Riding toys cleaned weekly or as needed	
- Water toys—disinfect table daily	
- Water toys—clean and disinfect daily	
- Large toys—disinfect weekly	

TABLE 3.7   CONTINUED

Tasks	Dates (daily unless otherwise stated)
BATHROOM - Clean sink. - Clean taps. - Clean counters. - Clean toilet seat. - Clean potty chair. - Clean potty. - Clean flushing handle. - Clean toilet bowl (inside and outside). - Clean doorknobs. - Clean walls every six months or as needed. - Clean changing table.	
OTHER - Launder mops and cleaning cloths. - Launder dry mops weekly.	
PETS - Clean animal cages.	
KITCHEN - Clean stove. - Clean dishwasher. - Clean countertops. - Sweep floors. - Wash floors. - Clean fridge weekly or as needed. - Clean sinks. - Clean cupboards weekly or as needed.	

TABLE 3.8   **YEARLY TASKS**

Task	Dates
1.	**Sand**
	Turn sand over to depth of 45.7 cm.
	Replace sand every two years.
2.	**Inspections**
	Ventilation system
	Furnace

- Clean walls and deep-clean carpets every six months.
  - Windows and screens should be washed and cleaned as needed.
  - Wash any mats regularly.
  - Wash dress-up clothes and dramatic props such as tablecloths, doll clothing, and doll bedding regularly
  - Clean tabletops and other surfaces with disinfectant solution (see Figure 3.9) as needed
- Clean and disinfect toys.
  - Toys that have been mouthed or sneezed on should be set aside immediately and disinfected before other children can use them (Figure 3.10)
  - Toys for older children should be cleaned once a week. As older children are not as likely to put toys in their mouths, the disinfection time (Figure 3.10) can be reduced.
  - Choose only stuffed toys that can be machine-washed.
  - Hard plastic toys can be washed in the dishwasher.
  - Water tables and water toys should be disinfected with bleach solution (Figure 3.9) every day. Water should be thrown out after water play is finished. Do not allow children with open wounds or sores to play in the water area.

FIGURE 3.10   **Washing Toys**

To wash and disinfect hard plastic toys:

- Scrub toy in warm soapy water.
- Rinse toy in clean water.
- Immerse toy in disinfectant solution (see Figure 3.9) for 10 to 20 minutes.
- Rinse toy well in cool water.
- Air-dry toy.

Source: Family Management (2003).

- Organize storage areas to avoid clutter of old furniture and refuse. Ensure that area is clear of clutter so that it is easy to keep floors and shelves clean.
- Ensure that equipment is clean and in good working condition. Clean riding toys and climbing equipment regularly. Rake sandboxes. Cover outside sandboxes when not in use. Change sand regularly.
- Maintain cleaning supplies and keep brooms, vacuum cleaner, dry and wet mops, cleaning cloths, and cleaning supplies locked away from children. If possible, have a second sink for cleaning. Launder wet mops and cleaning cloths daily and dry mops twice a week. Store sponges in bleach solution between uses.
- Ensure that the environment is protected from pests.
    o Protect windows and doors with screens.
    o Use licensed exterminators for pesticide control if needed.
- Ensure that pets are housed and cared for appropriately.
    o Keep animals away from food-handling areas.
    o Clean animals frequently; wash hands after cleaning.
    o Wash hands after handling animals.
- Maintain a clean kitchen.
    o Wear clean clothes and maintain high personal hygiene.
    o Clean and disinfect all surfaces.
    o Keep hair covered during food preparation.
    o Wash all dishes and utensils in a commercial-grade dishwasher.
    o Clean fridge and freezer regularly.
- Dispose of garbage daily or as needed.
    o Use plastic liners in garbage cans with tight lids.
    o Store garbage in water- and rodent-proof containers.
    o Disinfect garbage cans after garbage removal.
- Provide laundry arrangements.
    o Laundry should be washed at a temperature higher than 60 degrees Celsius.
    o Store laundry supplies in locked cupboards.
    o If no laundry facilities are available, develop written procedures to handle emergency situations (for example, items that need to be washed due to contagious illness) and send clothing and bedding home to be washed.
- Sanitize bathroom facilities.
    o Clean and disinfect taps, doorknobs, and toilet fixtures at least daily
    o Clean potty with soap and water after each use; rinse, disinfect, and air-dry.
    o Wash hands.
    o Provide liquid soap dispensers and paper towels within easy reach of children.
    o Label all personal items—toothbrushes, hairbrushes, face clothes—and store them so that items do not touch each other and can be air-dried.
- Ensure proper ventilation and heat.
    o Have systems checked and cleaned at least once a year.
    o If finances permit, install an ultraviolet disinfection unit within the air ducts. This unit will inactivate any airborne pathogens.

D) **EMERGENCY PROCEDURES** All staff should have up-to-date training in first aid and cardiopulmonary resuscitation (CPR) irrespective of licensing requirements, which vary across jurisdictions in Canada. When an emergency occurs, timely interaction is critical. In many situations, such as choking or allergic reactions, the individual nearest the child needs to react and intervene quickly. There is no time to find and wait for the individual with training to deal with the situation.

- *Emergency contacts.* An emergency plan (see Figure 2.2 on page 54) should be posted in a central location for easy and quick access. All staff should know where the information is posted and should be thoroughly versed in the specified procedures.
- *Isolation.* To minimize exposure to infectious disease, an isolation area within the child-care environment must be set up while waiting for the child to be picked up (see page 75).

SUMMARY

Child-care providers have an important role to play in protecting the children within the daycare setting from illness. Aspects of this role include gaining knowledge of symptoms and management of disease, providing a sanitary environment, and engaging in preventative practices.

- Child-care providers need to have knowledge of the symptoms and transmission of disease and of the symptoms of ill health in young children to take prompt and appropriate action when children become ill.
- Child-care providers can effectively reduce the risk of communicable disease by following appropriate personal and environmental sanitary practices.
- Child-care providers need to be aware of and practise sound preventative practices based on established health guidelines and requirements.

KEY POINTS

Spread of illness

- Illness is transmitted by pathogens to susceptible hosts via air, contamination, direct contact, or indirect contact.

Communicable diseases

- Airborne—colds, chicken pox, fifth disease, influenza, measles, meningitis, mononucleosis, mumps, rubella, streptococcal, tuberculosis
- Contamination—AIDS, hepatitis, giardiasis, pinworm, salmonella, streptococcal
- Direct contact—AIDS; athlete's foot; conjunctivitis; CMV; hepatitis B; hand, foot, and mouth disease; head lice; herpes; impetigo; ringworm; roseola; infantum; scabies; cold sores
- Indirect contact—colds, dysentery, E. coli, encephalitis, head lice, impetigo, influenza, malaria, rabies, ringworm, Rocky Mountain Spotted Fever, tetanus, West Nile Virus, SARS

Reduce risk of spreading disease by:

- learning to recognize symptoms
- posting list of symptoms in accessible place
- sharing and discussing symptoms of disease and control measures with staff and families

- offering workshops to increase understanding of diseases and control measures

Universal precautions

- Take universal precautions when in contact with contaminated surfaces and items or when cleaning any blood or substances containing blood.
- Wash hands, use disposable latex or rubber gloves, avoid contact with skin when removing gloves to avoid contamination, wash hands again, and disinfect surface.

General symptoms of ill health

- Behavioural—fussiness, hard to soothe, easily upset, listless, tired, lack of interest, lack of appetite, behaviour change
- Physical—hot or cold clammy skin, flushed, dry or hot skin, loose bowels, smelly bowels, distended abdomen, itchy skin, complaints of pain

Management of ill health

- Soothe child, set and follow procedures for the child-care centre, check and record symptoms, call family, take child to hospital if symptoms are severe.
- Ensure health of staff members—regular medical checkups, immunization as required.
- Set up an isolation area within the centre.
- Establish emergency routines and sanitary routines and review them periodically.

Record keeping

Develop and keep records of:
- ill health
- administration of medication

- permission to share health information
- immunization
- diapering information

Allergies

- Allergy—reaction to contact with a foreign object
- Anaphylactic shock—body response involving more than one organ; possibly fatal
- Common allergies—respiratory, skin, bites, food, chemical, medical

Immunization

- Creates antibodies to fight disease
- Reasons for not immunizing—personal beliefs, fear, feeling it is not natural
- Variation of requirements across Canada; check local immunization schedule
- Establish immunization policy for child-care centre, collect and maintain records, provide information

Sanitary practices

- Handwashing
- Diapering routines
- Disinfecting solution and procedure
- Toileting routines
- Sanitizing the environment—cleaning, disinfecting, organizing, maintaining cleaning supplies, protection from pests, care for pets, kitchen routines, garbage disposal, laundry, bathroom routines, annual checks, sanitization checklist

EXERCISES

1. Develop a chart, including a diagram, to show how disease is spread.

2. Explain why it is necessary to know the method of transmission of infectious diseases.

3. In small groups, discuss what strategies you might use to increase public awareness on how to reduce the spread of contagious disease.

4. Knowledge of the symptoms and control of communicable diseases is an important aspect of early childhood education. What strategies might you use to:
   a) become more familiar with the information presented in Table 3.2?
   b) make others—families and other professionals—more aware of the importance of good control for disease prevention?

5. Review the control strategies for communicable diseases presented in this chapter. Develop a checklist of common control mechanisms that all child-care centres should use (see chart below). Visit a community daycare centre and interview the centre's supervisor to find out how these strategies are implemented. Compare results with other groups in your class. Develop a large chart to include all of the different strategies. Post the chart.

6. Universal precautions are the best protection against becoming infected. Reflect on your feelings about the need to use universal precautions.
   a) Do you agree that they are necessary?
   b) When should they be used?
   c) Review the universal precautions. How many of these strategies do you currently use?
   d) Which steps or strategies do you need to add to your routine?

CHART 1

Common Control Strategies	How Implemented

7. Compare the common symptoms of ill health and the symptoms of various contagious diseases.

   a) How are they similar?
   b) How are they different?
   c) Why is it important for you to be able to recognize and continue to observe the symptoms of ill health?

8. Interview a parent of young children. Use Figures 3.2 and 3.3 in your interview and bring the completed forms to class. In small groups, discuss the results of your interviews.

   a) What are the common contagious diseases?
   b) Were the same control mechanisms used?
   c) What steps might have been missed?
   d) Were these significant? Why?

9. Survey the class to find out what allergies your fellow students have. List the symptoms and treatments. Discuss how these allergies affect an individual's lifestyle. Develop a list of strategies to help control allergies within a daycare centre.

10. How are allergies similar to asthma? How are they different? What strategies need to be used to protect children from an asthma attack?

11. A family wants to register its two children at your daycare. When you request immunization records, you find out that the children have not been immunized. When you state that it is the centre's policy to accept only children that have been immunized, the children's mother indicates that immunization is against the family's religious belief. How might you deal with this situation?

12. You work with an individual who does not understand the importance of many of the sanitary practices. Her philosophy is that children need to be toughened up and that exposure to disease will help them gain immunity. In a small group, discuss how would you deal with this situation.

*Glossary

Allergens (page 76) Allergy-producing substances that cause a reaction when they come in contact with a foreign body.

Anaphylactic shock (page 76) An allergic response of the body that involves more than one organ and may be life threatening.

Antibodies (page 81) Substances produced by the body in response to a bacterial or viral attack to destroy the disease-carrying viruses or bacteria.

Immunization (page 81) A process that helps build defences against disease caused by viruses and bacteria. Individuals receive an injection that builds antibodies within the body to fight disease.

Pathogen (page 62) A virus, bacteria, or parasite (fleas, lice, ticks) that causes a particular disease such as measles or meningitis.

Reye's syndrome (page 73) Flu-like symptoms or upper respiratory problems. In severe cases, it can lead to death.

Susceptible host (page 62) An individual (human or animal) who becomes infected by a pathogen and exhibits symptoms of a particular illness such as measles or meningitis.

Universal precautions (page 64) Procedures to protect individuals from accidental exposure to harmful infectious organisms.

Vaccine (page 81) Tiny amounts of disease-causing viruses and bacteria injected to build antibodies within the body to fight off the disease.

REFERENCES

Aronson, S., & Spahr, P. (2002). *Healthy young children: A manual for programs.* Washington, DC: National Association for the Education of Young Children.

Canadian Paediatric Society. (1999). *Children and youth new to Canada: A health care guide.* Ottawa: Canadian Paediatric Society.

Canadian Paediatric Society. (2001). *Handwashing for parents and kids.* Mississauga, ON: Canadian Paediatric Society.

Canadian Immunization Awareness Program. (2003). *Canadian immunization program.* http://www.immunize.cpha.ca, accessed 8 July 2003.

Family Management. (2003). *Practices to reduce disease and injury washing and disinfecting toys.* http://www.familymanagement.com, accessed 22 May 2003.

Gestwicki, C., & Bertrant, J. (2003). *Essentials of early childhood education.* Scarborough, ON: Thomson Nelson.

Health Canada. (2002a). *Canadian immunization guide.* Sixth edition. http://www.hc-sc.gc.ca, accessed 20 May 2003.

Health Canada. (2002b). *Immunization schedule.* Division of Immunization and Respiratory Diseases. http://www.hcsc.gc.ca, accessed 9 March 2003.

Health Canada. (2003). *How to breathe easier dealing with allergies and asthma.* http://www.hc-gc.ca, accessed 10 January 2003.

Maclean's. (2003). Waiting for West Nile. *Maclean's, 116,* 16–23.

Marotz, L., Cross, M., & Rush, J. (2001). *Health, safety and nutrition for the young child.* Albany, NY: Delmar.

Pimento, B., & Kernested, D. (1996). *Healthy foundations in child care.* Scarborough, ON: Nelson Thomson Learning.

Shapiro Kendrick, A., Kaufman, R., & Messenger, K. (1995). *Healthy young children: A manual for programs.* Washington, DC: National Association for the Education of Young Children.

Shiel, W., Lee, D., Hecht, F., Hecht, B., Marks, J., & Schoenfield, L. (1995). *Allergies.* http://www.MedicineNet.com, accessed 25 May 2003.

Shore, P., & Sears, W. (2002). *Medical emergencies & childhood illnesses.* Toronto: Parent Kit Corporation.

Warrick, J., & Helling, M. (1997). Meeting basic needs: Health and safety practices in feeding and diapering infants. *Early Childhood Education Journal 24*(23), 195–199.

4

CHAPTER

The Learning Environment

"Children's growth and development are continually shaped and influenced by their environment. Growth is enhanced through nurturing and responsive caregiving, good nutrition, homes and schools that are clean and safe, access to health care, and communities that are free of drugs and violence. Opportunities for learning, experiencing new challenges, and positive social interaction are important for promoting children's intellectual and psychological development. Thus, there are many aspects of children's environments for teachers and parents to consider. Every effort must be made to create physical, cognitive, and psychological environments that have positive effects on children's growth and development." (Marotz, Cross, & Rush, 2001: 158)

Chapter Outcomes

After reading this chapter, the reader will:

1. Describe why and how safety and learning are interconnected.

2. Identify critical aspects of physical safety for:
   • infants
   • toddlers
   • preschool children
   • school-age children

3. Identify the relationship between developmental appropriateness and safety for:
   • infants
   • toddlers
   • preschool children
   • school-age children

4. Identify critical aspects of emotional security for:
   • infants
   • toddlers
   • preschool children
   • school-age children

5. Discuss why and how adult/child ratios are important to the well-being of young children.

6. Explain why and how group size influences the well-being of young children.

7. Explain why education is important in developing safe, quality programs for young children.

8. Discuss how the quality of programs and the well-being of children can be enhanced through family involvement.

9. Identify relevant resources that relate to the well-being of children.

Photo 4.1

Interconnection of Safety and Learning

Quality learning experiences for young children depend on the interactions between individuals, materials, and environments. To grow and develop optimally, children depend on safe and responsive environments. "Quality child care programs must be built upon a foundation that ensures the physical, emotional, and nutritional health and well-being of every child." (Goelman, Doherty, Lero, LaGrange, & Tougas, 2000: 4) Children learn through active play (Kieff & Casbegue, 2000; Shipley, 2002; Crowther, 2003; Watson, Watson, Cam Wilson, & Crowther, 2000; Gestwicki, 2003). They explore their environment by:

- using all of their senses (photo 4.1)
- interacting with each other and with the adults and materials within learning spaces (photo 4.2)
- engaging in activities that challenge their coordination, strength, and endurance (photo 4.3)
- manipulating objects to discover how they work (photo 4.4)
- transforming objects and materials (photo 4.5)
- seeing the results of their actions (photo 4.6)
- learning to take acceptable risks (photo 4.7)

Children feel confident in their abilities to explore and manipulate materials and equipment in their environment when the adults in that environment ensure that:

- the learning environment is safe from physical harm
- the learning activities and materials are **developmentally appropriate**
- an atmosphere of trust and respect has been established between all participants—families, children, staff, other professionals

✱ **Developmentally appropriate**

Photo 4.2

Photo 4.3

Photo 4.4

Photo 4.5

Photo 4.6

Photo 4.7

Infants

1. Physical Safety

Aleah can sit up by herself, if she is helped into a sitting position. Her actions are still a little shaky and she easily loses her balance and falls over. A quilted blanket is placed under her to protect her in case she falls. Her favourite toys are placed in front of her, close enough so she can reach them by herself (photo 4.8). When Aleah picks up a toy, she looks at it carefully, turning it around to examine it from several perspectives (photo 4.9). Finally, she puts it in her mouth (photo 4.10). Aleah's caregiver responds to her efforts: "Good for you, you picked up the butterfly." As Aleah looks at her toy, her caregiver watches very carefully to see what Aleah is looking at in order to provide appropriate verbal labels.

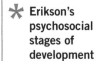

✳ Erikson's psychosocial stages of development

Aleah gains confidence in her ability to explore objects of her choice through reaching, grasping, and exploring the objects with her tongue and mouth. Aleah is at the first of **Erikson's psychosocial stages of development**, Trust versus Mistrust (Table 4.1).

Aleah develops confidence in her abilities because her learning environment provides safety for her to explore that environment based on her abilities. Her caregiver helps her into a sitting position. Her immediate environment is clear of any sharp or hard objects and a blanket is provided to cushion any potential falls. Her toys are placed near her, so she can reach them. The toys are soft and will not harm her if she puts them in her mouth.

In contrast, Kirstin, who is at the same psychosocial stage of development as Aleah, is placed in the middle of a small wading pool containing a few inches of water and floating plastic ducks. When Kirstin tries to grasp one of the ducks, she pushes it under the water. It slips out of her grasp and bobs up in a different spot. This moves the other ducks a little farther from Kirstin's reach. Kirstin leans over to try to grasp another duck. She has to reach too far and falls face down in the water, which makes her very upset. After she has been calmed down, her caregiver asks her if she wants to

Photo 4.8

Photo 4.9

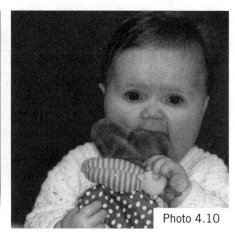

Photo 4.10

TABLE 4.1   **ERIKSON'S PSYCHOSOCIAL STAGES OF DEVELOPMENT**

Age	Stage	Explanation
Infancy Birth to 1 year	1: Trust versus Mistrust	- Infants gain a sense of whether the world is a safe place through positive interactions with caregivers, the environment, and materials.
Infants and toddlers 1 to 3 years	2: Autonomy versus Shame	- As children develop increased motor skills and mental capacities, they gain independence and confidence in their abilities. Autonomy is developed by providing choices and encouraging children to solve problems.
Toddlers and preschoolers 3 to 6 years	3: Initiative versus Guilt	- Children's growing competence in motor, social, language, and cognitive skills leads to an increased ability to learn through experimentation, observation, imitation, and participation with peers and adults.
Preschoolers and school-age children 6 to 11 years	4: Industry versus Inferiority	- Continued development and skills in all domains and increased ability to think more abstractly, compute, write, and read leads to ability to work independently and cooperatively. - Children begin to learn to value and take pleasure in productive work and completion of tasks.

Source: Schickedanz, Schickedanz, Forsyth, and Forsyth (2001: 12–13).

try again. Kirstin hides her head in her caregiver's shoulders and stiffens her body. Her caregiver correctly interprets the signal that Kirstin does not wish to repeat the experience. Kirstin clearly shows her reaction to a negative experience—she does not want to try again. She has learned to mistrust her experience in the wading pool.

It is critical that caregivers provide appropriate experiences within a learning environment that is safe to explore. Infants must develop confidence in their ability to explore their environment. Positive experiences will lead to further explorations and a resulting increase in continuous learning. Negative experiences often lead to withdrawal from situations that are perceived as "hurtful" or dangerous. Infants who are continually put into situations in which they are likely to hurt themselves will cease to explore. They will learn to mistrust that their actions will lead to a satisfactory experience. This may lead to lifelong effects to learning in all domains—physical, social, emotional, and cognitive (McCain & Mustard, 1999).

2. Developmentally Appropriate Experiences

Aleah's learning experience was developmentally appropriate for her age. Her caregivers provided her with opportunities to:

- make realistic choices (photo 4.8)—It was appropriate to limit the number of choices. Young infants are easily distracted when presented with too many choices.
- manipulate materials—The toys given to Aleah were ideal for her development: bright to capture her attention, soft to aid grasping with her whole hand, detailed to encourage looking at it, safe to put in her mouth, easy to care for (washable), and soft so that shaking it will not inadvertently cause injury to her (photo 4.9).

Kirstin's learning experience was not developmentally appropriate for her age. Kirstin was put at risk of a poor learning experience by:

- placing her in the centre of the wading pool—Kirstin's balance was not yet steady enough. It was predictable she would fall. Although her fall was cushioned by water, she landed face down in the water. The pool is slippery and she had to be rescued from a frightening experience.
- inappropriate choice of toys—The plastic ducks were too hard for Kirstin to grasp. She still uses a full **palmar grasp** (using the whole hand as a unit to pick up items; see Figure 6.2 on page 170). When she attempted to pick up a duck, it slipped out of her grasp and bobbed away. The movement of the water moved the other ducks out of her immediate reach.

Palmar grasp

In summary, providing developmentally appropriate learning experiences to infants ensures that infants will continue to:

- manipulate materials safely
- explore without risk
- have pleasurable learning experiences
- develop trust in their individual ability

3. Emotional Security

Both infants' emotional needs were met appropriately. Aleah's efforts were noticed and praised. Her caregiver watched carefully to see what Aleah was doing in order to provide language stimulation. Kirstin's caregiver responded quickly to her negative experience in the pool. She provided emotional support to Kirstin so that Kirstin would get over her scare. She also acknowledged Kirstin's feelings by not putting her in the same situation again.

Emotional security implies that children feel safe within the learning environment to engage freely in a variety of tasks. The atmosphere of an emotionally secure space requires:

* caregivers trained in early childhood development who are able to use developmentally appropriate guidance techniques
* caregivers who respect a child's efforts—Aleah's caregiver acknowledged her interests by following her lead; she watched Aleah's efforts and responded to what she was doing
* caregivers who respond to the child's actions in a timely fashion—Both Aleah and Kirstin had caregivers who responded promptly to their different needs

In summary, there is a strong connection between healthy growth and development and a safe and secure environment (Figure 4.1). Healthy brain development demands that infants are encouraged to explore the environment freely, without risk of:

* physical harm—falling and hurting themselves, choking on small parts, pulling objects down on themselves
* physical abuse—physical punishment
* emotional abuse—harsh language, ignoring the child's needs, ignoring the child's efforts
* inappropriate materials—too small, sharp, hard, hard to grasp (Begly, 1997; Nash, 1997; Shondoff & Phillips, 2001; McCain & Mustard, 1999)

FIGURE 4.1

Infant Development and Safety

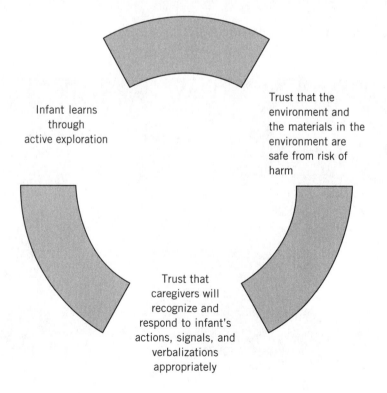

Infant learns through active exploration

Trust that the environment and the materials in the environment are safe from risk of harm

Trust that caregivers will recognize and respond to infant's actions, signals, and verbalizations appropriately

Toddlers

1. Physical Safety

Rashawne has been playing with a set of frogs. He suddenly gets up, goes to a cupboard, and brings out a set of silver bowls. He places the frogs in the bowls, hides them under the bowls, and finally discovers that he can put the bowl on his head to wear as a hat. He becomes distracted when he hears the phone ring. He stops his play and watches his father answer the phone (photo 4.11). When his father finishes talking, Rashawne runs to him and hands him a bowl. Rashawne holds out his hand and his father hands him the phone. Rashawne climbs onto his father's lap and watches as his father places the bowl on his head (photo 4.12). Rashawne giggles with delight when the bowl falls off his father's head. He watches it fall to the ground and starts to get off his father's lap to retrieve the bowl but notices that he still has the phone in his hand. He starts to talk on the phone. Rashwane's father pretends to talk back to him (photo 4.13).

Rashawne has gained increased independence. He knew where the bowls were kept and was able to get them to enhance his play with the frogs. Rashawne engages in a lot of **imitative play** (watching others and copying actions immediately or at a later time)—making the frogs jump, talking on the phone. He is also able to represent one object with another symbolically (**symbolic play**)—using the bowl as a hat. He is at Erikson's second psychosocial stage of development, Autonomy versus Shame (see Table 4.1 on page 103). Rashawne is showing his growing autonomy by:

* making his own choices—play with the frogs, bowls, and telephone; involving his father in play
* solving his own problems—He needed support material for his frog play; he knew where the bowls were kept and fetched them.

✳ **Imitative play**

✳ **Symbolic play**

Photo 4.11

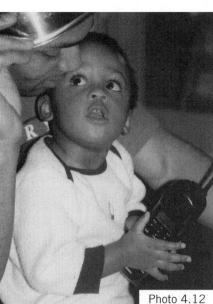

Photo 4.12

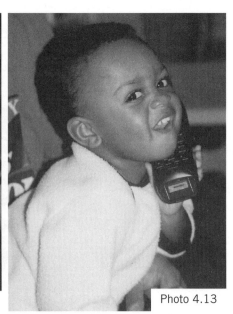

Photo 4.13

Rashawne's growing independence was nurtured in several ways. His parents have provided:

- a large open space in which Rashawne can play—He spread his bowls and frogs around the room. By providing a large, uncluttered space, it is safe for him to explore materials by dumping, spreading them out, and running to find other materials without danger of tripping over objects or running into furniture.
- accessible storage—The cupboards that contain safe materials for Rashawne to play with were within reach and left unlocked. Cupboards that contain materials that are potentially dangerous to Rashawne are kept locked.
- materials that are safe to use—The frogs are large enough to prevent choking if mouthed, and the bowls are not breakable.

In contrast, Toruk, who is at the same psychosocial stage of development as Rashawne, hears three children giggling and laughing as they each try on a hat. He quickly runs over to join them. He looks for a hat but cannot find one. Toruk spies a plastic bowl on the floor, quickly puts it on his head, and runs to join the children. Melanie, an early childhood educator, stops him and says, "This is a bowl. It is to put things in. Let's take it over to the sand area and put some sand in it." Toruk follows her and watches as she puts sand in the bowl. "Now it's your turn, would you like to try?" Toruk shakes his head and wanders back to the drama area. He watches the other toddlers play and again looks for a hat. When he can't find one, he runs to the cloakroom and brings back a hat. Melanie sees him and says, "That is not your hat, Toruk! It is John's hat. You will have to put it back." Toruk runs to the cloakroom and throws the hat on the floor. He then returns to the drama area and takes one of the other children's hats. Toruk is told that it is "not nice to take a friend's hat" and redirected to the quiet area to look at a book.

Toruk's caregivers are also concerned about safety issues in the centre. To provide a safe environment they:

- enforce rules—A bowl should be used appropriately. Toruk was guided to use the bowl correctly. When Melanie was asked why she reinforced this rule she said she thought Toruk might not be able to distinguish a breakable bowl from a nonbreakable bowl and would use the wrong bowl next time. If it fell and shattered, he could get hurt.
- protect children's health—Children are to wear only their own hats because of the danger of head lice. Play hats are plastic and are washed after every use.
- protect others—Toruk was redirected to the quiet area because he took someone's hat. Melanie was trying to prevent an outburst and possible hitting of other children.

Both adults were concerned with the safety of the children in their care. Rashawne was encouraged to be independent and responsible for his choices. The environment was set up to encourage him to look for his own resources (finding the bowls to support his play). His father supported his actions (symbolic play by wearing the bowl as a hat, imitative play with the bowl and the telephone).

Melanie was concerned with the safety of the toddlers (possibility of the bowl breaking, head lice). She tried to ensure Toruk's safety by controlling his actions. She told him to stop using the bowl as a hat and redirected his play when it became disruptive to the other children (taking another child's hat). Toruk is learning to comply with external rules rather than to solve problems by himself.

2. Developmentally Appropriate Experiences

Rashawne's learning experiences were developmentally appropriate for his age. His parents provided him with opportunities to:

- use realistic props—bowls were nonbreakable, shiny, and noisy (especially attractive to toddlers); a real telephone under supervision
- use materials in alternate ways—bowls used as a hiding place for the frogs and as a hat (encourages symbolic play)
- imitate behaviours previously seen—encouraging Rashawne to use the phone by pretending to talk to him on it, imitating Rashawne's actions by wearing the hat

Toruk's learning experiences were age appropriate. He was involved in:

- symbolic play—using the bowl as a hat
- imitative play—trying to imitate the other children's play with hats
- increased mental process—remembering where he could find a hat
- seeing the world from his own perspective—taking someone's hat (if I see it and I want it, I will take it)

However, Melanie's interactions were not developmentally appropriate for Toruk. She missed opportunities to:

- reinforce Toruk's learning—symbolic play, finding a hat
- reinforce Toruk's choice to become involved in imitative play with his peers
- model appropriate language—Her statement indicated that it was not nice to take something from a friend. What should have been stressed is that it is inappropriate to take someone else's toy away. By inference, children can conclude that it is permissible to take a toy from someone who isn't "my friend."
- provide real choices—Not enough hats were available for all the children to engage in play.

In summary, learning experiences and environments need to be carefully set up to safely reinforce toddlers' growing independence. To maximize autonomy, caregivers should:

- provide safe materials that are readily accessible and lock away hazardous materials
- provide enough materials for all toddlers to use—Toddlers see the world from their own perspective and are attracted to what goes on around them. By providing duplicate materials, negative behaviours such as grabbing or hitting can be avoided.

3. Emotional Security

Rashawne's actions were supported by his father. His father followed Rashawne's lead, wearing the bowl and talking on the telephone. He recognized Rashawne's need to be close to him when Rashawne wanted to sit on his lap. Rashawne gained emotional security by learning that:

- his actions and behaviours were appropriate and important—His father imitated his actions.
- he could solve his own problems—finding the bowls, using them in different ways
- he could successfully initiate activities—climbing on his father's lap, imitating his father on the telephone

Toruk, on the other hand, learned to follow someone else's directions. He learned that he needs to follow someone else's lead. He was not provided with an opportunity to gain self-confidence in his own actions or his ability to solve his own problems.

In summary, toddlers who are given opportunities to engage in developmentally appropriate learning activities in a safe physical environment will:

- increase their self-confidence in their own power to act
- initiate learning activities of choice
- learn to solve problems
- gradually learn to become more self-reliant (Figure 4.2)

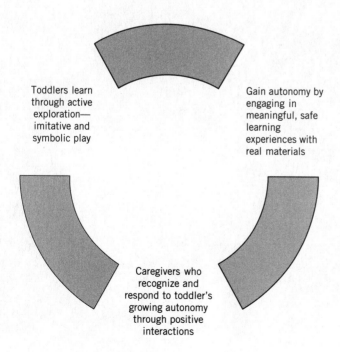

FIGURE 4.2

Toddler Development and Safety

Toddlers learn through active exploration—imitative and symbolic play

Gain autonomy by engaging in meaningful, safe learning experiences with real materials

Caregivers who recognize and respond to toddler's growing autonomy through positive interactions

Preschool Children

1. Physical Safety

Photo 4.14

Braelyn, a preschooler, has become fascinated with feelings. She is the first to notice when someone is upset or sad. She will immediately run to that individual and try to console him or her. One morning she discovers the book *Hot, Cold, Shy, Bold: Looking at Opposites* (Harris, 1995) and is fascinated by the various expressions on the children pictured in it. Braelyn decides to write her own book on feelings. She discusses her plan with Mandy, her early childhood teacher. With Mandy's help, Braelyn makes a list of items she will need (Figure 4.3). She decides she will cut out the cover herself (photo 4.14). She completes the cover, calling her book *Braelyn's Feelings*. This activity alone takes several days. Mandy takes pictures of Braelyn's face whenever she is asked to. The expressions in Braelyn's book include happy, happier, silly, mad, angry, frustrated, sticking out tongue, and sad (photo 4.15). She identifies this particular picture with "This is my sad face." The entire book-making process takes several weeks. When it is finished, a copy is made to send home with Braelyn and the original is placed in the preschool library.

Braelyn is at the third of Erikson's psychosocial stages of development, Initiative versus Guilt (see Table 4.1 on page 103). She has been provided with an opportunity to initiate activities that will direct her learning.

Jenna, who is at the same psychosocial stage of development as Braelyn, participates in a different preschool program, where she engages in a similar task. All the children

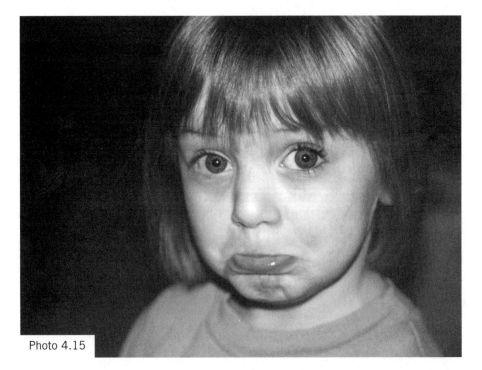

Photo 4.15

Mandy takes pictures of my face

White paper for the cover

Pink paper for the inside pages

Page protectors so it won't wreck

Paint to decorate the cover

Binder

FIGURE 4.3
Braelyn's Book List

in this program create Feelings Books. The books themselves are prepared for the children. All books are the same size and colour. The children decorate the covers of their books by using crayons, markers, and pencil crayons. When children arrive in the morning, they are asked to draw how they are feeling in their books. The caregiver then writes the feelings the child has expressed verbally in the book (Figure 4.4). If the child wishes, the caregiver will discuss the feeling with the child.

Braelyn gained many skills through her interactions with the learning environment and the individuals within that environment. She initiated skill development tasks such as cutting and decorating that gave her valuable practice in using fine motor skills (cutting on a line, colouring within a confined space) and transfer of skills (using different media such as crayons, pencil crayons, pastels, markers, and paint to decorate the

FIGURE 4.4
Feelings Book

cover of her book). She became more self-reliant as she worked on her project from start to finish—planning what to use and how to put it together, implementing her plan (putting the book and photos together), and cleaning up (cleaning surfaces and handwashing).

Braelyn's physical environment was set up to consider safety aspects and to accommodate her developing skills. She was able to use a variety of utensils of choice:

- scissors—The scissors she used were checked to ensure that they were sharp enough to cut. Braelyn and Mandy reviewed rules about how to use scissors appropriately (hold scissors by handles, put away when not using, don't point scissors at anyone). These rules, with appropriate pictures, were posted in the creative area.
- markers and paint—Washable paint and markers were used. This not only made it easier to wash Braelyn's clothing, but it also prevented dye from being absorbed through her skin.

Braelyn's safety was also enhanced by the following practices in the child-care centre:

- Children wash their hands when they become dirty.
- Children help clean up areas that become dirty through use of glue, paint, markers, or scarps.
- The learning environment is set up to encourage safe use of materials—a rack for scissors; baskets that can be carried to various places in the room for each of markers, crayons, and pencil crayons; painting areas set up at easels and at a table.

In contrast, Jenna's environment was set up to maximize cleanliness and physical safety. The children used crayons, markers, and pencil crayons because these are less messy, and in this way their books will remain neat. The staff feels that neatness is a skill children must learn when using books. The Feelings Books were prepared for the children because use of scissors is not encouraged. The staff feels that "good scissors" (scissors that cut) are too dangerous for little fingers and that plastic scissors do not cut as well.

Jenna worked in her Feelings Book over time. She added many drawings to her pages (Figure 4.4) and transferred some skills by copying what she had done in her Feeling Book to other settings (photo 4.16). Some of her behaviour was controlled externally. She could not experiment with various media to create her own book. Her "neatness" was a result of how the learning situation was set up (prepared book, limits on what could be used in the book).

Both experiences had a focus on learning. Braelyn was encouraged to take "initiative." She enjoyed the process of completing her book. She worked to create something of interest to her, sustained by her, and accomplished by her. Jenna also initiated some of her activity. She could repeat her activity in another setting. However, Jenna missed the opportunity to create something initiated by her, sustained by her, and accomplished by her.

Children can be creative within limiting tasks. As adults, we have great control over the actions of children. Adults can direct children to do almost anything. Children are very eager to please adults and will willingly engage in tasks and enjoy them. However, if one reflects on the experiences of Braelyn and Jenna, it becomes evident that for

Photo 4.16

children to develop and expand their skills to the maximum, they must be empowered to take charge of their own learning. In this way, they gain the self-confidence to:

- initiate and sustain efforts
- use their own creativity and talents
- persist in a task
- take pride in their accomplishments

2. Developmentally Appropriate Experiences

Braelyn's learning experiences were safe and developmentally appropriate. She had opportunities to:

- use materials that were at her developmental level—scissors, decorative materials
- work in an environment that nurtured her creativity and provided realistic choices—carrying needed items to where she wanted to work
- engage in experiences that were physically safe—washable colouring materials, scissors that cut, safety rules established, supervision provided

Jenna's learning experiences also were safe and developmentally appropriate. She had opportunities to:

- use materials that were at her developmental level—some decorative materials
- work in an environment that nurtured her creativity and transfer her skills from one area to another—copying her work at the easels
- engage in experiences that were physically safe—washable colouring materials, supervision provided

However, some of Jenna's experiences were not developmentally appropriate. She had limited opportunity to:

- explore her own creativity through a wide range of materials—limited creative materials
- make meaningful decisions about her work—Activity was pre-set, all children worked with same materials.
- control her own behaviour—Activity was adult-directed (what to use and when to do it).

In summary, preschool children will become empowered to initiate more learning activities if the environment provides developmentally appropriate materials, safe experiences, and opportunities to make realistic choices, and sustains learning activities over time.

3. Emotional Security

Braelyn's learning activity was initiated by her and sustained over time by her. Mandy facilitated the process by helping Braelyn as needed—developing her planning list (see Figure 4.3 on page 111), taking photographs of Braelyn, and adding Braelyn's book to the preschool library when it was finished. Through this learning experience, Braelyn satisfied her emotional needs to:

- make decisions about her own learning—develop a book about feelings
- work cooperatively with an adult—discuss and prepare the book together
- enjoy the opportunity to complete a project over time—Braelyn set her own pace and decided when her project was complete
- take pride in her accomplishment—Other children read her book and several decided to write their own books to put in the preschool library.
- become self-reliant—Braelyn made all decisions on what to put in her book, how to arrange it, and how to create it.

Jenna also had some of her emotional needs met. The adults in her environment set up the learning situation to ensure that the feelings expressed in the children's books were private. Children could share their work with their peers, but did not have to. The staff also acknowledged that children might not wish to share some of their feelings. Children did not have to discuss their feelings if they did not want to. Jenna could work over time and could initiate other related tasks. She took pride in her accomplishments. When she completed her "happy" picture, the staff took a photo of her accomplishment and hung it on the display board (photo 4.16).

In summary, preschool children will initiate more of their own learning when they are given opportunities to:

- engage in relevant tasks of their choice
- interact with adults and peers in relevant ways
- work in an environment that provides materials that are developmentally appropriate and safe to use
- interact with each other and adults within a respectful, nurturing environment (Figure 4.5)

FIGURE 4.5

Preschool Development and Safety

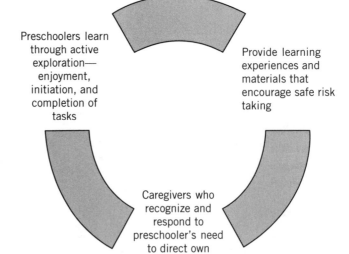

Preschoolers learn through active exploration—enjoyment, initiation, and completion of tasks

Provide learning experiences and materials that encourage safe risk taking

Caregivers who recognize and respond to preschooler's need to direct own learning within a secure environment

School-Age Children

1. Physical Safety

Stephanie has gained many skills that help her accomplish tasks. She can read, write, compute, and has much greater control and coordination of her motor skills. Stephanie uses a combination of her skills to spontaneously create scenarios that uplift her spirits and serve to nurture herself. She creates a large picture. Later, she sits down and writes a story about it (Figure 4.6). She asks Kaya to help her spell several words. When she is finished, she asks Kaya to take a photo of her with her poster (photo 4.17).

Photo 4.17

Stephanie is at Erikson's fourth psychosocial stage of development, Industry versus Inferiority (see Table 4.1 on page 103). During this stage, she develops greater skills in all domains and increased ability to think more abstractly. This leads to greater ability to work more independently and cooperatively. She begins to value and take pleasure in productive work.

Stephanie was able to move around the room to find the materials she needed for her creative effort. The arrangement of the environment helped her find materials readily. The room is divided into several learning areas and children can move around these areas to complete work as needed. Stephanie worked with markers at the drawing area, then moved to the writing area to complete her work. Safety was encouraged by providing a clear system of organization. This is especially important since there are a large number of people in Stephanie's program (32 children and 3 adults). Children need to access materials readily to keep the environment clean and tidy enough to continue to work in it.

In contrast, Jonathan, who is in the same psychosocial stage of development as Stephanie, is required to do a piece of creative writing every day. He has a writing book for this purpose. The book must be covered with blue construction paper, have a centred title—Creative Writing—and have his name in the bottom right corner. Jonathan must write so that all letters fit appropriately on the correct line. The title of each piece must be in the centre of the page and underlined twice. The date must appear on the second line in the upper right corner. If he does not complete his writing in class, he must finish it as homework. His teacher marks his work every day. Corrections are made with a red pen.

Jonathan must complete his creative writing at his desk. Children are given 15 minutes to write. His teacher has imposed the following rules to encourage the writing process:

- no talking—She has explained that talking interferes with the creative process and with thinking about what one is going to write.
- homework preparation—Children are encouraged to read books, magazines, and newspapers or to think about a topic they would like to write about before they return to class the following day.
- length—Each piece of writing should be a minimum of half a page and a maximum of one page.
- rewards—Good work will be read aloud to the class and receive a star.

FIGURE 4.6
Stephanie's Story

My Dream Poster

I wanted a dream poster for my room.

I wanted it to be a nice, sunny day with fluffy clouds in the air
and the water flowing and the grass growing to play in.

Jonathan has excellent verbal skills. However, he finds it very difficult to organize his thoughts on paper. He prefers to talk about things first to get ideas. He spends his 15 minutes chewing on a pencil, staring out the window, scratching his head, and slumping in his seat. He quickly closes his book and puts it in his desk when the 15 minutes are up. He has to be reminded to bring his book to the teacher for marking (Figure 4.7).

Safety for school-age children is more concerned with establishing rules for different settings and reinforcing these rules. Often rules are designed to help deal with

FIGURE 4.7
Samples of Jonathan's Writing

Sports You forgot to underline.

March 15, 1995
Date should be on the first line

I don't like sports!! Try to make your numbers
stay on the line!

You will have to complete this work at home.
You do not have enough detail. Write at least
six more sentences!

Sp

Sports make you swetty. Sports are
boring. Sports are stupid. I don't
see why I have to play sports! My
friend hates them too. I hate
writing about sports.

This is a poor effort. The writing is messy. You
have just strung sentences together.
You will need to improve your effort!!!

larger groups of children. The rules are in place to encourage appropriate behaviours. Jonathan had a set of rules imposed on him. These included:

- how much he needed to write
- how long he needed to write for
- how he was to behave while writing
- the consequences of not doing an adequate job

Jonathan often has to finish his writing in an after-school program. He grumbles and complains about having to do "this stupid work." He is often encouraged to try harder. Jonathan replies that he is no good at writing no matter how hard he tries.

In summary, school-age children understand and follow established rules (with occasional reminders). To encourage children to become more industrious, adults should:

- involve children in setting realistic rules
- involve children in monitoring their own behaviour

2. Developmentally Appropriate Experiences

Stephanie's learning activity was developmentally appropriate. She was encouraged to become more "industrious" by:

- providing appropriate time frames—Stephanie could monitor her own time to complete her picture and add more detail (writing her story) later.
- having materials set up to encourage interactions and choice—various interest areas, variety of materials within each area, free movement between areas to complete a task
- being given the freedom to choose what she wanted to accomplish—making her poster and writing about it

Jonathan's learning activity was not developmentally appropriate. The only choice he was given was what to write about. He could not interact with other children to make the process easier for him. He was tied to the resources within his own space (his desk). He had no interactions with adults to facilitate the process. The rules were set externally and actually interfered with Jonathan's creative process.

3. Emotional Security

Stephanie had a very positive experience. She received satisfaction from her creation (poster) through:

- positive interactions with Kaya—having her photo taken and posted on the bulletin board with her story, asking for and receiving help (photo, spelling) as needed
- personal satisfaction—completing a poster to hang in her room, completing a story to post, having her picture taken and posted

- reflecting on what she had accomplished—finishing her poster, writing a story to accompany her artwork

Jonathan continually had negative experiences. His work was always covered with red comments from his teacher. He never received a star for his efforts. His concerns were not listened to ("I'm no good at writing no matter how hard I try."); he was simply asked to try harder. Jonathan developed very poor self-esteem about his ability to write.

In summary, to become more industrious, children need opportunities to:

- work on something they enjoy doing
- have developmentally appropriate resources available to them
- establish rules that are developmentally appropriate
- work within realistic time frames to complete tasks
- work in an environment that encourages creative efforts
- work with adults who listen and respond appropriately
- work with adults who help facilitate appropriate problem-solving skills (Figure 4.8)

There is a close interconnection between safety and learning. Children of all ages need to have the security to work and play in environments that keep them safe physically and emotionally. Children will actively explore and learn through these explorations. It is common sense that children who interact in environments that cause them physical harm or ridicule their efforts will tend to avoid these circumstances. The cornerstone of all positive learning experiences is that they are safe and rewarding for all individuals involved.

Quality Care in Canada

The children discussed in the previous examples have had varying qualitative experiences. It was easy to see what changes needed to be made to give all of the children

FIGURE 4.8

School-Age Development and Safety

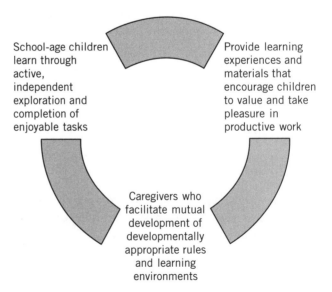

experiences of equal quality. These are obvious changes that are easy to implement. Less obvious are underlying factors that ensure quality growth and development. These factors include child to adult ratios, group size, caregiver qualifications and characteristics, quality programs, family involvement, and resources and referrals.

1. Child to Adult Ratios

The ability of adults to provide appropriate experiences for children is directly related to the number of infants under their care. This in turn directly influences the well-being of young children. The more children there are:

- the fewer the one-to-one interactions
- the harder it is to supervise children to keep them safe
- the more difficult it is to observe children's interactions
- the greater the amount of time spent in group situations with group control
- the more structured the program becomes
- the more uniform the creative expressions of children become

Adult to child ratios are determined by each province and territory in Canada (Table 4.2). These requirements vary greatly and are only minimum requirements necessary to protect the well-being of children. "Ideally, high quality child care programs provide one full-time teacher for every seven to eight children three to six years of age. Programs serving children with disabilities should have one teacher for every four to five children, depending on the age-group and severity of their limitations. If children younger than two years are included, the staff/child ratio should be no more than one full-time teacher per three to four children. A list of substitutes should be available in the event of teacher illness or other absence." (Marotz, Cross, & Rush, 2001: 164)

2. Group Size

Group size refers to the maximum number of children per age group for which a child-care centre may be licensed. Group size has been shown to influence the way children and caregivers behave. Children in larger groups tend to be more apathetic and are more easily upset. Children in smaller groups show more positive characteristics (Roopnarine & Johnson, 2000). Children in smaller groups:

- talk more
- are more involved in play activities, especially dramatic play
- are more creative
- are more cooperative

Group size also influences how caregivers behave. Studies on increases in group size (Roopnarine & Johnson, 2000) have shown that caregivers:

- are less sensitive to children's needs
- are more adult-directed
- are less likely to engage in social interactions
- provide fewer language stimulation activities

TABLE 4.2   ADULT TO CHILD RATIOS

Age Category	Age	Lowest Ratios	Highest Ratios
Infants	Birth to 18 months	1:3	1:5
	13 to 18 months	3:10	1:4
	13 to 24 months	1:4	
Toddlers	19 to 35 months	1:5	1:6
	18 months to 2 years	1:5	
	25 to 35 months	1:4	1:6
	Birth to 3 years	1:4	
	17 months to 5 years		1:7
Preschool children	17 months to 5 years	1:8	1:15
	4 to 5 years	1:8	1:10
School-age children	6 to 12 years	1:10	1:20
	57 to 84 months	1:12	
	84 to 144 months	1:15	
	5 to 11 years	1:10	

Large group sizes have an impact especially on the quality of the social, emotional, and language interactions within early childhood education programs. Any interaction pattern of poorer quality negatively influences the healthy growth and development of children. As a result, many jurisdictions throughout Canada have regulated the maximum group size for each age group for which a centre may be licensed. Maximum group sizes for:

- infants vary from 6 to 12
- toddlers vary from 8 to 15
- preschool children vary from 16 to 20
- school-age children vary from 20 to 30

However, some jurisdictions do not specify maximum groups sizes for any age group.

3. Caregiver Qualifications and Characteristics

"Recent brain research has found that the emotional tone of adult-child interactions was a strong predictor of certain biochemical reactions in the brain. For example, babies who were exposed to caregiving that was characterized as cold, distant and disorganized showed significantly elevated levels of cortisol which is associated with the 'dampening' of higher-brain functioning. The researchers concluded that 'these data strongly suggest that sensitive, responsive, secure caretaking plays an important role in buffering or blocking elevations in cortisol for infants and young children.'" (Goelman, Doherty, Lero, LaGrange, & Tougas, 2000: 4; Dunn, 1993)

It is clear that caregivers play a critical role in the healthy growth and development of young children. Many individuals who work with children already have some of the characteristics identified as critical—they are warm, nurturing, and responsive. However, research has shown that with specialized training in early childhood education, individuals gain the skills to meet all children's needs—social, emotional, language, cognitive, and physical—more adequately. According to numerous studies, training caregivers in early childhood education affects quality in the following ways (Goelman, Doherty, Lero, LaGrange, & Tougas, 2000; Dunn, 1993; McCain & Mustard, 1999):

- Caregivers are more likely to provide more sensitive caregiving.
- Caregivers are more likely to have specialized training (for example, infant and toddler training) and therefore are more responsive to children's needs.
- Caregivers engage in more social interactions with children.
- Caregivers provide more social stimulation.
- Caregivers provide less restrictive behaviour management techniques.

Additionally these studies also conclude that training in early childhood education is a predictor of:

- higher quality child care overall
- higher cognitive competence of children
- higher quality impacts on the learning environment

Requirements across Canada for qualified early childhood educators are inconsistent and in many cases do not meet even minimum standards. Training requirements vary from:

- no requirements—within daycare and **family day home** (care provided in a home by an individual with or without children of his or her own) settings
- minimal requirements—30 hours of professional development every 3 years, one orientation course in early childhood education (30 to 60 hours)
- maximum requirements—10 months and 500 hours of supervised work, 2-year diploma from a community college, approved degree
- post-diploma specialization—Some jurisdictions require specialization to work with children with special needs or with infants and toddlers.
- additional requirement—Usually at least one staff member with training must be assigned to each age group; program supervisors require diploma and experience; many jurisdictions require first aid and CPR training and a clear criminal reference check.

Family day home

4. Quality Programs

All quality programs for young children ensure that children learn through active play. Active play implies that children will explore the environment using all of their senses and interact with individuals within that learning environment. Quality programs should ensure that children's needs are met in all domains in both indoor and outdoor environments:

- cognitive—curiosity, spontaneity, construction, experimentation, manipulation, math and science concepts, reasoning, problem solving

- aesthetic—learning to appreciate beauty in nature and the arts
- social/emotional—developing positive feelings of self-worth and self-confidence, interacting with others, developing respect for others, developing social skills, emotional security, mental health
- language—vocabulary, conversations, reading, writing, communicating effectively, alternate forms of communication (Braille, signing, music)
- physical—nutrition, safety, skill development, health

Quality programs are based on three principles—development, implementation, and review. The development, implementation, and review processes of the program should involve interaction between all key individuals—staff, other professionals, families, and children—and should represent all we know about how children learn best. There are several tools on the market to help early childhood educators in this process.

1. Measure of Success (Elliott, 1995) is a rating scale that identifies various components of quality within programs for young children. The scale identifies the following areas of competence:

   - knowledge, interaction, and communication
   - curriculum—review, development, and implementation
   - preparation of the physical environment

2. Early Childhood Environmental Rating Scales. Harms, Clifford, and Cryer have developed a number of rating scales to help early childhood education programs move toward excellence. The scales are developed for various situations (Table 4.3):

   - Early Childhood Environment Rating Scale, Revised Edition (ECERS–R)—tool to identify quality components within preschool day-care settings (Harms, Clifford, & Cryer, 1998)
   - Infant/Toddler Environment Rating Scale (ITERS)—tool to identify quality components within infant and toddler environments (Harms, Cryer, & Clifford, 1990)
   - School-Age Care Environment Rating Scale (SACERS)—tool to identify quality components within school-age settings (Harms, Vineberg Jacobs, & White, 1996)
   - Family Day Care Scale (FDCS)—tool to identify quality components within family daycare settings (Harms & Clifford, 1989)

Many of the licensing requirements in Canada are based on minimum standards. These requirements often revolve around physical safety, mental health, and nutrition. "Quality cannot occur without the dimension of safety and basic care." (Goelman, Doherty, Lero, LaGrange, & Tougas, 2000: 4) However, this is only one aspect of care. "If the child care program is limited to this one dimension, which is often referred to as custodial care, it cannot be considered quality care." (Goelman, Doherty, Lero, LaGrange, & Tougas, 2000: 4) As a result, a number of jurisdictions in Canada have adopted the Harms, Clifford, and Cryer rating scales as part of their licensing and review procedures. It is but one attempt to improve the quality of child care in Canada.

TABLE 4.3   **COMPONENTS OF EARLY CHILDHOOD ENVIRONMENTAL RATING SCALES**

Setting	Components Measured
Infants/toddlers—ITERS	- Furnishings and display for children - Personal care and routines - Listening and talking - Learning activities - Interactions - Program structure - Adult needs
Preschool children—ECERC-R	- Space and furnishings - Personal care routines - Language and reasoning - Activities and interactions - Program structure - Parents and staff
School-age children—SACERS	- Space and furnishings - Health and safety - Activities - Interactions - Program structure - Staff development - Special needs supplementary items
Family day care—FDCRS	- Space and furnishings for care and learning - Basic care - Language and reasoning - Learning activities - Social development - Adult needs - Supplementary items: Provisions for exceptional children

5. Family Involvement

Family involvement is critical when providing services to children since families know their children best. Families have a vested interest in the care of their children and will continue to be the primary support for those children long after they leave the child–care centre. In addition, children need to be raised within an environment that has congruent expectations at home and within the daycare centre. Family involvement helps all partners (children, families, staff, and other professionals) become more knowledgeable about the care of children. To facilitate a smoother integration between home and daycare environments, many programs across Canada, such as the following, offer additional support to families:

- workshops—nutrition, health, breast-feeding, child guidance, immunization, child development, financial management
- periodic newsletters and pamphlets on special topics—special needs, health concerns such as head lice and impetigo, safety concerns such as sun safety, West Nile Virus protection, toy safety
- interaction with children within the program on a regular basis
- on-site services—checkup or consultation with nurse, dentist, speech and language specialist, resource consultant, social worker

These supports often include families, other professionals, and staff.

6. Resources and Referrals

Early childhood educators will encounter a variety of problems during interactions with children and families. It is impossible to be an expert in all areas. In fact, it is better to direct families to appropriate information sources or to refer them to other specialists when more serious problems are involved. Each child-care facility should be aware of the services and resources in their community, including:

- health-related services—health department, dental clinics, medical clinics, immunization clinics, pregnancy clinics
- nutrition-related services—dietitians, Canada Milk Board
- physical safety—fire department, police department
- social problems—social services, Children's Aid Society, community development councils, local politicians
- legal problems—Legal Aid Society
- subsidies—social services, subsidized housing agencies
- special needs—resource consultants, regional chapters for services for special needs children, speech and language clinics, physiotherapy clinics, National Institute for the Blind

SUMMARY

In summary, any learning environment for young children should:

- maximize all areas of development—social, emotional, cognitive, language, and physical

- optimize safe and healthy practices
- use developmentally appropriate practices
- provide high-quality services to all children and their families
- involve families as partners

KEY POINTS

Interconnection between safety and learning

- Ensuring physical, emotional, and nutritional health and well-being so children can gain the trust necessary to actively explore the learning environment

Infants

- Physical safety—develop trust that developmentally appropriate materials, environments, and learning experiences are safe to explore
- Developmentally appropriate experiences—explore materials that are safe to manipulate; exploration that is risk free, pleasurable, and develops infant's trust in his or her own abilities
- Emotional security—use of developmentally appropriate guidance techniques, respect of infant's efforts
- Response in timely fashion

Toddlers

- Physical safety—open play spaces, accessible storage, hazardous materials locked away or safely out of reach
- Developmentally appropriate experiences—realistic props, materials that can be used in alternate ways or encourage imitation of behaviours previously seen, duplicate materials available
- Emotional security—developmentally appropriate guidance techniques; opportunities to initiate activities, solve problems, and become more self-reliant

Preschool children

- Physical safety—materials provided are safe to use, establish and reinforce simple safety rules, encourage good health practices (handwashing, cleanup of environment)
- Developmentally appropriate experiences—materials that encourage sustained effort, realistic choices, physically safe experiences
- Emotional security—developmentally appropriate guidance techniques, opportunities to make decisions about own learning and take pride in accomplishments, increased opportunity to become more self-reliant, interaction with adults and peers in a respectful, nurturing environment

School-age children

- Physical safety—involvement in setting realistic rules and monitoring own behaviour
- Developmentally appropriate experiences—appropriate time frames to complete tasks, materials that encourage interactions, problem solving and choice
- Emotional security—personal satisfaction in work accomplished, self-reflection, solving own problems

Erikson's psychosocial stages of development

- Stage 1: Trust versus Mistrust
- Stage 2: Autonomy versus Shame
- Stage 3: Initiative versus Guilt
- Stage 4: Industry versus Inferiority

Quality care in Canada

- Adult to child ratios—large group size associated with fewer one-to-one interactions, harder to supervise and observe individual children, more emphasis on group control, more structured program and greater uniformity of children's efforts, variation in ratios across Canada
- Group size—influences how children behave (talk, play, creativity, cooperation), influences how adults behave (less interactive and sensitive, less stimulation, more adult-directed), variation in group size across Canada
- Caregiver qualifications and characteristics—characteristics (sensitive, responsive, warm, nurturing); qualified caregivers more likely to be sensitive, have specialized training, engage in social interactions, provide less restrictive guidance; qualifications are a predictor of higher quality overall, higher quality learning environment, higher cognitive competence in children; variation in qualifications across Canada

- Quality programs—provide active play; interaction of sound practices in safety, health, nutrition, learning
- Family involvement—congruency between home and daycare; support families through workshops, information sharing, interaction, on-site services, resources, referrals
- Resources and referrals—physical safety, social problems, legal aid, subsidies, special needs

EXERCISES

1. Observe two different environments—infants and toddlers, or toddlers and preschoolers, or preschoolers and school-age children. Compare safety aspects in the two environments observed. Use the chart provided below. Bring results to class to compare and discuss with other students.

CHART 1

Aspect	Age Group:	Age Group:
Physical safety		
Developmentally appropriate experiences		
Emotional security		

2. Explain why health, safety, and learning are essential considerations in developing a quality program for young children.

3. Using Erikson's psychosocial stages of development (see Table 4.1 on page 103), identify how each of the following changes with the age of the child:
   a) physical safety
   b) developmentally appropriate experiences
   c) emotional security

4. Jennifer, an infant, arrives at the child-care centre in the morning crying. Her mother seems very upset. When she puts Jennifer on the floor, Jennifer starts to scream. What can you do to offer emotional security to both mother and child?

5. Justin, a seven-year-old, walks with a limp. You notice that he is often involved with other boys in active play—floor hockey, football, soccer. He often seems to get hurt during these activities because he cannot move quickly enough to avoid accidents. What strategies might you use to minimize accidents in the future?

6. Olia, a toddler, sees Suchart, another toddler, playing in the sand with a bucket and shovel. She immediately

runs over and tries to grab the pail and shovel. Suchart hangs on to both, shouting, "Mine!" How would you handle this situation? Explain your strategies.

7. Explain how child to adult ratios affect the following:
   a) supervision of children
   b) interactions with children
   c) setting up learning activities

8. Consider the following two scenarios.
   a) You are responsible for 15 preschool children ages 3 to 5 years
   b) You and another early childhood educator are responsible for 16 preschool children.

   Reflect on these two situations. Identify the different strategies you would have to use to ensure the health and safety of the children in each group.

9. Group size seems to influence the behaviour of both children and adults. In a small group, discuss at least five reasons why you think larger group size leads to less overall quality in settings for young children. Explain your answers.

10. Explain why education is of critical importance for early childhood educators.

11. Obtain copies of two of the rating scales listed below. Identify the health and safety rating items in the two scales (see below). Evaluate two settings using the items selected. What differences did you find between the two age groups?
    ITERS—items 11, 13, 14, 29
    ECERS–R—items 13, 14, 30, 31
    SACERS—items 13, 14, 15, 31
    FDCRS—items 12, 13, 26

12. Attend a support service offered to families in your area (workshop, on-site service). Identify the overall effectiveness of your choice.

13. Using the chart provided, identify the resources in your area.

CHART 2

Resource	Description	Contact Name	Address/Phone Number

*Glossary

Developmentally appropriate (page 100) Activities, materials, experiences, interactions, and learning environments based on the abilities and developmental level of the child.

Erikson's psychosocial stages of development (page 102)
- Stage 1: Trust versus Mistrust—Infants gain a sense of whether the world is a safe place through positive interactions with caregivers, the environment, and materials.

- Stage 2: Autonomy versus Shame—As toddlers develop increased motor skills and mental capacities, they strive to gain autonomy.

- Stage 3: Initiative versus Guilt—As preschool children develop competence in motor, social, language, and cognitive skills, they start to initiate learning through experimentation, observation, imitation, and participation with peers and adults.

- Stage 4: Industry versus Inferiority—School-age children work more independently and cooperatively. They begin to value and take pleasure in productive work.

Family day homes (page 121) Care of children provided in a home by an individual with or without children of his or her own.

Imitative play (page 106) Play that involves watching others and copying actions immediately or at a later time.

Palmar grasp (page 104) Using the whole hand as a unit to pick up items

Symbolic play (page 106) Play that involves representing one object with another (for example, a bowl becomes a hat).

REFERENCES

Begly, S. (1997). How to build a baby's brain. *Newsweek, 28,* 28–32.

Crowther, I. (2003). *Creating effective learning environments.* Scarborough, ON: Nelson Thomson Learning.

Dunn, L. (1993). Proximal and distal features of the day care quality and children's development. *Early Childhood Research Quarterly, 8,* 167–192.

Elliott, B. (1995). *Measures of success: The educator in practice for those who care for young children.* Toronto: Association of Early Childhood Educators, Ontario.

Gestwicki, C. (2003). *Developmentally appropriate practices.* Second edition. Scarborough, ON: Nelson Canada.

Goelman, H., Doherty, G., Lero, D., LaGrange, A., & Tougas, J. (2000). *You bet I care! Caring and learning environments: Quality in child care centres across Canada.* Guelph, ON: Centre for Families, Work, and Well-Being, University of Guelph.

Harms, T., & Clifford, R. (1989). *Family day care rating scale.* New York: Teachers College Press.

Harms, T., Clifford, R., & Cryer, D. (1998). *Early childhood environment rating scale.* Revised edition. New York: Teachers College Press.

Harms, T., Cryer, D., & Clifford, R. (1990). *Infant/toddler environment rating scale.* New York: Teachers College Press.

Harms, T., Vineberg Jacobs, E., & White, D. (1996). *School-age care environment rating scale.* New York: Teachers College Press.

Harris, P. (1995). *Hot, Cold, Shy, Bold: Looking at Opposites.* Toronto: Kids Can Press.

Kieff, J., & Casbegue, R. (2000). *Playful learning and teaching: Integrating play in preschool and primary programs.* Needham Heights, MA: Allyn and Bacon.

Marotz, L., Cross, M., & Rush J. (2001). *Health, safety, and nutrition for the young child.* Albany, NY: Delmar Thomson Learning.

McCain, M., & Mustard, F. (1999). *Early years study final report.* Toronto: Publications Ontario.

Nash, M. (1997). Fertile minds. *Time, 149,* 48–56.

Roopnarine, J., & Johnson, J. (2000). *Approaches to early childhood education.* Toronto: Prentice-Hall of Canada Inc.

Schickedanz, J., Schickedanz, D., Forsyth, P., & Forsyth, G. (2001). *Understanding children and adolescents.* Fourth edition. Needham Heights, MA: Allyn & Bacon.

Shipley, D. (2002). *Empowering children*. Scarborough, ON: Nelson Thomson Learning.

Shondoff, J., & Phillips, D. (2001). *From neurons to neighborhoods: The science of early childhood development*. Washington, DC: National Academic Press.

Watson, L., Watson, M., Cam Wilson, L., & Crowther, I. (2000). *Infants and toddlers*. First Canadian edition. Scarborough, ON: Nelson Thomson Learning.

5 Nutrition Guidelines

CHAPTER

"Eating of course fuels children's physical growth. But it also helps them grow in other ways. Through food, your child will encounter the large world: She'll get more skilled at using her hands, mouth, and senses; learn to make choices; start to assert her independence; and learn to enjoy herself." (Dowshen, Izenberg, & Bass, 2001: 375)

Chapter Outcomes

After reading this chapter, the reader will:

1. Describe the importance of good nutrition for young children.

2. Describe how food attitudes are established in infants, toddlers, and preschool children.

3. Discuss how individual differences affect planning mealtimes for infants, toddlers, and preschool children.

4. Describe healthy eating habits for infants, toddlers, and preschool children.

5. Discuss how culture influences eating habits.

6. Describe how mealtimes can be established as pleasant experiences.

7. Describe routine health practices in the kitchen.

8. Describe routines for cooking.

9. Describe Canadian guidelines for healthy nutrition for:
   • infants
   • toddlers and preschool children

10. Describe food safety precautions that should be taken with:
    • infants
    • toddlers and preschool children

11. Describe individual differences in the eating habits of infants, toddlers, and preschool children.

12. Describe how food preparation can become part of a curriculum/program for young children.

The Importance of Good Nutrition

Good nutrition is a vital part of growing up. Young children are particularly in need of good nutrition because of the rapid growth of every part of their body and all their body systems. Children also need to learn to establish healthy eating habits just as they learn about other aspects of their lives, such as interacting with others and developing language. It is important that appropriate nutritional practices become part of all programs for young children in order to:

- provide children with the energy and essential nutrients they need to grow, develop, and be active
- provide opportunities for children to develop their sense of taste, acceptance, and enjoyment of different types of foods from a variety of cultural perspectives
- contribute to children's sense of well-being and feeling good about themselves
- provide opportunities for children to develop appropriate attitudes and practices that will form the basis for lifelong health-promoting eating and activity patterns (Office of Nutrition Policy and Promotion, 2002b)

Children whose meals follow Canada's Food Guide to Healthy Eating (Figure 5.1; Office of Nutrition Policy and Promotion, 2002b) are more likely to receive all of the vital minerals and vitamins they need. If children are eating well, growing normally, and are healthy, they should not need to take any vitamin or mineral supplements (Office of Nutrition Policy and Promotion, 2002a).

Shaping Healthy Habits

1. Early Development of Food Attitudes

At birth, an infant already has certain food preferences. Newborns have a highly developed sense of smell, and infants will recognize the scent of their mother's milk. "The well-developed sense of smell found in newborns, and their ability to learn quickly to recognize certain smells is seen in their rapid identification of their own mothers' milk and body." (Schickedanz, Schickedanz, Forsyth, & Forsyth, 2001: 99) Newborns prefer fluids that are sweet to those that are sour or bitter. They also prefer sweet water to plain water. "Newborns demonstrated these preferences by sucking less when offered fluids with sour or bitter and salty tastes, and sucking more when offered sweet tastes." (Schickedanz, Schickedanz, Forsyth, & Forsyth, 2001: 99) As infants grow and mature, more preferences are established. A one-month-old infant prefers milk with a vanilla flavour. At four months the infant prefers salty water to plain water. Additionally, a fussy infant will be soothed and calmed when given a sugar and water solution.

FIGURE 5.1

Canada's Food Guide to Healthy Eating

Health Canada   Santé Canada

CANADA'S

Food Guide

TO HEALTHY EATING
FOR PEOPLE FOUR YEARS
AND OVER

Enjoy a variety
of foods from each
group every day.

Choose lower-
fat foods
more often.

Grain Products
Choose whole grain
and enriched
products more often.

Vegetables and Fruit
Choose dark green and
orange vegetables and
orange fruit more often.

Milk Products
Choose lower-fat milk
products more often.

Meat and Alternatives
Choose leaner meats,
poultry and fish, as well
as dried peas, beans
and lentils more often.

Canada

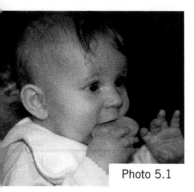

Photo 5.1

It is easy to see how, right from the start, we can influence a child's attitude toward food. Many parents are hesitant to give an infant sugar water but do not hesitate to give the infant a limited amount of fruit juice. This is a common practice in Canada. So, at a very early age, adults are already reinforcing and perhaps establishing new food preference patterns.

Infants usually start to eat solid foods between four and six months. At this point, a whole new set of experiences is presented to the infant. Prior to this, the infant has developed preferences mainly through smell and taste. Once the infant starts eating solid foods, new dimensions are added—colour, new flavours, and texture. At this stage, it is most important to watch the infant's signals to try to determine likes and dislikes (photo 5.1).

Suzanne and Jenna are discussing their experiences with their infants. Both mothers are still breast-feeding their six-month-olds but have recently introduced puréed vegetables to their children. Suzanne started with spinach, because she thought that spinach would have the greatest nutritional value for her daughter. She is disappointed that her daughter does not like the taste, making a face and promptly spitting it out. Jenna says that she started with carrots. She noticed that her son likes bright colours and picked carrots for that reason. Her son absolutely adores the taste. Suzanne says that she has tried more than once to feed spinach to her daughter, but now she won't even open her mouth to try it. Suzanne feels that she maybe should have switched to a new vegetable and is afraid that her daughter will not try a new vegetable at this point. Jenna urges Suzanne to try carrots with her daughter, and comments that it would be interesting to try spinach with her son to see if she gets the same reaction from him.

Jenna buys some fresh spinach on the way home to cook and try with her son, Jason. She carefully observes him as he takes his first taste. "How will you like this, my little man? This is spinach. Yummy!" Jason tries the first spoonful and makes a strange face, indicating that this is a new taste for him. He does not eat the spinach with the same gusto as he does carrots, but finishes what Jenna has prepared for him.

Suzanne worries all the way home. She buys some puréed carrots but is not sure whether to try them or to go back to the cereal her daughter, Samantha, has eaten before. She finally decides to try the carrots. As Suzanne offers the first spoonful, Samantha promptly turns her head away. Suzanne is ready to give up when her husband walks in. He assesses the situation and says, "Carrots, yum, yum!" He takes a spoonful of the carrots and smacks his lips. Next he offers Samantha some. She takes a tentative nibble and looks at her mother. Suzanne smiles at her and says, "Good." Samantha decides to try a few more spoonfuls.

These two experiences show:

- individual differences in food preferences
- how important the interactions between adults and children are
- how much interactions influence what a child may try to eat
- how individual values influence food choices

2. The Role of Daycare in Developing Food Attitudes

Children come to daycare with many food attitudes already in place. They already have definite ideas about food, some of them formed through actual experiences or by imitating behaviours they have observed. Children's attitudes about food include:

- likes and dislikes
- reluctance to try something new because they have heard that it is not good or because someone else told them that they did not like it or simply because they do not like the smell or the look of the food
- wanting to eat only one thing—Christopher, age three, likes bananas. He wants to eat no other fruit than bananas. After a few weeks of eating bananas, he suddenly decides that he likes green grapes better and now wants to eat only green grapes.
- wanting to drink only if they can pour their own cup
- eating certain foods only on certain days and not on others—Jamie: "Is today Monday?" Jane (teacher): "No, today is Thursday." Jamie: "Could you call Mom and see if it is Thursday there too? 'Cause on Monday I get to eat some raisins."

Toddlers and preschool children actively explore their environment and the materials in that environment. They are naturally curious and often involve their senses in exploration. Food is a natural part of this exploration. When children are encouraged to become involved in food exploration, they gain experience and learn about:

- which foods need to be cooked before eating
- how foods change when cooked
- how to prepare foods—peeling, cutting, boiling, baking, frying
- texture of food—mashed potatoes, mashed cooked vegetables, mashed fresh fruit; differences in texture of food before and after cooking
- the taste of new food—Children involved in preparation of food are much more likely to try new tastes.

Much of what a young child learns about the world is through imitation of behaviours seen or heard previously. It becomes critical for adults to model healthy eating habits, which include:

- providing a variety of foods and appropriate ways to eat them—finger foods; cutting your own meat with a knife; spreading your own butter onto bread; serving yourself with tongs, spoons, ladles, and serving forks; using culturally specific utensils such as rice bowls and chopsticks
- providing opportunities to examine and talk about food before eating—cutting open a vegetable to see what it looks like inside, opening a sandwich to see what is inside
- presenting foods from the four food groups to ensure that children receive the essential nutrients and energy
- providing opportunities to try foods from other cultures

- making mealtime a pleasant, relaxed time—allow children to make choices about how much they will eat and whether they will try a new food, provide ample time to eat (avoid rushing children through mealtime because of a schedule)
- providing appropriate modelling—how to use utensils, table manners, enthusiasm about various foods, discussion about colour, texture, and taste of food

3. Establishing Healthy Eating Habits

A) EARLY ESTABLISHMENT Healthy eating habits need to be established right from the start. Mealtimes should become associated with:

- a pleasant atmosphere—The following is a reflection of two adults about mealtimes as a child:

  - Adult One: "I can remember dreading suppertime. We all had to sit around the table. I had to remember so many rules—sit straight, both hands on the table, never put your elbows on the table, don't speak with a full mouth, don't wave your fork or knife or spoon around, don't cut your vegetables with a knife even if they are too hard to cut with a fork. I was both proud to be able to eat with adults and so afraid I would forget something. My mother served us and we were expected to eat what was on our plate. Failure to do so meant you got no dessert. I can remember several times that I had to leave the table because I had to vomit. As a grown-up, I made sure that mealtimes were fun, relaxing, pleasurable times. I am proud that my family enjoys our mealtimes together."

  - Adult Two: "Mealtimes were so much fun at our house. Both of my parents worked, so we all pitched in to help plan, shop for, and prepare meals. It was a fun time. We got to plan different kinds of meals, sometimes picking up odd-looking foods at the grocery store to try them. As we shared mealtime tasks, we discussed the highlights of our day. By the time the meal was on the table, we were usually laughing and joking. We all served ourselves. If something new was served, there were gentle hints that encouraged us to try it. Even today, family gatherings involve shared planning, preparation, and cooking."
- a time to develop independence—what I want to eat, how much I want to eat, what I might want to try
- developing respect—having my choices respected and acknowledged
- enjoyment—looking forward to social time with others

B) THE ROLE OF CHILD CARE Healthy eating habits start in infancy. If infants are breast-fed, child-care centres should provide an open, hospitable environment for mothers to come and nurse their infants during program hours, if possible. This is an opportunity to establish a pleasant interaction with the infant. A comfortable area should be established for feeding the infant (bottle-feeding or nursing). A comfortable adult-sized chair with a table beside it for storage of such things as the bottle, a receiving blanket, tissues (to wipe up spills or regurgitated milk), and a covered garbage can should be set up. The infant should always be held when bottle-feeding. This is a wonderful opportunity for the adult to relax and engage in one-to-one interactions with the infant. This sets up a pattern of pleasant mealtime experiences.

Toddlers and preschool children are very curious about the food they eat. They want to know why they need to eat something, where it comes from, and why you cook it, and will have many interesting perceptions to share. "Milk comes from a carton from a store. It does not come from a cow." "My teeth are fine, look," smiling and pointing to her teeth, "so why can't I have another cookie?" Children need to learn the basics of nutrition. They need to know what it is, learn about the various food groups, and learn the effects of healthy nutrition on their bodies. Some suggestions for promoting awareness of good nutrition include the following:

- Establish a snack area within the housekeeping area. Encourage children to help prepare their own snacks by cutting up soft fruit for a fruit salad or spreading peanut butter on a piece of bread or a cracker.
- Create a child-sized version of the Canada Food Guide and hang it near the meal area. Children can identify and discuss the food groups included at mealtimes.
- Plan meals with children. Focus on including items from the four food groups. In doing this, you can incorporate children's choices and increase their awareness of healthy eating habits.
- Invite visitors to speak about or go on field trips to understand food sources and how they are produced.
- Grow a vegetable/fruit garden with children so they gain an understanding of the process—planting, maintaining, harvesting, preparing to eat, and eating.

4. Cultural Dimensions

All children enjoy familiarity in their environment. Toddlers and preschoolers need to have security and structure in their lives that are consistent in their home and child-care environments. This extends to mealtime activities. "Most prefer meals and snacks on a regular basis on a regular schedule and in familiar surroundings. Many toddlers insist on having milk in a certain cup, their food cut in preferred shapes, or the same food for lunch over several days. New foods may be refused with the common refrain such as, I don't like it, or I've never tried it. As preschoolers get older, they tend to be more willing to try unfamiliar foods that are prepared and served in different ways." (Office of Nutrition Policy and Promotion, 2002b: 3)

Include family members in meal planning to ensure that there is continuity between the home and child-care environments. This also provides for opportunities to create menus that encompass a variety of cultural food experiences.

5. Making Mealtimes a Pleasant Experience

We are very influenced by what we see and what we smell. Food involves both of these senses. If a smell is not familiar, we tend to be suspicious of a food item. If food does not look appealing, we tend not to want to try it. So much depends on our experiences with foods. For example, milk has a definite, recognizable smell. We associate spoiled milk with a sour smell. Buttermilk has a sour smell, and many individuals will not try it because of its smell and the association of that smell.

Food presentation has a great deal to do with what we will try and how much we will eat. Many famous cooking schools around the world provide training in food presentation. If it looks attractive, most of us will want to try it. Children will also be more likely to try things that look attractive. When providing servings to children, some simple techniques can be used to encourage children to try new foods and to encourage dialogue. These include:

Photo 5.2

- serving vegetables in attractive patterns to encourage children to pick their own pieces and sometimes create their own patterns (photo 5.2)
- creating small points of interest on food, such as an interesting design on a bed of mashed potatoes (photo 5.3)
- serving fruit and vegetables attractively displayed in a colour wheel (photo 5.4)
- adding fun to meals by creating different food shapes to eat (photo 5.5)
- adding items to the table that children can use to garnish their own meals, such as tomato slices, green onions cut into small pieces, vegetable chunks or slices, vegetable rounds such as carrots and cucumbers, or fruit slices or rounds (photo 5.6)

Not only is food presentation important, but the table setting also needs careful consideration. The table should be an attractive place to eat. Some suggestions for a more aesthetically pleasing table setting include the following:

- Ensure that the table is clean.
- Provide placemats or a tablecloth (either commercially purchased or created by children and then laminated). Interesting seasonal shapes such as flowers, birds, or

Photo 5.3

Photo 5.4

Photo 5.5

rabbits in the spring can be scattered on the tablecloth. Placemats can be changed regularly to reflect seasonal changes. This gives children additional topics to talk about at mealtimes (photo 5.7)

•   Children can help with setting the table. This provides experience with counting and one-to-one correspondence.

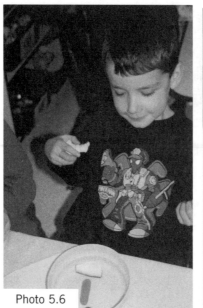

Photo 5.6

Photo 5.7

- Give thought to purchasing attractive dinnerware that is durable and attractive.
- Create centrepieces as points of interest. Children can help create these, or families often will bring in attractive centrepieces. For example, the children decided that the weather was warm enough to eat outside. One of the families had brought in a large flower. Samia thought that the flower would look great on the picnic table (photo 5.8). The children were disappointed when they realized that it was too big to be a centrepiece. Eventually they moved the picnic table under a tree and hung the flower from the tree. The children had great fun discussing the "giant flower growing in a tree."
- Create opportunities for more formal eating, such as around Thanksgiving or cultural occasions (photo 5.9)

Photo 5.8

Photo 5.9

Mealtimes are ideal times for development of children's skills. Children are able to practise skills, transfer skills from another situation, and apply skills in real settings. These skills include:

- increasing independence—setting the table, serving oneself, clearing the table, making choices about what to eat
- fine motor coordination—using utensils, spreading butter, pouring milk
- cognitive skills—one-to-one correspondence such as placing one plate on each placemat and one spoon beside each plate
- counting—how many plates are needed, how many peas to eat
- developing concepts about what we eat—beans are green or yellow, vegetables become soft when cooked, potatoes grow under the ground, egg whites become fluffy and stiff when whipped
- learning about new tastes and textures of food
- social skills—interacting in a small group around the meal table, learning about mealtime etiquette, taking turns serving oneself

Routines for Eating

Some routines about food and eating are important to reinforce with young children. These routines include good health, cooking, and personal hygiene practices.

1. Health Practices

Routine health practices are concerned with developing a clean and sanitized environment in which to cook and eat. Kitchens should be well removed from washrooms and have doorways that can be closed to protect wandering children from danger. Children should be in the kitchen only under close supervision. Common routines in the kitchen include the following (Shapiro Kendrick, Kaufman, & Messenger, 1995):

- All perishable foods should be kept in covered containers and in a refrigerator at a temperature below 4.4 degrees Celsius.
- Medication that needs refrigeration should be in containers with lids that prevent spillage.
- All non-perishable foods should be stored in labelled insect- and rodent-proof containers with tight lids.
- All cleaners and other poisonous substances should be stored in their original containers and out of reach in a locked cupboard.
- Any sharp objects such as cutting knives should be stored out of reach with child-safe locks.
- All dishes and eating utensils should be crack-free and washed in a commercial-grade dishwasher (which has higher temperatures to disinfect dishes) after every use.
- A fire extinguisher should be securely mounted on the wall.

- Good safety habits should be established—all staff knowing how to use the fire extinguisher, pot handles turned to the back of the stove, stable stepping stool to retrieve out-of-reach items, garbage kept well away from food preparation areas in containers with lids, regular disinfection of countertops.

2. Cooking Practices

Appropriate cooking practices help protect children from food contamination. Such practices include:

- washing hands before any food preparation
- preparing all food on clean surfaces that are free from cracks
- cleaning all vegetables and fruit with water prior to giving them to children
- serving hot foods at a temperature of 60 degrees Celsius or higher; lower temperatures will cause bacteria such as salmonella to multiply, which can lead to stomach upset or gastrointestinal disorders
- cleaning and disinfecting all counters and sinks immediately after preparing food

3. Personal Hygiene Practices

Personal hygiene practices encourage children to develop routines that will eventually become automatic. Children should:

- wash their hands thoroughly before and after eating
- brush teeth after eating

Canadian Guidelines for Healthy Infants

Infants' families bring the required food—bottles, cereal, and puréed foods—to daycare. Not until infants start to eat finger foods does the daycare begin providing some of the food for them. At that point, it is important to involve families in planning meals. The meals planned should be an extension of what the infant is used to and eats at home.

Infants should be encouraged to start to eat by themselves as soon as they are able. Infants should be encouraged to eat using a spoon or their fingers and to drink from a cup or their bottle independently. When infants are about one year old, foods from the four food groups should be introduced. "Safe finger foods include:

- bread crusts,
- dry toast,
- pieces of soft cooked vegetables and fruit,
- soft ripe fruit such as bananas,
- cooked meat and poultry, and
- cheese cubes." (Canadian Paediatric Society, Dietitians of Canada, & Health Canada, 1998: 29)

1. Infants and Food Safety

A) RISK FROM PATHOGENS The two major risks from pathogens to infants are infant botulism and salmonellosis, both of which are associated with food preparation. Infant botulism is caused by honey. Salmonellosis is caused by raw egg products. It is recommended that:

- infants under one year not be fed honey
- all eggs be well cooked and products containing eggs be avoided
- all surfaces used to prepare eggs be disinfected (Canadian Paediatric Society, Dietitians of Canada, & Health Canada, 1998)

B) UNSAFE FOODS "Hard, small and round, smooth and sticky foods can block a child's airways." (Canadian Paediatric Society, Dietitians of Canada, & Health Canada, 1998: 31) Foods that are not safe for infants include:

- popcorn
- hard candies
- gum
- cough drops
- raisins
- peanuts or other nuts
- sunflower seeds
- fish with bones
- peanut butter served alone
- snacks with toothpicks or skewers in them (Canadian Paediatric Society, Dietitians of Canada, & Health Canada, 1998)

Some infants may be allergic to milk. In this case, the infant will have an allergic reaction to the proteins in milk. The infant could develop a skin rash, hives, or gastrointestinal disturbances. As the child matures and starts to eat different foods, additional allergies such as milk food allergies (cheese, butter, milk, yogurt, cream, ice cream), soy protein allergies (soy is contained in many commercially prepared foods such as vegetable broth, vegetable shortening, and various soy products), egg allergies, or peanut or nut allergies may start to develop. Food allergies are usually identified prior to a child entering a daycare situation. Foods that the child is allergic to should be avoided. Prior to using any foods, labels should be read carefully. In some cases, if the allergy is severe and there is a danger of anaphylactic shock, the food or any food products containing that food should be avoided within the daycare setting.

2. Safety Recommendations

When feeding infants, some general safety recommendations should be followed at all times:

- Ensure safe food preparation (Table 5.1).
- Never leave an infant with a propped-up bottle (choking hazard).

TABLE 5.1 SAFE FOODS

Food	Preparation
Wieners	Diced or cut lengthways
Carrots	Grated
Hard fruit such as apples	Grated
Fruit	Remove pits
Grapes	Chopped
Peanut butter	Spread thinly on crackers or bread

- Always supervise infants while they are eating.
- Check for allergies and avoid foods containing these products.

3. Infants and Individual Differences

Infants tend to have individual eating schedules. As they get older and start to eat solid foods, these schedules gradually become more similar and more regular. Individual differences also are noted in:

- how often infants are fed
- how much they eat at a time
- food preference
- when they start eating solid foods
- types of food they are used to (cultural differences)

Individual differences should be noted and care should be taken to respect individual schedules and to avoid foods the child actively dislikes. Family members can help by indicating the types of foods the child is eating at home. Preparing some culturally different food for all infants provides opportunities for infants to try different foods and ensures a smoother transition from home to the daycare setting for all infants.

Canadian Guidelines for Healthy Toddlers and Preschool Children

Healthy development demands that children follow a healthy diet. Foods should be chosen carefully to meet the children's needs for energy and healthy growth and development. Foods should include choices from all four food groups (Figure 5.2; Office of Nutrition Policy and Promotion, 2002a):

- grain products—5 to 12 serving per day
- vegetables and fruit—5 to 10 servings per day

FIGURE 5.2

Number of Servings per Day

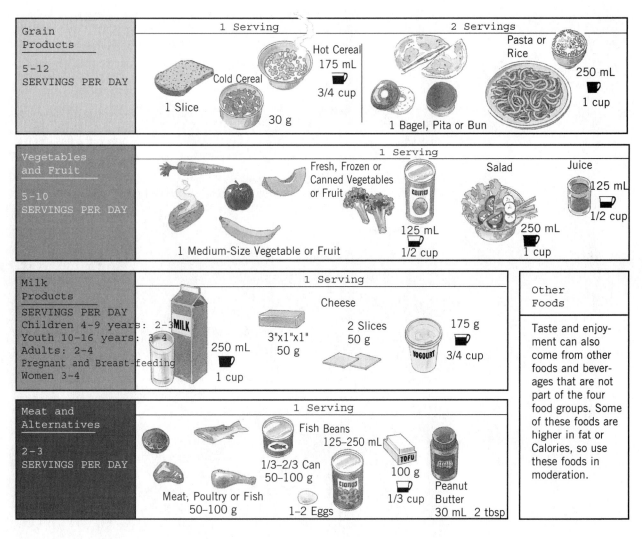

Source: Office of Nutrition Policy and Promotion (2002a).

- milk products—2 to 3 servings per day; 2 cups or 500 ml of milk per day (good source of vitamin D)
- meat and alternatives—2 to 3 servings per day

1. Individual Differences

The amount of food eaten by children varies not only with age but also between children. Some children have better appetites than others. Some children are more active and seem to require more nourishment. "Generally the size of portion increases with age.

For example, a two-year-old may eat a half a slice of bread, whereas a four-year-old is more likely to eat a whole slice of bread. Both can be counted as one child-sized serving of Grain Products." (Office of Nutrition Policy and Promotion, 2002b: 10)

Table 5.2 lists some examples of serving sizes.

Toddlers and preschoolers have developed much more extensive food preferences. This age group is very susceptible to the modelling they are exposed to. They will imitate behaviours they have seen or heard. As a result, it may be much more difficult to encourage children to eat greater varieties of foods because of exposure to:

- eating habits from home—cultural differences, family choices
- poverty—inability to afford healthy foods
- modelling of others—individuals of significant influence such as friends or family members who are observed eating less healthy foods or have expressed strong opinions about certain foods
- television—constant bombardment with advertising for less healthy foods (fast food, snack foods)
- lifestyles—families encouraging children to eat less healthy foods (fast food, snack foods)

TABLE 5.2   SAMPLE SERVING SIZES

Grain products	1/2 to 1 slice of bread 15 to 30 g cold cereal 75 to 175 ml (1/3 to 3/4 cup) hot cereal 1/4 to 1/2 bagel, pita, or bun 1/2 to 1 muffin 50 to 125 ml (1/4 to 1/2 cup) pasta or rice 4 to 8 soda crackers
Vegetables and fruit	1/2 to 1 medium-sized vegetable or fruit 50 to 125 ml (1/4 to 1/2 cup) fresh, frozen, or canned vegetables or fruit 125 to 250 ml (1/2 to 1 cup) salad 50 to 125 ml (1/4 to 1/2 cup) juice
Milk products	25 to 50 g cheese 75 to 175 g (1/3 to 3/4 cup) yogourt Preschool children should consume a total of 500 ml (2 cups) of milk every day
Meat and alternatives	25 to 50 g meat, fish, or poultry 1 egg 50 to 125 ml (1/4 to 1/2 cup) beans 50 to 100g (1/4 to 1/3 cup) tofu 15 to 30 ml (1 to 2 tbsp) peanut butter

Source: Office of Nutrition Policy and Promotion (2002b: 11).

2. Encouraging Children to Try New or Different Foods

Many people are hesitant to try new foods, especially if something about the food (texture, colour, smell) is not appealing to that individual. Children may be particularly hesitant to try new foods and need to be encouraged to do so. Some strategies that might be used follow.

1. Children are influenced by the significant adults in their lives. Caregivers are therefore in an ideal position to encourage children to try new foods by being models. Caregivers need to sit with children during mealtimes. Discussions about the texture or taste of new foods and encouraging children to express opinions about taste are effective ways to motivate children to try a variety of different foods.

2. Food presentation is an important factor. If food looks attractive, is presented in an attractive manner, and is served in appropriate quantities, children are much more likely to eat it. Vary food offerings by providing different textures, colours, and shapes. For example, offer sandwiches in different shapes (circular, triangular, rectangular, square) and garnish these to create excitement.

3. Involve children in meal planning, shopping, and preparation. Encourage children to help in food preparation by asking them to create their own sandwiches or salads from choices provided (photo 5.10).

4. Introduce new foods one at a time. Too many new foods may cause children to become overwhelmed. As a result, they may not want to try anything.

Photo 5.10

5. Caregivers should not give up if some children will not try new foods the first time they are introduced. New foods should be introduced several times in different contexts—for example, raw fruit, the same fruit cooked, the same fruit in a milkshake, and the same fruit decorating a dessert.

6. It is critical that food is never used as a reward or punishment. For example, a child's cleanup efforts should not be rewarded with a cookie, or dessert should not be withheld because a child did not try a new food. Food is a necessity and should be treated as such.

3. Food Safety

Toddlers and preschoolers still have difficulty with certain foods that can present a choking hazard (see Table 5.1 on page 144). Children in this age range often eat too quickly and do not chew their food enough. As a result, large chunks could be swallowed, which can cause airway obstruction. Children should be supervised while eating, and appropriate chewing should be modelled and reinforced periodically.

Food allergies should be recorded and these problem foods should either be avoided for an individual child or, depending on the severity of the allergy, be eliminated from the environment altogether. Eight types of food are accountable for 90 percent of all food-allergic reactions. The foods that most commonly cause anaphylaxis (called *allergenic foods*) are:

- peanuts
- tree nuts (walnuts, pecans, etc.)
- shellfish
- fish
- milk
- soy
- wheat
- eggs (DEY, 2003: 1)

If the child-care environment needs to be free of a product such as nuts, this information must be posted at all entrances. All families and visitors must be informed of the situation (Figure 5.3).

FIGURE 5.3

Allergy Alert

> The .... room has a child with a severe allergy to ....
>
> This situation is **life threatening**. Please observe the following precautions:
>
> 1. Do not bring in any food items that contain .... products.
>
> 2. Check ingredients of food products before preparing special treats for children.
>
> 3. Do not enter the room if you have used a sap or shampoo containing ....
> products.
>
> 4. Children who have had .... before coming to daycare will not be admitted.
>
> Thank you for your help.

Sample Menu Plans

Menu planning can be a fun activity for everyone. Children can help create menus. Start by brainstorming different things children like for various meals (Figure 5.4).

When adults use a planning guide that incorporates food groups, it is easier to ensure that all food groups are being represented each day. It is also easy to slip in children's choices. Including children in the planning process has the following advantages:

- children become more aware of the various types of foods they should be eating
- children become skilled at picking appropriate foods—The children that planned the menus in Figure 5.5 had been doing so once a week as a regular part of their program, usually in small groups and based on interest in this activity. A child's pictorial version of Canada's Food Guide was used to facilitate appropriate choices.
- children are more likely to eat food when they are given choices and involved in the planning process

---

What we want to eat for breakfast

Jimmy—blueberry muffins, maybe three times

Josh—cornflakes

Ben—Cheerios

Leah—hard-boiled egg, but only on Monday and Friday

Yannis—red grapefruit every day

Bakang—bananas every day

Mohammed—toast and peanut butter on two days

We would like milk or orange juice this week.

What we want for snacks

Crackers and cheese every day 'cause some of us don't want fruit every day

Grapes, apples, oranges—all of them on Monday and Tuesday and Friday

Fruit salad with yogourt—two days

Drinks—water or orange juice

Vegetables and dips in the afternoon—carrot sticks, celery sticks, and broccoli

Meat skewers

What we want for lunch

Meat loaf

Chicken

Spaghetti and meatballs

Fish sticks

Chicken vegetable soup that we will help make

Vegetables—you can pick what goes with stuff

Note: This program offers breakfast to children.

FIGURE 5.4

Children's Food Brainstorming List

FIGURE 5.5   **Sample Menus Based on Children's Planning and Providing Choices at Each Meal**

Breakfast

Food Groups	Monday	Tuesday	Wednesday	Thursday	Friday
Grain products	Blueberry muffins Cornflakes or Cheerios	Toast and peanut butter Cornflakes or Cheerios	Blueberry muffins Cornflakes or Cheerios	Toast and peanut butter Cornflakes or Cheerios	Blueberry muffins Cornflakes or Cheerios
Vegetables and fruits	Red grapefruit pieces Banana slices Orange juice	Red grapefruit pieces Banana slices Orange juice	Red grapefruit pieces Banana slices Orange juice	Red grapefruit pieces Banana slices Orange juice	Red grapefruit pieces Banana slices Orange juice
Milk products	Milk Hard-boiled egg	Milk	Milk	Milk	Milk Hard-boiled egg

Morning Snack

Food Groups	Monday	Tuesday	Wednesday	Thursday	Friday
Grain products	Crackers and cheese	Crackers and cheese	Crackers and cheese	Crackers and cheese	Crackers and cheese
Vegetables and fruits	Grapes, apples, or oranges Water Orange juice	Grapes, apples, or oranges Water Orange juice	Fruit salad Water Orange juice	Fruit salad Water Orange juice	Grapes, apples, or Orange Water Orange juice
Milk products			Yogourt	Yogourt	

FIGURE 5.5   Continued

Lunch	Monday	Tuesday	Wednesday	Thursday	Friday
Grain products	Small dinner roll	Small dinner roll	Small dinner roll	Small dinner roll	Small dinner roll
Vegetables and fruits	Mashed potatoes Peas or green beans	Boiled potatoes Salad (which children make) Salad dressing	Baked potato Corn or broccoli	Spaghetti Peas or green beans	Rice or mashed potatoes Salad (which children make) Salad dressing
Milk products	Milk Water	Milk Water	Milk Water	Milk Water	Milk Water
Meat and alternatives	Baked chicken	Meat loaf	Chicken vegetable soup	Meatballs	Fish sticks

Dessert—Different JELL-O Jigglers each day

Afternoon Snack

Food Groups	Monday	Tuesday	Wednesday	Thursday	Friday
Grain products	Crackers		Crackers		Crackers
Vegetables and fruits		Carrot or celery sticks Orange juice Water		Carrot or celery sticks Orange juice Water	
Milk products		Sour cream and onion dip		Sour cream and onion dip	
Meat and alternatives	Hot dog Kebabs		Chicken cold cuts Kebabs		Hot dog Kebabs

Sample Cooking Activities for Children

Many cooking activities involve an adult doing most of the work while children take turns pouring or stirring. It is much more motivating when children can make a recipe from start to finish. When children are encouraged to do more of the cooking by themselves, a number of skills are developed. Cooking activities:

- reinforce appropriate routines—cleaning surface before you prepare food, washing hands before handling food, wearing an apron, tying back hair
- reinforce appropriate safety habits—using a knife correctly, learning how to cut, using new tools such as a cutting board
- develop skills—fine motor control, coordination of activities (cutting and holding), independence
- develop children's self-confidence in ability to do things by themselves
- develop pride in accomplishment

The following are a few suggestions of cooking activities children can do by themselves with minimal adult involvement.

1. Salad

Adults should cut harder vegetables such as carrots, celery, or cucumbers into appropriate-sized pieces. These could be placed into small bowls or arranged on a larger platter and set out on the table. Children can:

- separate the lettuce leaves
- wash and dry the leaves
- shred the leaves into a large bowl
- serve themselves from the choices at the table—lettuce and vegetable choices

2. Fruit Salad

Adults should cut harder pieces of fruit such as apples, remove pits from fruit, and place into individual bowls. Children can:

- peel fruit such as oranges or mandarins (you may have to start to peel the fruit)
- cut fruit such as bananas, orange slices, peaches, or other soft fruit and place into individual bowls
- create own combination of fruit salad in individual bowls
- add toppings such as pudding, yogourt, or JELL-O cubes

3. Innovative Snacks

A) STUFFED CELERY STICKS Adults cut celery into appropriate-sized chunks. Children spread peanut butter or light cream cheese into the groove of the celery chunks. Add raisins or chopped green onions to the top ("flies on a log" or "frogs on a log").

B) FUNNY FACE SANDWICH Adults put ingredients into small bowls around the table. Children can create their own sandwiches by:

- spreading a thin layer of peanut butter (choose an easy-to-spread type), Miracle Whip, butter, or mayonnaise on a piece of bread (help may be needed with the peanut butter)
- adding eyes and nose with fruit or vegetable rounds (banana, tomato, cucumber)
- adding mouth with slivers of carrots, green onions, or tomato
- adding hair with sprouts (bean, onion, watercress)

C) SHAPED SNACKS Children can add toppings to small different-shaped slices of bread or crackers. They match the appropriate-sized slice of cheese or cold cut to bread or a cracker and then garnish with olive slices, green onion pieces, and other small pieces of vegetables.

Learning Activities to Reflect Nutrition

There are numerous ways that nutrition can become part of the program within the daycare setting. Children need to transfer knowledge from one setting to another. When children read about foods, sort food groups into categories, and then use fruits and vegetables to prepare a snack, the learning becomes reinforced and is more likely to be remembered. Table 5.3 provides some suggestions of such learning activities.

TABLE 5.3 LEARNING ACTIVITIES AND NUTRITION

Activity	Description of Activities
Books	**Cooking books** for children with pictures and instructions that are easy to follow. Examples: Oetker, Dr. (1993). *Let's cook*. Toronto: Canadian Manda Group. Robins, D., & Stowell, C. (1994). *The kids' around the world cookbook*. New York: Kingfisher. **Books about food** with descriptions of how food grows or details about its appearance. Examples: Mettler, R., Bourgoing, P, & Jeunesse, G. (1990). *The egg*. London, England: Moonlight Publishing Ltd. Valat, P., Jeunesse, G., & Bourgoing, P. (1990). *Fruit*. London, England: Moonlight Publishing Limited. **Storybooks** Davis, A., & Petričić, D. (1998). *The enormous potato*. Toronto: Kids Can Press. Palazzo-Craig, J., & Nagano, M. (2001). *The magic peach: A story from Japan*. New York: Troll. Rattigan, J., & Hsu Flanders, L. (1993). *Dumpling soup*. Boston: Little, Brown and Company.

TABLE 5.3 LEARNING ACTIVITIES AND NUTRITION

Activity	Description of Activities
Web site resources	Cooking with Young Children, http://members.aol.com/sgrmagnlia/ Cooking with Children Can Be Easy, http://members.aol.com/amcpr2000/cooking.html Cooking for Children, http://dmoz.org/Home/Cooking/For_Children/ Cooking with Children: Kids in the Kitchen, http://www.nncc.org/Curriculum/fc46_cook.kids.html Cooking with Kids, http://www.childrensrecipes.com/
Music	Raffi. (1980). "Biscuits in the Oven." *Raffi*. Willowdale: Baby Beluga/MCA Music Entertainment Ltd. Raffi. (1980). "Oats and Beans and Barley." *Raffi*. Willowdale: Baby Beluga/MCA Music Entertainment Ltd. McMillan, B., & Raffi. (1989). *Everything grows*. New York: Crown Publishers, Inc.
Water/sand	Provide practice in skill development by pouring liquids and sand, measuring, and creating mixtures Provide measuring cups, moulds, funnels, whisks, spoons, scoops, small pitchers, and containers for pouring into Pretend garden—plant, irrigate, water
Housekeeping/drama area	Create own playdough (see recipe in Figure 5.6) Provide opportunities to pretend cook—use realistic objects such as playdough that can be shaped into foods and cut Provide water for pouring Set up store with nutritious foods on sale
Writing	Encourage children to create and write recipes (Figure 5.7) Dictionary cards—pictures of food with words printed beside them Children create own books about good food
Manipulatives	Puzzles—fruits, vegetables Matching games such as matching similar foods Sorting games such as sorting by fruits or vegetables
Gardens	Grow vegetables such as lettuce, carrots, squash, peas, and beans, and fruit such as strawberries and raspberries. Plant long-term items such as fruit trees or grape bushes (these have an added advantage in that they provide shaded areas)
Resources	Web site resources Dairy Farmers of Ontario, http://www.milk.org/ A Nutrition and Hygiene Pathfinder for K–8th Grade, http://www.northlakecollege.edu/nlcl/kids/pathfinders/nutrition.htm Healthy Eating Strategy for Island Children and Youth, http://www.gov.pe.ca/photos/original/hss_hea_2002.pdf

Ingredients

1 cup	Flour
1/4 cup	Salt
1/4 to 1/2 cup	Water
	Food colouring or drink crystals

Instructions

Draw outlines of measuring cups:

- 1/4 cup and place on a mat
- 1/4 cup and place on a second mat
- 1 cup and place on another mat

Have one eyedropper per container of food colouring, or one measuring spoon per separate bowl of drink crystals.

FIGURE 5.6

Recipe for Playdough

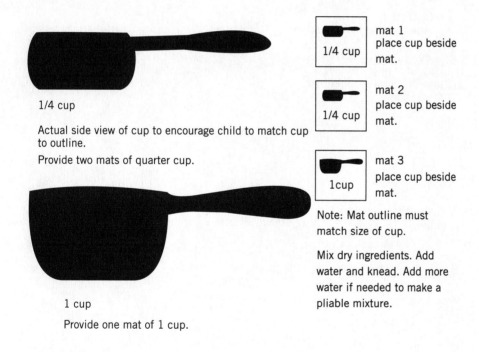

1/4 cup

Actual side view of cup to encourage child to match cup to outline.

Provide two mats of quarter cup.

1 cup

Provide one mat of 1 cup.

mat 1
place cup beside mat.
1/4 cup

mat 2
place cup beside mat.
1/4 cup

mat 3
place cup beside mat.
1cup

Note: Mat outline must match size of cup.

Mix dry ingredients. Add water and knead. Add more water if needed to make a pliable mixture.

Place mixing spoons and mixing bowls on the table.

Place four mats on a table with ingredients—flour, salt, water, food colouring or drink crystals—placed in separate bowls or containers on each mat with the measuring cups

Initially children will want to pour everything. Adults need to ensure that the quantities placed on the table require measuring but are not too large if dumped out by children.

Some valuable experiences are gained. Children can problem-solve:

- what to do if mixture is too dry
- what to do if mixture is too wet
- how to get more intense colours
- how to follow a recipe

FIGURE 5.7

Stephanie's Recipe

My Fruit Salad

5 pieces of apple

1/2 of a banana cut into round circles

2 strawberries cut in half

5 peanuts

3 spoonfuls of strawberry yogourt

Mix it all up and eat it.

Making Fruit Salad

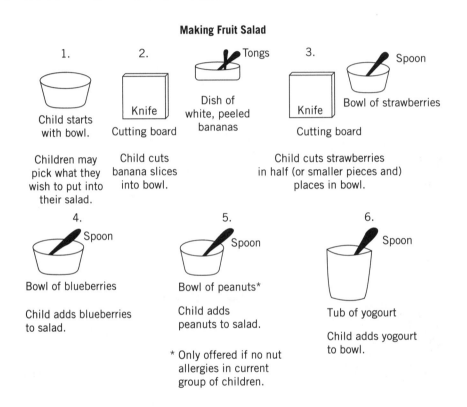

1.

Child starts with bowl.

Children may pick what they wish to put into their salad.

2.

Knife   Cutting board

Child cuts banana slices into bowl.

Tongs

Dish of white, peeled bananas

3.

Knife   Cutting board

Spoon

Bowl of strawberries

Child cuts strawberries in half (or smaller pieces and) places in bowl.

4.

Spoon

Bowl of blueberries

Child adds blueberries to salad.

5.

Spoon

Bowl of peanuts*

Child adds peanuts to salad.

* Only offered if no nut allergies in current group of children.

6.

Spoon

Tub of yogourt

Child adds yogourt to bowl.

SUMMARY

Appropriate nutrition is a cornerstone of healthy growth and development. Child-care settings play a key role in providing:

- nutritious food from each of the food groups, following Canada's Food Guide to Healthy Eating
- opportunities to develop appropriate attitudes toward food
- opportunities to establish healthy eating habits
- age-appropriate learning activities about types and health-related values of different foods
- an atmosphere that respects children's individual food tastes and aesthetic appreciation

KEY POINTS

Importance of nutrition

- Provide energy and nutrition
- Develop sense of taste and preference
- Contribute to well-being
- Develop appropriate attitudes

Food attitudes

- Newborns prefer sweet liquids and mother's milk
- Individual differences
- Importance of interactions about food
- Interactions influence what child will eat
- Individual values influence choices of food
- Smell and appearance of food
- Behaviour of child, such as wanting to eat only one thing
- Children need to learn about food—preparation, taste
- Modelling—eating variety of foods, talking about food, examining food, how to eat, pleasant mealtimes

Healthy eating habits

- Pleasant atmosphere
- Develop independence
- Respect choices
- Create enjoyment around mealtime
- Learn about foods—kitchen part of housekeeping area, child-sized version of Canada's Food Guide, children help plan meals, visit food sources, invite "food experts" to talk to children, grow vegetable/fruit garden

Cultural aspects

- Need representation of cultural aspects of eating—various foods, eating utensils
- Include families in planning meals

Making mealtimes pleasant experiences

- Present food in attractive ways
- Have attractive table settings
- Use mealtime as opportunity to develop new skills

Healthy practices

- Clean, sanitary environment
- Kitchen routines—perishable foods refrigerated, mediation in closed containers in fridge, non-perishable foods in labelled closed containers, toxic and sharp materials out of reach, eating utensils in good repair, fire extinguisher available, good safety habits used by staff

Cooking routines

- Handwashing
- Disinfecting surfaces
- Heating foods appropriately to prevent spread of bacteria

Canadian guidelines for healthy infants

- Involve families in meal planning when child starts to eat finger foods
- Food safety—risk of botulism (no honey under one year of age), salmonellosis (cook egg and egg products well)
- Unsafe foods—small, round, sticky, and smooth foods are choking hazard, food allergies
- Safe food preparation—cut into small pieces, grate, remove pits, spread sticky substances thinly
- Individual differences—how often and how much infants eat, when they eat, what they like, when they start solid foods

Canadian guidelines for infants and toddlers

- Eat from four food groups every day—grains, vegetables and fruits, milk and milk products, meat alternatives
- Individual differences—amount of food eaten, type of food eaten, financial means of family to provide adequate nutrition, influences on eating habits (friends, family, media)
- Encourage children to try new foods—modelling, food presentation, children involved in planning and

preparation, introducing new foods slowly and one at a time; never use food as reward or punishment

- Food safety—children need to learn to chew properly; dice, chop, or grate smooth, slippery, hard, or round foods; avoid foods to which children are allergic and if severe allergy exists, create environment free of that food
- Planning weekly menus—include children so they become more aware of different foods, become more skilled at picking out new foods, and are more likely to try them
- Sample cooking experiences with children—children need to be fully involved, such as by creating their own salads or snacks

Learning activities to reflect nutrition

- Books—recipe books, books about food products, Web site resources, stories about food
- Music—songs about food
- Water/sand—skill development through measuring, moulding, and pouring; planting vegetables
- Housekeeping/drama area—create own playdough, create dramatic situations such as a store
- Writing—dictionary cards, stories
- Manipulatives—puzzles, matching games, sorting games
- Outdoor garden—vegetables, fruits, long term and short term

EXERCISES

1. Using Canada's Food Guide to Healthy Eating, reflect on your own eating habits. Do you maintain a healthy diet? What changes would you need to make to model appropriate eating habits?

2. In a small group, list your unhealthy eating habits. Discuss why you have developed these habits, and why thy might not be good for you.

3. Interview parents of an infant, toddler, and preschooler. Ask the parents which items in the four main food groups—grain products, vegetables and fruit, milk products, meat and alternatives—they use to plan their weekly menus. In a small group, compare your results. Are the children getting an appropriate diet? What in their diet needs to be increased/decreased?

4. Create a checklist you could use to identify and keep track of healthy eating habits for infants, toddlers, and preschoolers.

5. Interview individuals from different cultures in your area to describe how their eating habits differ from yours. Use Canada's Food Guide to assist you. Develop a guide of alternative foods that could fit into the four food groups for a different culture.

6. Develop a plan for how you might increase children's independence at mealtimes.

7. In a daycare environment, children eat in small groups of about six per table with one adult at each of two tables and one table that is monitored at a distance. When lunch arrives from the kitchen, each plate already has the serving on it and juice is already poured. Plates and glasses are placed in front of children on the table and adults distribute required cutlery to the children. The following problems have been identified: Children complain that they are not hungry and do not wish to eat. Some children pick at their food, but much of it is thrown out. Dialogue around the table seems to be about finishing what is on the children's plates or trying a bit of the food. The staff does not like lunchtime, and the tendency is to rush children through their meals. Why might this not be a healthy situation? Discuss what changes should be made and why.

8. Using Canada's Food Guide, plan a healthy weekly menu for infants (on solid foods) and for toddlers and preschoolers.

9. Develop a poster that could be hung in a kitchen to illustrate food safety. Identify potential dangers and list some solutions.

10. Develop a safety checklist for food preparation. Implement your checklist in a child-care centre.

11. Discuss how individual differences might influence meal preparation. What adjustments might need to be made?

12. Go to a library and/or the Web and develop a resource list that can be used to provide appropriate books and music to children about cooking and food experiences, and storybooks related to cooking or eating.

13. Visit toy stores and look through catalogues of children's toys to develop a resource list to identify appropriate learning materials that could be purchased to support nutritional activities in the child-care setting.

REFERENCES

Canadian Paediatric Society, Dietitians of Canada, & Health Canada. (1998). *Nutrition for healthy term infants.* Ottawa: Ministry of Public Works and Government Services Canada. http://www.hc-sc.gc.ca, accessed 10 October 2002.

DEY. (2003). *Allergic reaction central.* http://www.allergic-reactions.com/home/sitemap.html, accessed 10 October 2002.

Dowshen, S., Izenberg, N., & Bass, E. (2001). *Kidshealth guide to parents.* New York: McGraw-Hill.

Office of Nutrition Policy and Promotion. (2002a). *Canada's food guide.* Ottawa: Health Canada. http://www.hc-sc.gc.ca, accessed 10 January 2002.

Office of Nutrition Policy and Promotion. (2002b). *Canada's food guide to healthy eating focus on preschoolers—Background for educators and communicators.* Ottawa: Health Canada. http://www.hc-sc.gc.ca/hpfb-dgpsa/onpp-bppn/food_ guide_preschoolers_e.html, 8 September 2003.

Schickedanz, J., Schickedanz, D., Forsyth, P., & Forsyth, G. (2001). *Understanding children and adolescents.* Fourth edition. Needham Heights, MA: Allyn & Bacon.

Shapiro Kendrick, A., Kaufman R., & Messenger, K. (1995). *Healthy young children: A manual for programs.* Washington, DC: National Association for the Education of Young Children.

6 Physical Fitness

CHAPTER

"Child care providers play an important role both as role models and by giving young children positive experiences with active play. By encouraging large-motor play and by making physical activity a priority every day, children and caregivers will experience the fun of movement and the benefits of good physical health. Parents who see the importance of active play for their children in preschool and day care settings will advocate for physical education programs when their children are in school." (Belfry, 2003: 4)

Chapter Outcomes

After reading this chapter, the reader will:

1. Define the nine principles of developmentally appropriate physical activities for young children and explain why each is important to overall physical growth and development.

2. Outline developmentally appropriate outcomes for each of the following age groups:
   • infants
   • toddlers
   • preschool children
   • school-age children

3. Define and identify the three movement concepts.

4. Explain how children's self-confidence and self-concept increase with increased physical skill development.

5. Define fitness and identify how children gain understanding of the importance of fitness activities.

6. Describe how the physical environment and activities should be set up to increase children's physical skills.

7. Describe the adult's role in fostering physical growth and development.

The Importance of Physical Activity

With advances in new technology, children in our society have become more passive. Children watch more television—an average of 26 hours a week—and play more computer and video games. Canadian children are 40 percent less active than they were 30 years ago (Belfry, 2003). In addition, because of efforts to reduce costs due to decreased educational funding, many elementary schools have cut physical education programs. Health Canada (2002) identified that:

- half of Canadian children—38 percent of girls and 48 percent of boys—are not active enough for optimal growth and development
- the number of children who are overweight has doubled and the number of those who are obese tripled between 1981 and 1996

As a result, Health Canada has developed a guide for physical activities for children (Figure 6.1). Children who engage in regularly scheduled physical activities as outlined in the guide will receive the following benefits:

- optimal healthy growth and development
- healthy weight management
- improved fitness
- lifelong patterns of healthy living and exercise
- increased strength of muscles, bones, and heart
- maintained flexibility
- improved posture and balance
- improved physical self-esteem
- increased relaxation
- increased opportunities to socialize (Health Canada, 2002)

Developmentally Appropriate Activities

A program of physical activity, just like any other, needs to be built on strong foundations that are sensitive to children's abilities and needs. Developmentally appropriate programs for physical activity for young children ensure that the following nine principles are met for all children (Graham, Holt/Hale, & Parker, 1998):

1. *Planned physical activities are based on developmentally appropriate outcomes.* Physical activities need to be based on outcomes that are appropriate for all children. "It includes a balance of skills, concepts, games, educational gymnastics, rhythm, and dance experiences designed to enhance the cognitive, motor, and physical fitness development of every child." (Graham, Holt/Hale, & Parker, 1998: 8)

2. *Children are encouraged to gain awareness of the concepts of movement.* When children engage in regular gross motor activities, they begin to understand the concepts of movement, which include:

   - body awareness—Mikayla learns about how to control her body (photo 6.1) by climbing on a tree. She needs to balance her body on the branch, she needs to coordinate her leg and hand movements to climb up the branch, and she has to decide how high is comfortable for her to climb.

Photo 6.1

FIGURE 6.1

Canada's Physical Activity Guide for Children

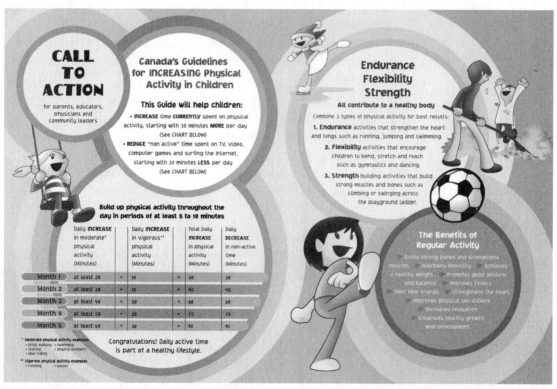

Photo 6.2

Photo 6.3

- space awareness—Jonathan learns how to use the space around him effectively by playing basketball (photo 6.2). He learns how close he needs to be to successfully throw the ball into the net and how high and hard he needs to throw the ball.
- understanding how much effort is needed—Giancarlo has noticed that some of the children can navigate the rings by using only every second ring, and he is determined to do the same. However, Giancarlo is much shorter than the children who have succeeded at this activity. As a result, it takes a number of trials before he succeeds (photo 6.3).
- understanding the relationship between movement and its results of movement—When Grace moves her body in a certain way, the Hula Hoop will rotate around her neck (photo 6.4).

3. *Children gain skill and develop self-confidence in their abilities to engage in a variety of gross motor tasks*. Gross motor tasks include:

   - **non-locomotor tasks** (anchored movement such as balancing, twisting, rocking, or swinging arms)—Niko has built a horizontal structure using the foam blocks. She decides to see if it is long enough to fit her. When she tries to balance on it she loses her balance at first. Eventually she manages to balance on her structure (photo 6.5). She holds this posture for a few minutes.

✳ **Non-locomotor tasks**

Photo 6.4

Photo 6.5

- **locomotor tasks** (moving from place to place such as running, walking, skipping, or climbing)—Eventually, Niko decides to balance on her structure by walking over it and jumping off at the end (photo 6.6).

- manipulative—Niko has used both her fine muscles and her gross muscles to manipulate the blocks to create her structure (photos 6.5 and 6.6).

4. *Children begin to understand the concept of fitness.*

   - A variety of daily gross motor activities, both indoors and outdoors, provides opportunity to practise and reinforce motor skills in different settings.
   - Adults must ensure that there is opportunity to engage in both active and restful activities (warm-up, active, and cool-down activities).
   - To gain understanding, children need opportunities to discuss the value of physical activities and the benefits of physical activity to their bodies.

5. *Physical activity is an integral part of the program.* Children gain understanding of the various concepts of their activities by discussing the activities they are engaged in with peers and adults. Mikayla (photo 6.1) found it easier to balance by climbing the branch on her knees. Tommy tried it on his knees but said it was "too unbalanced." He thought he had more control by shimmying up the branch. Jonathan (photo 6.2) said he needed to "line up the ball" to be able to get it into the basket. These children were able to articulate concepts about movement. Grace was twirling the Hula Hoops around her body (photo 6.4). She then decides to try to fit the two hoops she was using together (photo 6.7). Her activity attracts other children, who work together with their teacher, Komela, to create

Photo 6.6

Photo 6.7

Photo 6.8

Photo 6.9

a structure with all the hoops (photo 6.8). These children are engaged in a social problem-solving activity that extends their movement activities.

6. *Physical activities provide opportunities to develop positive self-concepts.* Giancarlo (photo 6.3) was extremely proud of his accomplishment on the rings. He asked to have a picture taken of his success. Grace (photo 6.4) managed to twirl one hoop around her neck. She was then proud of her ability to twirl two hoops around her neck and called out for everyone to "quickly watch."

7. *All physical activities are set up to encourage practice and maximize the children's abilities to succeed at different motor tasks.* Niko had enough room to encourage her to build and test her structure (photo 6.9). Toddlers love to transport large items (photo 6.10). The ball is large, light, and easy to hold and the covered outside deck provides ample room to carry the ball, throw it, roll it, or kick it. The ball is light and will not hurt if it accidentally lands on another child.

8. *Active physical activity is inclusive and scheduled on a daily basis.*

   • Material and equipment that encourages a variety of skill levels should be used (photos 6.11 and 6.12).

Photo 6.10

Photo 6.11

- The environment should be adapted for children with physical challenges. For example, there should be wider pathways and ramps for wheelchair accessibility, and handrails or holds on transfer points such as platforms to allow children to get in and out of wheelchairs. Access to items such as rings or bars should be low enough for those with physical challenges. Also, elevated sandboxes should be provided.
- Activities should be set up to encourage children to engage in active play continuously. A variety of choices should be presented, such as climbing equipment, riding paths, balancing activities, and activities that test strength, endurance, or coordination.

9. Physical activities are bias-free.

- Boys and girls should have equal access to all activities.
- All activities should encourage individual and/or group play.
- All activities should provide opportunities for collaboration and cooperation.
- Activities and games should include cultural variation.

Photo 6.12

Developmentally Appropriate Outcomes

The early years build the foundations for all later skills. As children progress through various ages and stages of normal development, a predictable, universal sequence may be observed for most children. Each of these ages and stages of normal development is associated with specific developmentally appropriate outcomes. "Refinements in motor development depend on maturation of the brain, input from the sensory system, increased bulk and number of muscle fibers, a healthy nervous system, and appropriate opportunities to practice." (Allen & Marotz, 2003: 23)

1. Infants

"During infancy, great advances in motor abilities occur. Motor development proceeds in two directions: 1) from the centre of the body out to the arms, hands, and fingers, and 2) from the top of the body downward. Development in the outward direction is known as proximodismal (literally, 'near' to 'far') development. This trend leads to ever-increasing skill in using the hands. Development in the downward direction is known as **cephalocaudal** (literally, 'head' to 'tail') development. This tends to eventually lead to using the legs to stand and walk." (Schickedanz, Schickedanz, Forsyth, & Forsyth, 2001: 128)

＊ Cephalocaudal

During the infant years, there is a critical interplay between gross and fine muscle development. For example, infants need to develop appropriate grasping techniques to pull themselves up to a standing position in order to learn to walk. By using developmentally appropriate outcomes that encourage both fine and gross motor development, adults can plan and implement activities to meet and enhance developmental motor skills for healthy growth and development (Table 6.1).

Photo 6.13

Photo 6.14

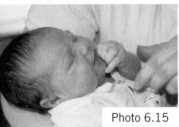

Photo 6.15

TABLE 6.1 **PHYSICAL DEVELOPMENT AND DEVELOPMENTALLY APPROPRIATE OUTCOMES FOR INFANTS**

Developmental Milestone	Developmentally Appropriate Outcomes
Grasping 1. Swatting without grasping intended item 2. Grasping intended item	**Grasping** 1. Develop eye–hand coordination to reach for and grasp intended item (photo 6.13) 2. a) Develop skill in handling intended item—transfer from hand to hand (photo 6.14) b) Practise reaching and grasping items to develop a variety of grasps (Figure 6.2)
Locomotor development 1. Lift head 2. Lift chest 3. Roll over 4. Sit with support 5. Sit and grasp 6. Sit alone, reach and grasp 7. Crawl 8. Stand with support 9. Walk with support 10. Stand alone 11. Walk alone 12. Walk and carry 13. Bend over, pick up object	**Locomotor development** 1. Support head when lifting or carrying infant (photo 6.15) 2/3. a) Place on stomach to encourage head lifting (photo 6.16) b) Place on stomach to encourage lifting of chest (photo 6.17) c) Place on floor to encourage rolling (photo 6.18) 4. Support child's back and sides to sit (photo 6.19) 5/6. Place objects within sitting child's reach to encourage reaching and grasping (photo 6.20) 7. Provide clear, unobstructed areas to encourage crawling and protect open areas with safety gates such as stairs or doorways 8/9. Provide sturdy objects to encourage pulling up to a stand and walking with support (photo 6.21) 10/11. Provide clear, unobstructed areas to stand and walk safely (photo 6.22) 12/13. Provide objects that are easy to pick up and transport (photo 6.10)

Photo 6.16

Photo 6.17

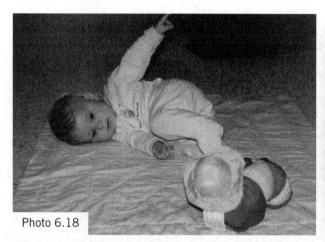

Photo 6.18

Photo 6.19

Photo 6.20

Photo 6.21

Photo 6.22

FIGURE 6.2
Variety of Grasps

Palmar grasp

Pincer grasp

Tripod grasp

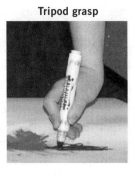

2. Toddlers

Toddlers are active explorers of their environment. They have mastered the skills outlined in Table 6.1. Toddlers' physical appearance has changed. Their body proportions are quite different from infants. This affects not only how they look, but also how they move. When children start to walk "they walk flat-footed with short, wide steps and a wobbly gait. Toddlers walk this way because top-heaviness, caused by their relatively large head, makes it difficult for them to keep their balance. They compensate, and thus maintain their balance, by placing their feet wide apart to create a wide base of support." (Schickedanz, Schickedanz, Forsyth, & Forsyth, 2001: 127)

As with infants, it is difficult to look at toddlers without considering both fine and gross motor abilities. Toddlers are constantly on the move—running, jumping, touching, and manipulating. Developmentally appropriate concepts for toddlers are outlined in Table 6.2.

3. Preschool Children

Preschool children practise skills attained during earlier years to perfect them. Fine and gross motor activities become more integrated and more coordinated. For example, preschoolers ride a tricycle effectively by pedalling with their feet, coordinating steering, and ringing the bell on their handlebar. The emphasis in the preschool years is to (Table 6.3):

- practise a variety of fine and gross motor skills
- refine existing skills such as throwing a ball to hit a target or land in a basket
- gain understanding and confidence in motor actions

4. School-Age Children

"Large motor skills include running, jumping, twisting, bending, and turning of the body. All of the maneuvers required to play baseball, basketball, tag, and soccer are gross motor movements. Quickness, balance, speed, and strength all continue to improve

TABLE 6.2 **PHYSICAL DEVELOPMENT AND DEVELOPMENTALLY APPROPRIATE OUTCOMES FOR TODDLERS**

Developmental Milestone	Developmentally Appropriate Outcomes
Manipulative skills	**Manipulative skills**
1. Scribbles	1. Provide opportunities to draw, paint, colour.
2. Feeds self	2. Provide opportunities to pour own drinks, serve self, use different cutlery to feed self.
3. Stacks toys	3. Provide toys that are easily stacked, such as foam blocks and small wooden blocks.
4. Fills and empties containers	4. Provide opportunities to fill and empty containers with objects, liquid, sand.
5. Throws objects	5. Provide objects that are safe to throw into, at, over, and through things.
6. Takes things apart and puts them together	6. Provide objects that fit together so they can be taken apart and put together.
Locomotive skills	**Locomotor skills**
1. Walks, runs—falls often	1. Provide opportunities to move at various speeds indoors and outdoors.
2. Pushes, pulls toys	2. Provide toys of various sizes to pull/push or ride.
3. Transports toys	3. Provide toys and containers to load and carry.
4. Climbs	4. Provide apparatus such as stairs and climbers to encourage climbing.
5. Stacks objects	5. Provide blocks of various sizes to build with.

during the school-age years. The acquisition of these basic skills enables school-aged children to play an increasing number of physical games." (Schickedanz, Schickedanz, Forsyth, & Forsyth, 2001: 415)

School-age children are capable of accomplishing increasingly more complex tasks. Their motor skills have become integrated and coordinated. They increasingly enjoy organized games and sports. Sudden growth spurts may cause some awkwardness in movements for short time periods. Much of the physical activity in this age group focuses on competitive sports. The proportion of girls competing in sports is lower than that of boys. "Sleek (1996) summarized research that demonstrates the benefits of having individuals focus on competing with themselves, with improvement as the measure of success, rather than competing against others, with winning as the measure of success. In addition to maintaining involvement for a longer time, those who focus on improvement enjoy the activity more and are more likely to develop a positive self concept." (Schickedanz, Schickedanz, Forsyth, & Forsyth, 2001: 415) Thus developmentally appropriate outcomes for this age group need to focus on:

- twenty minutes of vigorous physical activity per day
- new skills being demonstrated one at a time

TABLE 6.3   **PHYSICAL DEVELOPMENT AND DEVELOPMENTALLY APPROPRIATE OUTCOMES FOR PRESCHOOL CHILDREN**

Developmental Milestone	Developmentally Appropriate Outcomes
Manipulative skills 1. Develops tripod grasp 2. Uses a variety of manipulative skills such as pounding, cutting, drawing, sewing, or stringing 3. Begins to establish hand dominance	**Manipulative skills** Provide opportunities to develop various types of effective grasps for writing, cutting, and other manipulative tasks.
Locomotor skills` 1. Refines gross motor skills 2. Uses fine and gross motor skills to use equipment appropriately	**Locomotor skills** 1. Provide opportunity for active exploration to practise and refine gross motor skills such as climbing apparatus, riding toys, and space in which to run, walk, or ride. 2. Provide opportunity to practise and refine emergent skills with equipment such as balls, hoops, or skipping ropes.

- opportunity to practise new skills
- a cooperative skill development program
- opportunity for all children to participate equally
- opportunity for children to work on interpersonal skills through physical activity programs
- involving families to create a viable physical activity program

Movement Concepts

At the fetal stage of development, the fetus is in a state of constant movement. The fetus floats in amniotic fluid, moving his or her arms and legs, kicking and reacting to the mother's movements. "Fetuses react sharply to their mother's actions. 'We're watching the fetus on ultrasound and the mother starts to laugh, we can see the fetus, floating upside down in the womb, bounce up and down on its head, bum-bum-bum, mothers watch this on screen, they laugh harder, and the fetus goes up and down even faster.'" (Hobson, 1998: 47) As the fetus moves and responds to the movements of the mother, the fetus is already starting to learn to control his or her movements. The fetus has been observed in utero sucking a thumb or fingers, waving arms and hands, licking the uterine wall, and pushing off the uterus wall with the feet seemingly to walk around the womb (Belfry, 2003). At birth, infants are capable of jerky, uncontrolled movements of their limbs. Newborns already have some concept of movement and some rudimentary knowledge about their bodies. "Over the next four years, the brain progressively refines the circuits for reaching, grabbing, sitting, crawling, walking, and running." (Nash, 1997: 53) As children continue to grow and develop, they become more skilled at and more aware of the concepts of movement—body awareness, space awareness, and relational concepts.

1. Body Awareness

As young children gradually gain awareness of the various parts of their bodies, they begin to learn and understand:

* how to move each body part effectively
  * Newborns' jerky uncontrolled movements of legs and arms gradually become refined. The infant becomes aware of objects in his or her immediate vicinity. Initially that infant will swat at an item, often failing to make contact. Eventually the infant not only will make contact but also will be able to close his or her fingers around the object to grasp it. The infant has started to develop **eye–hand coordination** (ability to see an object, be able to reach and grasp that object, and use the object effectively; for example, the ability to reach for a rattle, grasp it, and shake it to make a sound).

    > ✳ Eye–hand coordination

  * Older infants learn to control leg and arm muscles to pull themselves into a standing position. They eventually learn to take their first tentative steps, which rapidly leads to the ability to walk and run.
  * Toddlers learn to navigate the environment through walking, running, and climbing. They learn to control their body to coordinate movements such as walking up stairs and holding on to railings, walking and carrying objects, and eating with a spoon.
  * Preschoolers refine their motor skills to coordinate movements such as cutting paper, pedalling and steering a tricycle, and eating with a knife and fork.
  * School-age children further refine their motor skills to become more skilled at coordinated movements such as dribbling a ball and running to avoid other players, writing, and drawing intricate diagrams.
* how to move with intent to achieve a specific action or goal
  * Once the infant has gained some control over arm and finger movement, he or she can reach for and grasp items. From this point on, infants are actively involved in making choices. The infant will choose what objects he or she wants if those objects are placed within reach (photo 6.23).
  * With control over mobility, children will actively explore their environment. Mobility (walking, running, climbing, drawing, and writing) opens up an ever-growing range of possibilities to explore and master.
* how movement, body position, and the environment are interconnected
  * To get from one side of a room to the other one needs to walk around objects.
  * To get to the top of the stairs or a climber one needs to climb up.
  * To operate a swing one needs to pump one's legs.
  * To prevent falling one must step over objects.

Photo 6.23

2. Space Awareness

Development of spatial awareness begins with movement. When infants reach to grab something, they learn about the position of their arms and fingers in relation to the object. When children start to move around their environment, they learn about the confines of space such as that doorways lead to other spaces (new rooms or an outdoor space), stairs lead to new areas on a different floor, walls confine a room, and fences confine a yard.

Children learn about space by active exploration. They learn about various spatial concepts such as on, over, under, around, through, up, down, in the middle, in front of, and behind. These concepts will be enforced as the child is able to navigate the environment and manipulate the materials in that environment.

3. Relational Concepts

Relational concepts are those that have a direct bearing on movement. These concepts include:

- speed—how fast the child can crawl or run, how fast a ball travels when thrown or rolled, how slowly one can ride a bicycle without falling over
- no movement—how quickly one can stop a moving object such as a rolling car, how quickly one can stop a tricycle or when running, how one can balance an object so that it does not move
- strength—children supporting their body weight in various ways (hanging by their feet or arms, doing push-ups), how much the child can lift, carry, push, or pull
- endurance—how long the child can engage in active physical activity; how long the child can run, jump, or skip; how quickly the child gets tired or winded during active physical activity
- balance—how well the child maintains his or her balance when engaging in active physical activity such as riding a bicycle, hopping on one foot, skating, walking on a line or a balance beam, climbing a branch of a tree, or running down a hill
- flexibility—how to use the joints and muscles to execute a full range of movements such as bending over, maintaining balance while reaching for an object, or stretching to touch the toes from various positions
- coordination—how well the child can do more than one thing at the same time such as climbing stairs with alternating feet, dribbling a ball while running, turning a rope while jumping, or controlling a stick and puck while skating

Skills and Self-Confidence

Children's self-confidence increases as their skill levels increase. Katie had slipped and fallen while running in the snow. Although she did not hurt herself badly, she now tends to walk very slowly and carefully while playing in the snow. One day, she observes several children joyfully running through the snow, squealing with delight.

Katie watches the children while they play in the snow. She watches as one child runs up and down a snowy hill. Katie joins the children as they run. With growing confidence she joins in the laughter and the play (photo 6.24). Eventually she also joins the children in running up and down the snowy hill. Katie has regained her self-confidence to try a new skill. She was successful as she ran tentatively through the snow. She did not fall again. Her new-found success prompted her to run faster and eventually run up and down the hill with the other children.

When Jeremy started kindergarten, he was 14 kilograms overweight. He refused to involve himself in most physical activities. He tired easily and even a moderate amount of exercise left him breathing heavily. Jeremy was often teased by the other children. He cried easily and seldom played with other children.

Jeremy's parents were concerned about his self-image. They talked to their family doctor about the problem. Jeremy started on a strict diet and joined a swimming program. Within six months, he had not only lost nine kilograms but also learned to swim. He enjoyed swimming so much he decided he would like to try a gymnastics program. Jeremy became much more active at school during outdoor playtime. He now enjoys using the climbing apparatus and has become quite skilled at using the monkey bars. The other children start to notice and admire his skill. He begins to form friendships and the teasing drops dramatically.

Jeremy not only gained confidence in his own abilities but also gained a more positive self-image. As he became more confident, he was teased less, he interacted with the other children more, and his social skills started to develop more positively. As Jeremy lost much of his excess weight, he was better able to participate in active physical activity. He did not tire as quickly and had more energy.

In summary, how well physical tasks can be accomplished depends on how healthy and fit the individual is. Since young children learn through active exploration, it is critical that children have an opportunity to engage in a variety of motor activities to increase their skills and confidence in the success of their actions.

Photo 6.24

Fitness Concepts

"Physical fitness is the capacity of the heart, blood vessels, lungs, and muscles to function at optimum efficiency." (Graham, Holt/Hale, & Parker, 1998: 34) Healthy young children in appropriate environments are naturally active. Children learn by doing. They will learn about the capacity of their bodies to engage in active physical activity. They will not learn to make connections between their actions and what is happening to their bodies unless their caregivers talk about these connections. Young children will start to make these connections if:

- they talk about their actions and how these actions affect their bodies—sweating, increased breathing, increased heartbeat
- they have opportunities to relate directly how their actions affect their bodies—feeling their heartbeat change with exercise, getting tired, feeling their muscles ache
- they listen to stories or songs about exercise and how it helps growing bodies
- they see adults participate in physical activity with children

Physical Activity as an Integral Part of a Program

An important measure of a quality environment for young children is active physical play both indoors and outdoors. Key components of making physical activity an integral part of the children's programs include scheduling and providing a safe environment for motor activity.

1. Schedule

- Regular indoor and outdoor activity should be scheduled for at least an hour each day.
- A program should include regularly scheduled free-play motor activity and skill-development gross motor activities such as music and movement.

2. Safe Environment for Motor Activity

The most critical element is to provide a safe environment for children to engage in active play. A safe environment includes:

- close supervision
- a fenced outdoor area
- gross motor equipment that is stable and in good repair
- appropriate footwear to prevent trapped toes or falls on slippery floors
- appropriate ground protection under gross motor equipment to cushion falls

Young children need to engage freely in a variety of gross motor tasks such as running, crawling, and riding. The younger the child, the less controlled are their actions and the more difficult it is for them to stop. Therefore, providing large, uncluttered, open spaces is another critical factor for appropriate gross motor play.

Children with special needs must be able to explore their environment freely. Therefore, the environment should be barrier-free by providing such elements as ramps, wider paved pathways, and raised sandboxes.

A variety of surfaces should be provided to encourage different skills:

- paved or tiled areas for riding or pushing toys
- sand areas for active sand play
- open grassy areas or large open spaces inside for group activities
- shaded, protected areas or quiet areas inside for relaxation or rest

Children should be protected from potential harm from the elements. Protection should include:

- windbreak—wooden barriers, hedges, sides of the building; equipment and play areas placed out of the main direction of the wind

- shelter from the sun—covered sandboxes, trees, archways covered with vines, umbrellas, playhouses, canopies, covered decks (photo 6.25)

Some features add to the ease of setting up, maintaining the outdoor environment, or providing greater comfort to children:

Photo 6.25

- outside water source for cleanup, water play, and drinking water (It is important to drink a lot of water while engaging in physical activity. Young children are especially vulnerable to dehydration and they do not know that they need to replenish their body systems.)
- convenient outside storage such as a shed or a storage room for gross motor equipment and other play equipment
- close access to washrooms

Much of the equipment in the outdoor space will be stationary. Stationary equipment is usually securely anchored for safety reasons and includes such items as slides, climbers, and swings.

Some outdoor equipment should be portable. Portable equipment provides opportunities to:

- maintain attention
- practise skills with different equipment such as riding toys, tunnels, securely attached ladders or nets on climbing equipment, large blocks and planks, balance beams, and tires to jump into, run around, and balance on

Play areas should be designed so as to not interfere with each other (Figure 6.3). They should have:

- large, clear areas around swings that have a well-defined border such as a raised lip to alert children to danger
- riding paths and paved areas separated from quiet play areas or other more stationary activities
- large, unobstructed, soft area away from other play areas for activities such as throwing, rolling, and kicking; should be approximately 40 percent of playground space (Canadian Standards Association, 2003)
- quiet area protected from other play areas
- clear spaces around potentially dangerous equipment such as teeter-totters, slides, balance beams; seating at periphery of these areas for children to observe play activities

Gross Motor Equipment

Gross motor equipment should be chosen to maximize children's opportunities to:

- stimulate a variety of motor skills (Figure 6.4)
- encourage a logical progression of skills such as crawling up a ramp, to climbing a set of steps, to climbing a ladder, to climbing a net or a pole
- experience success such as with steps that are spaced to allow the child to climb safely—the vertical rise for 18 months to 5 years should be at least 22.5 cm and for 5 to 12 years should be at least 30 cm (Canadian Standards Association, 2003)

FIGURE 6.3

Outdoor Playground

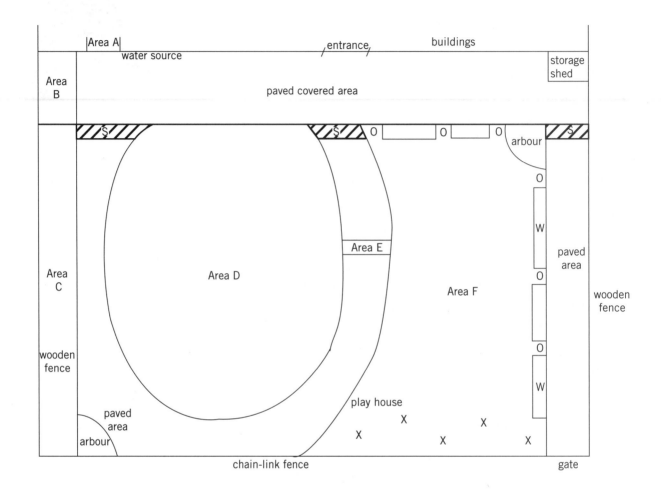

- encourage problem solving such as how to move through an obstacle course or how to stop a wagon from rolling down a hill
- encourage safe risk taking (photo 6.1)
- encourage transfer of skills from one situation to another such as by running on pavement, running up a hill, or running across a clatter bridge

Adaptations

Physical play spaces should be available for all children. Younger children should be separated from older children. If possible, separate playgrounds should be provided for infants and toddlers, preschoolers, and school-age children since each of these age

FIGURE 6.4
Equipment and Related Physical Skills

Area of Outdoor Playground (Figure 6.3)	Features and Benefits
• Area A	• Bathroom—access door to playground
• Area C, raised garden	• Garden—learn to plant, take care of growing plants—water, till, harvest • Children's garden—tomatoes, peas, beans, squash, pumpkins, green peppers, lettuce
• Wooden fences on two sides of play space	• Wind barrier
• Area E, bridge from small hill to larger hill over riding path	• Bridge—walking, crawling, running, observing

• Area F
  ○ X—mature trees
  ○ W—benches built into the hill at varying heights
  ○ arbour—grape vines with bench underneath
  ○ O—flowerpots between benches
	• Open, grassy, hilly area suitable for large group activity—uninhibited running, walking, crawling; throwing, hitting, kicking objects; resting; observing

• Area D, climbing equipment 	Climbing equipment encourages: • skills—climbing ladders, ramps, poles, rope; jumping from various heights; balancing on bars, poles; running, walking, or crawling along various surfaces • strength—hanging from rings, ropes, bars • endurance—practising skills at own pace • coordination—climbing, jumping, moving across rings, sliding down poles • socialization—practising skills together, demonstrating skills to each other, trying ideas suggested by peers

FIGURE 6.4

Continued

• Area B, protected rest area 	• Modelled after Japanese tea house (large Asian population in daycare, therefore culturally appropriate) • Shutters on two sides and large door on front to protect area from animals and windblown debris • Protected from the elements • Suitable place for soothing, restful activities
• Paved areas	• Riding to build strength and endurance, practise coordination • Pushing, pulling to build strength, endurance, problem solving
• Area S, crosswalks	• Following safety rules—riding is in one direction only, avoid hitting objects or people, vehicles must stop for pedestrians at crosswalks, pedestrians must watch for vehicles

FIGURE 6.4
Continued

- Mobile equipment

  ○ Balance Beams

- Can be created from items such as planks, row of tires, ladders on the ground, tree stumps in a row, patio stones in a row
- Children practise walking and balancing on different surfaces

  ○ Ball equipment

- Basketball
- Throwing balls into baskets, containers
- Throwing balls against a target—large bull's eye on fence or wall
- Kicking balls into nets

FIGURE 6.4
Continued

○   Other

- Teeter-totter

- Ramps, ladders, nets on climbers

- Water play—sprinklers

- Ice surface for skating

- Sliding, sledding when snowy

groups has very distinct needs. Separate play spaces can accommodate their particular skills and needs.

In some cases, separation of play spaces is not possible. Instead, outdoor and inside gross motor play is scheduled so that the various age groups are outside at different times. This presents a challenge to child-care providers. If only one set of equipment is available for all age groups, it is difficult to meet all of the needs of all of the children. In these cases, care must be taken to choose appropriate equipment. Equipment should:

- have various levels for skill development—ramps for crawlers; wider, lower stairs to climb for younger age groups; more advanced climbing opportunities such as ladders, ropes, and poles for older children
- be more mobile for younger children—climbers
- be supervised more closely to ensure safety of younger children and appropriate use by older children

For children with special needs and younger children, the following should be installed:

- wider pathways, ramps, platforms
- gentler slopes that encourage crawling or wheelchair access
- handrails at child height or wheelchair height
- guardrails to prevent falls from platforms
- wheelchair-accessible pathways to climbing equipment

Stimulation of Different Levels of Activity

All physical activity needs to include warm-up, a main activity, and cool down (Table 6.4). The early years are an ideal time to make children aware of appropriate physical practices in order to establish lifelong physical fitness skills.

TABLE 6.4   LEVELS OF ACTIVITY

Type of Activity	Purpose of Activity	Some Examples of Appropriate Practices
Warm-up activities	- Getting ready - Warming up muscles to start activity	- Stretches—reach to the ceiling, touch the floor - Related songs—head and toes can be done during transition times, tiptoe to the next room or outside - Walk slowly with arms held high, stand and swing arms. - With infants, make a game of it—move their arms way up high, to the side, to touch the chest.
Main activity	- Develop skills such as walking, running, balancing, climbing, throwing, catching; strength, coordination - Increase flexibility, endurance - Develop ability to listen to and follow directions - Increase cooperation with peers	- Active free play - Group play such as tossing games using bean bags - Running and stopping games—run to the fence, touch a tree, music and movement (follow the speed of the music—fast, slow, loud, soft; stop and start to the beat of the drum; musical team sports with older children) - Obstacle courses both indoors and outdoors

TABLE 6.4   CONTINUED

Type of Activity	Purpose of Activity	Some Examples of Appropriate Practices
Cool down activities	- Relax - Give muscles and body a chance to rest	- Gentle stretches - Lie down and concentrate on relaxing various body parts—hands, legs, head. - Listen to soothing music, keep beat with hands. - March to slowing drumbeat until finally sitting or lying; count to 10 before going to next activity.

Adult Interactions

When children are engaged in active free-choice play, it is critical for child-care staff to be actively involved. Active involvement includes the following principles:

1. *Supervision.* Adults need to be aware of potential danger so that they can intervene before an injury occurs. For example, a child is on the swing. Another child has kicked a ball, which rolls into the path of the swing. An adult can anticipate that a child will want to retrieve the ball and may run into the swing. If the adult is alert, this accident can be easily avoided. Many accidents can be avoided with careful supervision.

2. *Assistance with skill development.* Adults should carefully observe children to note what skills they already have, what skills are emerging, and which skills need reinforcement. Some skills can be reinforced spontaneously. For example, Jeremy was trying to throw the basketball into the net but was consistently missing. Maryam went over and talked to him. She told him that he might find it easier if he used two hands on the ball. After a few tries, Jeremy was successful. Other situations might involve setting up the environment to foster development of a skill. For example, Maryam noticed that the children were having difficulty with the spatial concepts of over and under. She set up both inside and outside equipment such as balance beams, stepping stones, small sturdy tables, adult-sized sturdy chairs, and a variety of hollow blocks. As the children used the equipment, Maryam indicated how they were using it—"You are under the table. You jumped over the block. You stepped over the rocks." Older children will need to know the rules of games such as baseball or soccer to participate in

them. They may also need some specific skill instruction, such as how to dribble a ball or how to kick effectively.

3. *Talk about what children are doing.* Children need to learn about the effects of physical activity on their body. By observing the children, the adult can interact with them to:

    - talk about the need to slow down—child may be hot, sweaty, or tired
    - talk about why the child is sweating, breathing hard, feels hot, or is tired
    - offer suggestions for cooling down—drinking water, walking around the room or playground, lying down and relaxing different parts of the body
    - talk about improvements made—the increased height a child climbed to, the increased number of times they rode their tricycle around the room or playground, the increased ability to move across the monkey bars without falling
    - talk about the new skills they have mastered—throwing the ball into the net, kicking the ball into the net

4. *Encourage social play.* Set up activities that encourage group participation without the need to wait a turn—obstacle courses, music and movement activities, moving to the beat of a drum, rolling balls to each other, or running to touch something in the room or yard.

Positive Self-Concept

Physical activity is a natural way for children to develop positive self-concepts. Young children develop positive self-concepts about themselves and their abilities. Infants learn to trust their actions when their actions become successful. For example, when infants are successful in pulling themselves up into a standing position, they can start to observe themselves and the world from a totally new perspective. The infants then quickly learn to use the new-found skill of standing to walk beside supportive structures. Not only can infants see more objects around them—on tabletops or on higher shelves—they also can travel toward these objects in an upright position, never losing sight of the desired object. When infants travel to the object and manage to get the object and therefore have their curiosity satisfied, they are gaining satisfaction in doing things for themselves.

Toddlers have a tremendous drive to do things independently. Satisfaction derived from pushing or pulling wagons up or down hills, riding toy vehicles, or solving problems by themselves leads not only to greater independence but also to a greater sense of pride in their accomplishments.

Preschoolers are continually refining motor skills. When preschoolers are successful in activities such as printing their own names, climbing to the top of a climber and down again, pedalling and steering tricycles, or hitting a target with an object, they gain practice in continually improving their motor skills and pride in improving those abilities and skills.

School-age children have developed many motor skills. The task for this age group is to further refine these skills to become increasingly more competent at more complex tasks, such as figure skating, playing hockey, downhill skiing, or ballet. As children become more competent, their pride in achievement increases and, as a result, their self-concept improves.

Maximize Success

All children need to engage in activities that are appropriate for their skill level and their age. Motor activities that are too difficult can become frustrating and a child eventually may avoid these activities altogether. Canadian society tends to push children into competitive activities and encourages them to play competitive sports long before they can understand the rules of the game. For example, during a T-ball game the following observations were made. The children needed a prop to hit the ball. As one child hit the ball, a coach had to tell the child where to run. Another coach took over once the child was on base and told the child when and where to run. A coach in the field told a child what to do with the ball she had caught. Even with coaching, some children ran to the wrong bases.

Competitive activities may encourage some children to strive harder, but may discourage other children from trying at all. As children mature they become increasingly aware of what they can or cannot accomplish. Children who are continually unable to achieve what they perceive they should be able to do often form a defeatist attitude. It is disconcerting to hear a four-year-old say that he or she cannot do something, or that he or she is no good, or that someone else is so much better, or to see him or her cease to try at all. For example, Jamie, who is four, sits at the side of the gym while other children engage in gross motor activity. When asked to join the other children, he shrugs his shoulders and says, "Can't." If pushed, he starts to cry. When his teacher talks to Jamie's father about this situation, he indicates that Jamie is not physically inclined like his two older brothers. He also says that he can't understand how Jamie can be so poor at sports since his brothers and father have always been good athletes. Jamie has already formed a negative impression of his motor skills. As a result, it takes a great deal of patience and continual encouragement to involve Jamie in motor activities.

Activities need to be planned to maximize success for all children. This can be done by ensuring that:

- equipment and materials are developmentally appropriate for all children
- activities are developmentally appropriate
- skill development moves from simple to more complex—carrying a ball, kicking or throwing the ball and other objects, rolling the ball, throwing balls or other objects into containers or at targets, playing catch, playing ball-related games
- equipment and materials are rotated regularly to maintain interest and provide opportunities for new skill development
- equipment and materials meet all physical requirements of children—endurance, strength, coordination, balance, flexibility, physical skills
- children practise skills in a variety of settings—indoors, outdoors, on field trips

- children's skills and abilities are carefully observed and recorded to ensure that appropriate equipment and materials are available to them
- competition among young children is avoided; they should be encouraged to improve their individual skills and abilities as opposed to being compared to someone else
- children's efforts are praised and encouraged

Bias-Free Physical Activity

All physical activities should be encouraged for all children equally regardless of gender, ability, skill, or culture. All children have the same need for physical activity for optimal growth and development (Table 6.5).

TABLE 6.5 CREATING A BIAS-FREE PHYSICAL ACTIVITY PROGRAM

Activity	Purpose	Guidelines for Appropriate Activities
Establishing positive attitudes	- Develop positive attitude toward physical activities - Develop acceptance of individual differences - Develop acceptance of personal growth - Develop acceptance of diversity in physical activities	- Ensure that all activities, equipment, and materials are appropriate for all children. - Avoid competitive games—those that identify winners or losers. - Avoid games that encourage waiting your turn or that eliminate players (duck, duck, goose; musical chairs). - Encourage children to talk about how they have improved. - Encourage children to demonstrate newly acquired skills. - Talk about individual strengths and needs. - Read books and stories about individuals of varying abilities. - Encourage activities from other cultures such as variations of hopscotch, musical games (for school-age children, *Children's Games from Around the World* (Kirchner, 2000) is an excellent reference. - Help children set own goals toward self-improvement in physical activities.

TABLE 6.5 CONTINUED

Activity	Purpose	Guidelines for Appropriate Activities
Encouraging equality	- Everyone gets a turn at doing what they like to do, regardless of ability or skills.	- Have enough equipment so that everyone can engage in activity. - Help children recognize that they will get a turn when equipment is available. - Involve all children in activities, regardless of gender or age. - With older children, ensure that everyone plays the sport position they prefer. - With older children, talk about good sportsmanship.

SUMMARY

Canadian children are facing a fitness crisis. Lack of physical exercise influences all developmental areas. Children who are not fit may be overweight, may lack energy to actively participate, and may face future cardiovascular problems. It is critical that physical activity becomes an integral part of every child's daily routine. Through active physical activities, children:

- learn about their bodies
- learn about concepts such as movement, speed, space awareness, and relational concepts that will affect understanding in math and science
- develop self-confidence in their abilities
- develop positive self-esteem
- establish lifelong skills related to appropriate physical fitness

KEY POINTS

Canadian children are less fit

- Half of children not fit enough
- Overweight doubled and obesity tripled between 1981 and 1996

Developmentally appropriate activities

- Developmentally appropriate outcomes
- Awareness of motor concepts

- Increased self-confidence
- Understanding fitness concepts
- Integral part of program
- Develop self-concepts
- Maximize success
- Inclusive and part of daily routines
- Bias-free

Developmentally appropriate outcomes

- Infants—directional development, critical interplay between fine motor (grasping) and gross motor (locomotor development control)
- Toddlers—interplay between manipulation and locomotor movement
- Preschool children—practice of motor skills, refine existing skills, start to gain understanding and confidence in physical actions
- School-age children—increasing refinement to accomplish complex tasks, motor skills become integrated and coordinated, increased competitive focus

Movement concepts

- Body awareness—moving body parts effectively
- Space awareness
- Relational awareness—speed, lack of movement, strength, endurance, balance, flexibility, coordination

Skill and self-confidence

- Increased motor ability leads to increased skill leads to increased self-confidence

Fitness concepts

- Optimal functioning of all body systems

Integral part of program

- Schedule—indoors and outdoors, regularly scheduled physical activity
- Environment—safety, variety of spaces (open and confined), variety of surfaces (hard and soft), barrier-free, protection from the elements, convenient features, stationary and portable equipment, lack of interference between play areas
- Gross motor equipment—stimulate variety of skills, logical progression of skills, maximize success, encourage problem solving, encourage safe risk taking, encourage transfer of skills

Adaptations

- Separation of space for various age groups and needs—various levels of skills, mobile equipment, close supervision
- Adaptations for children with physical handicaps—wider pathways, gentle slopes, handrails, guardrails, accessible pathways to all areas

Stimulation of a variety of activity levels

- Warm-up activities—get ready, prepare muscles
- Main activity—encourage active physical activity individually and in groups to increase skills and related concepts
- Cool down activities—relax muscles, rest

Adult interactions

- Supervision—safety, prevention of accidents
- Assist in skill development—spontaneous, planned
- Talk about what children are doing
- Encourage social play—group participation, cooperation

Develop positive self-concept

- Succeeding at age-appropriate tasks
- Appropriate development of skills
- Encouragement

Maximize success

- Developmentally appropriate activities, materials, equipment
- Skill development from simple to complex
- Rotation of materials, equipment
- Practise skills in a variety of settings
- Observe and record skills to provide appropriate experiences
- Avoid competition
- Encourage and praise efforts

Bias-free physical activity

- Inclusive activities regardless of gender, ability, skill, culture
- Establish positive attitudes
- Encourage equality

EXERCISES

1. Using the nine principles of developmentally appropriate practices, reflect on your personal growth and development. How many of these principles were used in developing a physical activity program for you? How many were not in place? Why do you think some principles might have been missed?

2. Compare the developmentally appropriate outcomes for each age group. Identify how a maturational component is associated with each age. Why is it important to build on these outcomes?

3. Observe a group of preschoolers during outdoor play. Which movement concepts could you identify? How did the adults make the children aware of these movement concepts?

4. Reflect on some physical activities you do well or not so well. Which list is longer? Why do you think there is a difference between what you perceive you do well and what you perceive you do not so well?

5. In a small group, develop one activity per age group—infants, toddlers, preschool children, school-age children—to identify how you could make children more aware of their body movements or gain understanding of physical fitness.

6. Observe an outdoor playground. Identify how many relational concepts children can achieve in the playground. Which relational concepts are missing? What adaptations should be made to improve the play area or what additional components need to be added to meet all relational requirements?

7. In a small group, plan a gross motor activity for toddlers. The activity should include at least four of the following: development of strength, flexibility, balance, skill, endurance, coordination, and movement. Identify warm-up activities, main activity, and cool down activities.

8. Describe the adult's role in:
   • supervision
   • skill enhancement
   • increasing children's awareness of their activity
   • encouragement of social play
   • creating a bias-free physical activity program

9. You are one of three teachers in a daycare with mixed age groups (3 infants, 12 months to 18 months, all walking; 5 toddlers; and 8 preschoolers). All children use the same playground at the same time. What strategies would you have to put in place to be able to provide an effective physical experience for all three age groups? Use Figure 6.3 as your starting point.

10. Refer to the playground layout in Figure 6.3. A toddler's parent has complained that she finds your program very dictatorial. She does not understand why you would force children to travel one way around the riding path. She feels that the path is wide enough to accommodate two riders going in opposite directions. How might you respond?

✱ Glossary

Cephalocaudal (page 167) Development of bones and muscles proceeds from head to toes; infants learn to control their neck muscles first, then their trunk to roll over, and finally their leg muscles to learn to sit and walk.

Eye–hand coordination (page 173) Ability to see an object, be able to reach and grasp it, and use it effectively; for example, reaching for a rattle, grasping it, and shaking it to make a sound.

Locomotor tasks (page 165) Tasks that involve moving from place to place, such as running, walking, skipping, or climbing.

Non-locomotor tasks (page 164) Anchored movements such as balancing, twisting, rocking, or swinging arms.

REFERENCES

Allen, K., & Marotz, L. (2003). *Developmental profiles pre-birth through twelve*. Clifton Park, NY: Delmar.

Belfry, J. (2003). *Canadian children ace activity and fitness crisis*. Child and Family Canada. http://www.cfc-efc.ca/docs/cccf/00010_en.htm, accessed 22 September 2003.

Canadian Standards Association (2003). *Children's playspaces and equipment*.

Graham, G., Holt/Hale, S., & Parker, M. (1998). *Children moving: A reflective approach to teaching physical education*. Mountain View, CA: Mayfield Publishing Company.

Health Canada. (2002). *Canada's physical activity guide for children*. http://www.hc-sc.gc.ca/hppb/paguide/guides/en/children/index.html, accessed 22 September 2003.

Hobson, J. (1998). *Fetal psychology*. (Rep. No. 160).

Kirchner, G. (2000). *Children's games from around the world*. Toronto: Allyn & Bacon.

Nash, M. (1997). Fertile minds. *Time*, 149, 48–56.

Schickedanz, J., Schickedanz, D., Forsyth, P., & Forsyth, G. (2001). *Understanding children and adolescents*. Fourth edition. Needham Heights, MA: Allyn & Bacon.

7

CHAPTER

Physical Activity Programs for Various Age Groups

"Only 36% of schoolchildren today are required to participate in daily physical education. Yet researchers now know that exercise is good not only for the heart. It also juices up the brain, feeding it nutrients in the form of glucose and increasing nerve connections—all of which make it easier for kids of all ages to learn." (Hancock, 1996: 58)

Chapter Outcomes

After reading this chapter, the reader will:

1. Explain why it is important to provide physical activity programs for children.

2. Explain why physical activity is important to brain development.

3. Describe daily motor activities for
   • infants
   • toddlers
   • preschool children

4. Discuss how music can be used effectively to encourage physical activity.

5. Describe the components of a fitness program (warm-up, main workout, and cool down) and explain why each is important.

6. Describe fitness programs for preschool and school-age children.

Physical Activity and Brain Development

In 2003, a call for action to increase physical fitness for children living in Canada resounded across the country (Belfry, 2003; Health Canada, 2002). In November 2003, *Today's Parent* launched an initiative called Fat Action both via the Internet and in print. "We've heard it, read about it, and witnessed it. Now it's time to move on it. Our kids are on their way to early coronaries, diabetes and cancer because they eat too much and exercise too little. It's time for a radical societal solution." (Partridge, 2003)

Calls for action usually occur when a problem of concern and magnitude has been identified. Children in Canada have been identified as more obese and more sedentary than ever before. As a result, Canadian teenagers have now been identified as being at risk for heart problems. Most programs identified in the calls for action deal with older children. However, an effective preventative process needs to start at a much younger age.

Brain development clearly identities that stimulation of the brain is needed to form appropriate connections, known as "wiring of the brain" (Begly, 1997; Nash, 1997; Shore, 1997). Appropriate connections are formed when (Figure 7.1):

- a child is stimulated—Activities are provided that encourage active play such as running, jumping, climbing, crawling, reaching, and grasping.
- adults talk about and reinforce activities the child engages in—Connections are formed between specific movement and cognitive functions such as understanding and language.
- a child has opportunities to practise skills in a variety of settings—When children are given the opportunity to practise a skill over and over and transfer the skill from one situation to another, connections in the brain are strengthened and reinforced, which leads to more effective execution of skills.

✳ Myelinazation

The speed at which individuals respond to stimulation depends on another factor of brain development—myelinization. **Myelinization** is the "development of the myelin sheath around the axon, [which] allows the neuron to transmit its electrical impulses faster." (Kaplan, 2000: 288) Myelinization of the sensory structures is completed within the first year of life. "The increased speed of neural transmission allows the child to process information more quickly and efficiently." (Kaplan, 2000: 288)

Since the greatest brain development occurs in the first three years of life (McCain & Mustard, 1999), it is critical to start to act within the early years. All ages and stages are connected through one commonality—movement. At each stage of development the child is engaged in a variety of specific movements. As the child matures and develops, these movements become refined, specialized, and coordinated. As with any development, when opportunities for movement are not provided, children may experience developmental motor delays. The effects of the motor delays may be overcome if that infant is subsequently placed in a stimulating environment. If stimulating opportunities are not provided, that infant may never develop to his or her full potential.

Studies have been conducted with institutional infants who spent most of their time in cribs, were not given toys to play with, and were fed with bottles propped up in their cribs. "When babies managed to pull themselves into a sitting position, they were placed on the floor when awake, but were given no toys. Only 42% of the 1- and 2-year olds could sit up; none could walk. When they turned three, most of these children went to Institution II, where conditions were as bad. Only 15% of the children between 3 and 4 years of age at Institution II could walk." (Schickedanz, Schickedanz, Forsyth, & Forsyth, 2001: 137) A third institution modelled developmentally appropriate practices. The most severely motor-delayed infants in Institution I were transferred to Institution III. "By age 3, all children could walk alone (as compared to 8 percent at Institution I)." (Schickedanz Schickedanz, Forsyth, & Forsyth, 2001: 137) It is clear that infants need appropriate stimulation for optimal development to occur. They need daily opportunities to engage in physical activity both indoors and outdoors.

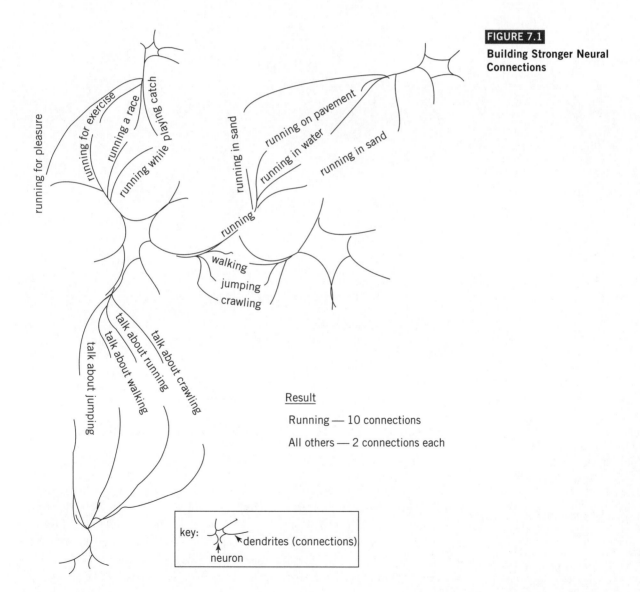

FIGURE 7.1

Building Stronger Neural Connections

FIGURE 7.1
Continued

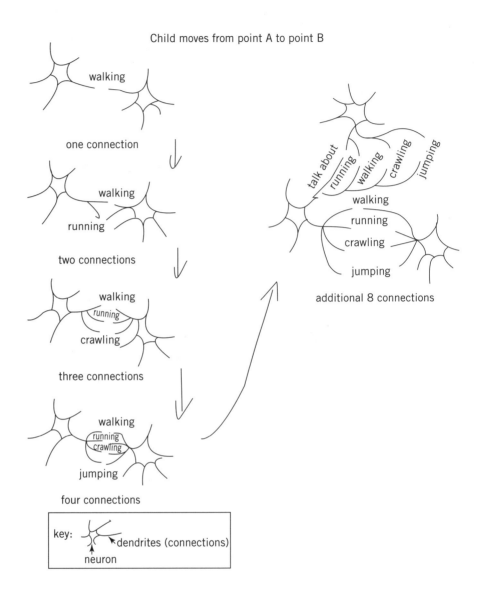

Child moves from point A to point B

walking

one connection

walking

running

two connections

walking

running

crawling

three connections

walking

running

crawling

jumping

four connections

talk about   running   walking   crawling   jumping

walking

running

crawling

jumping

additional 8 connections

key: dendrites (connections)
neuron

Physical Activity Programs for Infants

1. Non-mobile Infants

Much of a young infant's early learning is directly related to movement. Piaget identifies this as the **sensory motor stage** (birth to two years of age)—"Infant gradually becomes able to organize activities in relation to the environment through sensory and motor activity." (Papalia, Wendkos Olds, Duskin, & Feldman, 2001: 32) At birth, many of an infant's actions are **reflex actions**, or involuntary actions. These early reflex actions "play an important part in stimulating the early development of

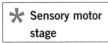

✳ **Non-mobile infant**

✳ **Sensory motor stage**

✳ **Reflex actions**

the central nervous system and the muscles." (Papalia, Wendkos Olds, Duskin, & Feldman, 2001: 135) Some of these reflexes, such as the sucking reflex, are needed for survival. Some reflexes, such as the rooting reflex (turning face toward a stimulus and trying to suck), disappear within three to four months. Other reflexes, such as the grasping reflex, become more refined with practice and maturation.

It is critical that infants be provided opportunities to use and practise their motor skills. Motor skills appear in an orderly sequence and skills build on each other. "Babies first learn simple skills and then combine them into increasingly complex systems of actions, which permit a wider or more precise range of movement and more effective control of the environment." (Papalia, Wendkos Olds, Duskin, & Feldman, 2001: 140) Activities that provide opportunities for movement can be divided into three categories—awareness of body parts, motivation to move, and control over movements. The major tasks that infants at this level of development need to master are:

- gaining control of their heads—Control of head muscles allows infants to look around the environment and gain a steady visual field. The infant can look at an object or event for longer periods of time. A steady visual field is a prerequisite to developing eye-hand coordination and balance (Wingert & Underwood, 1997).
- gaining sufficient upper body strength to pull themselves into a sitting position and then into a standing position

Table 7.1 provides descriptions of the movement categories along with sample activities to optimize infant motor development.

There is a close relationship between music and movement. Music provides opportunities to listen and react, such as moving in accordance with the speed of the music. Additionally, music can help set the mood, such as happy, sad, or curious. Movement is associated with feelings; we skip or dance when happy, or we may move slowly when sad. Providing music to move to helps establish natural **rhythm** (time-based concepts in music such as beat, length of sound, and tempo) or **beat** (the steady pulse that underlines a musical creation). All activities have a natural rhythm or beat. Some naturally occurring ones such as the heartbeat are already familiar to young infants. Others include such activities as walking, running, jumping, or relaxing. Table 7.2 provides some musical suggestions to implement with children.

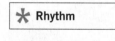

2. Mobile Infants

Mobile infants will start to move around their environment in various ways—rolling, crawling, pulling themselves up to walk, and finally walking independently. As infants learn to move independently, they develop confidence in their abilities. Motor skills are continually refined and infants become increasingly skilled in their ability to move around the environment. Although most infants follow a developmental sequence—crawling, pulling themselves up to stand, walking with support, walking unassisted—not all infants do. Some infants may walk before they crawl, for example. Physical activities for mobile infants are outlined in Table 7.3.

TABLE 7.1 DAILY MOVEMENT ACTIVITIES FOR NON-MOBILE INFANTS

Category	Activities
Awareness of body parts Infants need to learn about their body parts through observing them, feeling them, moving them, between a movement and its result (cause and effect).	- Attach noisemakers to wrists or ankles to attract attention to that body part when the child moves it (photo 7.1). - Play games that involve touching and talking about toes and fingers, such as This Little Piggy Went to Market. - Play games that involve moving the arms or legs into various positions—opening the arms, extending them wide, shutting them, bringing them across the chest, crossing them. - Massage various body parts (legs, back, arms) gently and talk about what you are massaging; also a good activity to relax infant. - Tickle various body parts; put the infant in different positions while tickling (photo 7.2). - Place items into hands to encourage grasping; talk about what the infant is doing/grasping (photo 7.3). - Use music such as classical music to gently move arms or legs in time (see Table 7.2 on page 201).
Motivation to move Infants need to explore movement by touching, grasping, kicking, and manipulating in a safe, stimulating environment. Since infants are so dependent on being carried, it is important to encourage them to move independently.	- Place infant on a blanket in a clear area on the floor to encourage unobstructed movement (photo 7.4). - Provide items within reach that child can grasp and manipulate (photo 7.5). - Model activities such as waving, clapping, or finger movements. - Dance to music while holding child in arms. - Provide toys that are easy to grasp, shake, touch, and manipulate (see photo 4.8 and photo 4.9 on page 102, and photo 6.14 on page 168). - Provide noisemakers such as rattles to shake (photo 7.5). - Provide items that encourage infants to swat at, grasp, and roll toward them (photo 7.6). - Play games such as Pat-a-Cake (photo 7.7). - Provide opportunities for water play; use wading pools or bathtubs with enough water to place infants safely on tummy or sitting; ensure water is warm and provide continual supervision; play with infant by splashing or swirling water around. - Help child pull himself or herself to a sitting or standing position (photo 7.8).

Photo 7.1

Photo 7.2

Photo 7.3

TABLE 7.1 CONTINUED

Category	Activities
Motivation to move	- When child is able to sit with support, provide pillows; when child can sit without support, provide soft area to sit on and clear area around child to prevent injury in case of a fall.
Control over movement By providing infants with materials that encourage different motor skills, such as **eye–hand coordination** (ability to reach for and successfully grasp an item), skills are refined and connections between cause and effect (for example, when button is twisted, toy makes a noise) are built.	- Provide toys that encourage reaching, twisting, pulling, turning, grasping, and shaking (photo 7.8). - Provide toys that are soft, fluffy, and sturdy to withstand biting; these are easy to pick up, transfer, and hold (photo 7.9). - Provide toys with harder edges and open surfaces that encourage different grasping skills—placing fingers around edges, different manipulation, releasing all fingers before transferring (photo 7.10) - When child is able to sit, place objects within reach and in front of child; helps with balance and moving while maintaining balance. - While the child is sitting, expand activities by playing games such as hiding a toy under a blanket (photo 7.11); helps child develop further control over balance, reinforces learning about **object permanence** (an object still exists even if it not in sight), helps child learn to coordinate actions (sitting, balancing, and reaching. and removing the blanket).

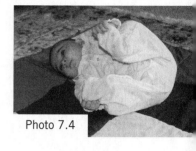

Photo 7.4

✳ **Eye–hand coordination**

✳ **Object permanence**

Photo 7.5

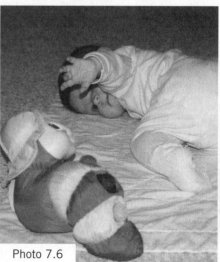

Photo 7.6

Photo 7.7

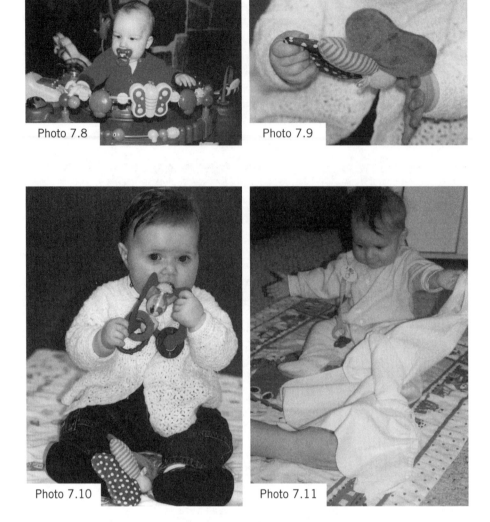

Photo 7.8

Photo 7.9

Photo 7.10

Photo 7.11

Physical Activity Programs for Toddlers

Toddlers are naturally active and very insistent on doing things by themselves. Toddlers walk and run with a wobbly, wide-footed gait. They often lose their balance and fall. "Toddlers walk this way because top-heaviness, caused by their relatively large heads, makes it difficult for them to keep their balance. They compensate, thus maintaining their balance, by placing their feet wide apart to create a wide base of support." (Schickedanz, Schickedanz, Forsyth, & Forsyth, 2001: 127)

Brain development continues throughout the toddler stage. Myelinization of motor structures is completed before the toddler is two years old. This means that the toddler will be able to process motor activity stimuli much more effectively. This may account for the rapidly evolving motor skills in the toddler stage.

TABLE 7.2   **MUSIC TO MOVE TO**

Purpose	Suggested Source and Actions
Moving infant's arms or legs in time to music Dancing to music with child in arms	*Lullabies: Cherished Bedtime Classics.* (2000). Don Mills, ON: Musical Reflections. *If You're Happy And You Know It Sing Along.* (2000). Arlington Heights, IL: Baby Reflections. *Countdown Kids.* (1998). Twinkle Twinkle Little Star. St. Laurent, QC: Madacy Entertainment. *Baby's First PlayTime.* (2003). St. Laurent, QC: St. Clair Entertainment.

Moving in time to music	Familiar songs to move to:
	
	"Here We Go Round the Mulberry Bush" (St. Clair Entertainment, 2003)—encourages walking and running around obstacles
	
	"I'm a Little Teapot" (St. Clair Entertainment, 2003)—strong walking beat
	
	"If You're Happy and You Know It" (St. Clair Entertainment, 2003)—following actions in the song, jumping, clapping
	
	"The Ants Go Marching Home" (Baby Reflections, 2000)—marching
	
	"Rock-A-Bye Baby" (Countdown Kids, 2003)—walking
	
	"Walking Up the Stairs" (Sharon, 2002)—climbing stairs
	
	Other music:
	
	"Chicken Dance" (St. Clair Entertainment, 2003)—combination of movements, walking, running, jumping, turning around
	
	Bach for Baby's Brain (Baby Reflections, 2003)
	  #1—tiptoeing, quiet walking
	  # 2—quiet, slow walking, speeds up to slow running
	  # 3—fast running, changes to skipping
	  # 6—stopping and starting, varied movements

Singing and encouraging action	"Ring Around the Rosie" "Hokey Pokey" "Itsy Bitsy Spider" "If You're Happy and You Know It" "Shake the Sillies Out"

TABLE 7.3 **DAILY PHYSICAL ACTIVITIES FOR MOBILE INFANTS**

Movement Category	Possible Activities
Pulling self up to stand As infants gain upper body strength, they use furniture, equipment, or the help of others to pull themselves up to standing. Infants gain new perspective from this position. They now can see more of what is on top of things and quickly gain the balance to hold on to a surface and grab items on that surface.	- Ensure that crib sides are securely locked since infants will pull themselves to standing. - Provide sturdy furniture and equipment to encourage children pulling themselves to standing (photos 7.12, 7.13, and 7.14). - Help children pull themselves to standing; provide hands but let children pull themselves up (photo 7.15). - Provide interesting substances or objects on surfaces to encourage children to pull themselves up to look; encourages children to balance while using one hand; the other hand can be used to touch or grab objects on surface (photo 7.16). - Provide opportunities for children to pull themselves to standing on various types of surfaces such as a rug, a bare floor, sand, grass, pavement, wood; skills are transferred from one situation to another and stronger brain connections are formed.
Walking with support Infants who have pulled themselves to standing quickly learn to walk while holding on to firm surfaces such as tables or chairs.	- Encourage infants to walk while holding your hands; stop and let them look at things around them; encourage them to pick up things while holding on to a hand for support. - Provide opportunities for children to walk along various surfaces both indoors and outdoors. - Provide sturdy toys that encourage children to hold on while walking; the push toy in photo 7.17 has weights attached to its bottom to make it stable enough to pull up on.

Photo 7.12

Photo 7.13

Photo 7.14

TABLE 7.3   CONTINUED

Movement Category	Possible Activities
Walking Once an infant stands without support or tries to get up to standing without support, walking unassisted soon follows (photo 7.18).	- Encourage walking by providing stable support as a starting point and someone else to walk to as a goal (photo 7.19). - Provide large, clear areas for walking both inside and outside. - Ensure transfer of skills by walking on different surfaces such as wood, rugs, grass, sand, and snow.
Crawling Crawling increases an infant's independence. Crawling makes it possible to move to a desired location or object.	- Encourage crawling in a variety of settings both indoors and outdoors by asking children to crawl to you. - Ensure that the environment is free of elements that could hurt crawlers—wood that splinters easily, carpets that could lead to carpet burn, small objects that could bruise or cut if crawled on. - Provide a variety of surfaces to crawl on or in—ramps, grass, wood, carpet, sand, water (photos 7.20 and 7.21).
Climbing When infants start to crawl, they also quickly learn to climb—stairs, ramps, and low platforms (photo 7.22).	- Provide opportunities for climbing both indoors and outdoors. - Provide close supervision, or safety gates when not able to supervise closely. - Teach infants to go down stairs backwards; many will attempt to go down head first. - Play games such as peekaboo as infants climb stairs.

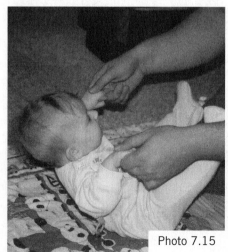

Photo 7.15

Photo 7.16

TABLE 7.3 CONTINUED

Movement Category	Possible Activities
Play with balls Many skills such as balancing, upper body control, arm and hand control, and eye–hand coordination can be developed through ball skills. Large exercise balls give infants a different movement perspective.	- Roll balls of various sizes toward each other, down ramps, and along the floor. - Throw balls and drop them into containers (photo 7.23). - Use alternative materials such as sock balls or beanbags to throw or roll. - Place infant tummy-down on a large exercise ball, hold infant by hands and sustain eye contact, and gently pull infant back and forth. - Encourage carrying balls and dropping them and watching them bounce.
Sliding/swinging Provides infants with experience in speed of movement and orientation of space	- Monitor the top of the slide to prevent children from tripping and falling down the slide; monitor the middle of the slide to ensure that speed is not too fast to scare children; monitor the bottom of the slide to prevent children from falling off and hitting their heads on the slide. - Use baby swings with supports on all sides; face infants when pushing them on swings to monitor comfort level at all times.

Photo 7.17

Photo 7.18

Photo 7.19

Photo 7.20

Photo 7.21

Photo 7.22

Photo 7.23

For optimal motor development to occur, toddlers need to engage in activities that will improve their balance, flexibility, strength, coordination, and spatial orientation. Toddlers learn through repetition. In fact, toddlers do things over and over again. Caregivers should use these **developmental teachable moments** (opportunities to expand learning taking place at a particular time that are based on knowledge of child development and observations of children using an activity a child is engaged in) to create opportunities for repetition in a variety of settings, both indoors and outdoors. For example, a toddler is delighted to roll a ball across the room and chase it. Developmental teachable moments that could result in response to this behaviour include engaging in a similar activity outside, rolling the ball to another individual, rolling the ball down a gentle hill, or kicking and chasing the ball outside. Additional activities that offer opportunities for developmental teachable moments include walking and running, speed of movement, squatting and bending, riding, climbing, jumping, and sliding and playing on swings.

✳ Developmental teachable moment

1. Walking and Running

Toddler should walk and run on a variety of open surfaces—hills (up, down, on top), gravel, sand, grass, pavement, carpeted areas, tiled floors, and ramps (up, down)—in various conditions—ice, snow, and water. Through these activities toddlers learn to navigate different surfaces appropriately (problem solving) such as by taking larger steps and walking carefully so they won't slip and fall (balance). They need to learn when it is safe to run and when it is more appropriate to walk (gaining understanding of speed of movement). Walking and running also improve **endurance** (the ability to sustain activity over time) and build up strength in the legs to climb up a hill or walk through more difficult terrain. Appropriate walking and running activities include:

* Endurance

* Spatial orientation

- directed running or walking—Play games in which children are directed to run to a fence, walk to a climber, or tiptoe down a hall. Children will become more aware of themselves and the space they are in (**spatial orientation**— where the toddler is in relation to the rest of the space, such as in the middle, at the side, or on top). This type of activity also provides opportunities for children to play in small groups, the beginning of shared social activities. When toddlers are involved in group activity, they can observe others doing similar activities to their own and thus gain understanding about actions as they relate to others.
- navigating simple obstacle courses that encourage walking or running (Figure, 7.2)— Adults should reinforce the direction of walking or running to prevent toddlers from colliding with each other. Toddlers learn to watch others as they engage in activities. Each area is set up to naturally encourage walking or running (gaining understanding of speed of movement)—open areas are usually used for running, whereas requiring children to go though something or around a corner (spatial orientation) slows them down to a walk.
- going for walks in the neighbourhood—walking on sidewalks or running in the park (gaining understanding of appropriate motor behaviour)
- playing hide and seek with individual children—Since toddlers have not yet fully developed the concepts of sharing, taking turns, or cooperation, this is a much better activity for one-on-one interaction (spatial orientation).
- ball activities—rolling, kicking, or throwing a ball and then chasing it. This activity works well indoors or outdoors. Be sure to use soft balls to prevent accidental harm and encourage children to throw or roll balls away from others. This activity provides opportunities for children to coordinate fine and gross motor activities and to be aware of others around them. It also increases flexibility (bending with balance to pick up and throw the ball), eye–hand coordination (aiming the ball), and awareness of speed (how fast the ball travels, how fast one has to run to catch up to it).
- bubble play such as chasing soap bubbles—Children can learn to blow bubbles and chase them, or try to catch bubbles blown by adults (photo 7.24). This activity

Photo 7.24

encourages eye–hand coordination (catching a floating bubble), awareness of speed (moving fast or slow enough to catch a bubble), and coordination of movements (running and catching bubbles).

- walking or running to the beat of a drum or in time to music (see Table 7.2 on page 201)—Toddlers learn to coordinate listening and moving, learn about speed of movement (fast, slow, no movement), and learn to interact with others at an individual level (each child moves according to his or her ability, but all children move together). Toddlers often engage in **swarming behaviour**—when they see or hear something of interest, they promptly join in—and this activity lends itself to their natural development.

✳ Swarming
behaviour

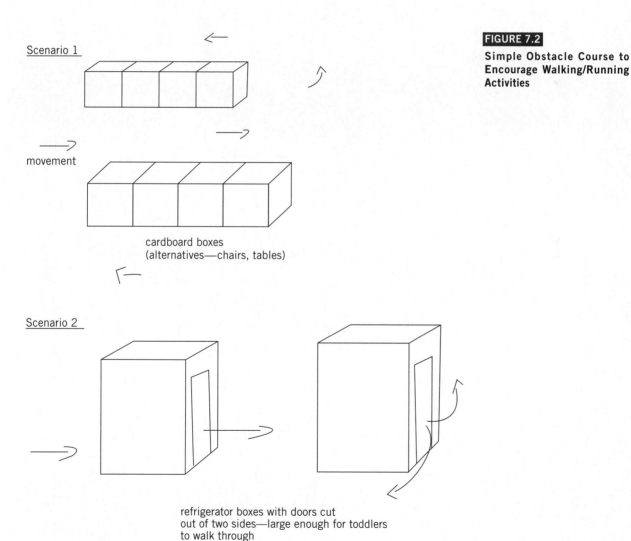

Scenario 1

movement

cardboard boxes
(alternatives—chairs, tables)

Scenario 2

refrigerator boxes with doors cut
out of two sides—large enough for toddlers
to walk through

FIGURE 7.2

Simple Obstacle Course to Encourage Walking/Running Activities

Scenario 3

Securely tape various shapes to the floor.
Children run or walk to a shape.

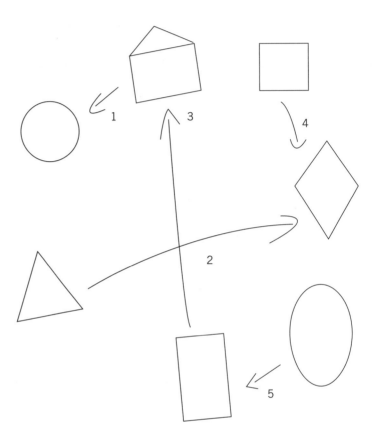

Activity appropriate for up to five toddlers.
There are more shapes than toddlers
to prevent accidents.

2. Speed of Movement

Many walking and running activities can be naturally adapted to opportunities to learn about speed of movement. Toddlers need to learn when it is appropriate to walk or run and *how to stop*. In general, large open spaces encourage running; corners, obstacles, or changes in the ground or floor such as inclines, sand, or snow will automatically signal changes in movement. It is much harder to run up a hill or through deeper snow or sand than it is on a clear, level surface. Barriers will signal stops and toddlers may actually use the barriers to stop themselves (running into a wall or fence to stop).

- Use natural activities to encourage running, walking, or stopping (increase understanding of appropriate speed of movement). Take children for a walk in the neighbourhood (walking on the sidewalk; stopping at a crosswalk; stop, look, and listen). Walk down a hall and in the daycare room. Run on the playground.

- When teaching children to move to music (see Table 7.2 on page 201), start with slower pieces that children can walk to. When the music stops, children stop. Be prepared that teaching children this rule will take some time. Toddlers get very enthusiastic about this activity and may continue walking when the music has stopped. Gentle reminders and practice help children learn to stop (increased understanding of speed of movement and coordination of listening and moving).
- Have children chase rolling toys such as balls. While the ball rolls, the child runs; when the ball stops, the child stops. This is a natural activity as the toddler naturally stops to pick up the ball when it stops rolling (gaining skill in stopping).
- Use push toys that children can ride. The harder you push, the faster you go. Encourage children to slow down and stop (increased balance, coordination, control over speed, endurance, strength, and awareness of spatial orientation).

3. Squatting and Bending

Toddlers spend a lot of time picking up items and carrying them from place to place. This activity requires them to bend down, pick up the item, and maintain balance to stand up again with the item in hand (photo 7.25). This type of activity increases a toddler's independence, agility, strength, coordination, and ability to solve problems. Activities that encourage squatting and bending include:

Photo 7.25

- placing toys on low, sturdy shelves—encourages toddlers to bend down to pick up items; toddlers can bend down while holding on to the side of the shelf to maintain balance
- providing baskets or other containers to place items in and carry them around with—helps toddlers gain control over their movements and increases coordination (walking with balance and carrying an object); toddlers enjoy filling and dumping so this becomes a natural activity for them
- providing large objects that require toddlers to pick up and carry them with both hands (photo 7.26)—increases flexibility, balance, and coordination of movement
- throwing, bouncing, rolling, and play with balls or beanbags—increases coordination of fine and gross motor control, increases eye-hand coordination, builds strength (photo 7.27)
- games such as peekaboo—encourages children to squat down to see and improves control over various body positions
- asking children to follow simple directions such as bend down and touch the ground, bend down and touch their knees, or find a ball and pick it up—encourages development of balance, flexibility, and coordination and serves to strengthen different muscle groups

4. Riding

Toddlers love to use riding toys, and they usually push themselves around rather than using pedals. Using riding toys encourages children to coordinate more than one

activity at the same time—balance, agility, pushing, and steering (photo 7.28). Activities that develop skills in riding include:

- using a variety of riding toys—toys that are pushed by feet, pedal toys
- using riding toys as a regular part of a program—during dramatic play, on walks, indoors and outdoors
- using riding toys in a variety of weather conditions—windy, wet, snowy
- riding in areas that encourage problem solving—going around corners, coasting down a short hill
- implementing realistic safety practices—posting stop signs to indicate when or where to stop before proceeding, posting one-way signs in narrow areas

5. Climbing

Climbing is an excellent way for toddlers to use their emergent motor skills. As Karson tries to climb on the rocking horse that has been firmly anchored to the ground (photo 7.29), he is expanding his ability to:

- solve problems—Karson tries several different ways to climb on the horse before he is successful.
- increase his agility—It is difficult for Karson to take the big step between the first and second rungs and to lift his leg high enough to put it over the back of the horse.
- increase his balance—The horse moves as Karson attempts to mount it and he finds it difficult to keep his balance as he tries to climb onto the saddle.
- coordinate his actions—Karson has to coordinate moving his hands and legs together, balancing on a moving surface, and moving his hands and legs in opposite directions to accomplish the task.

Photo 7.26

Photo 7.27

Photo 7.28

Photo 7.29

Additional climbing activities can be performed on:

- ladders or ramps on climbers (photo 7.30)
- steps in the diapering area
- a loft within the indoor environment (photo 7.23)
- sturdy furniture such as chairs, soft cubes, and ramps (photo 7.23)
- natural structures in the environment such as benches, hills, trees, or stumps

Photo 7.30

6. Jumping

Toddlers continually practise their emergent motor skills and continually expand their repertoire of skills. Much of toddlers' learning depends on imitating skills they have seen modelled. They are bombarded with examples of a variety of motor skills in their environment—watching older siblings or peers engage in more advanced motor activities, media promotion of sports, videos and stories about imaginary or real characters engaging in spectacular stunts, and toys that encourage imitation of these activities. One such motor activity is jumping from various heights. Toddlers have not yet developed the ability to judge whether a jump may be safe or not. They must be carefully supervised at all times.

Steven, two-and-a-half years old, is very interested in Spiderman. He often wears a Spiderman T-shirt and talks about the many feats Spiderman can accomplish. As Steven is using the outdoor climbing equipment, he suddenly decides to climb atop the railing at the top of the platform to "swoop down like Spiderman." One of Steven's teachers is alert enough to move into position quickly to catch him as he jumps.

Toddlers need to learn what is safe for them to do and what is not safe. They need to develop a sense of safe heights from which to jump. This learning can occur only if toddlers are given many opportunities to practise jumping. Activities that can help children develop greater competence in jumping include:

Photo 7.31

- jumping into or onto things—Jacob is jumping onto paper snowflakes (photo 7.31) in time to a song the preschool children created (Figure 7.3); the toddlers watched and imitated the older children.
- setting up an obstacle course in which children can jump into and out of items such as hoops, shapes (taped to the floor or ground), or tires
- setting up situations that encourage jumping—The toddlers discover that they can build a row of the large hollow blocks, walk along the top of these blocks, and jump off the end of the row (photo 7.32).
- playing jumping games such as jumping to music—for example, to "Popcorn" (Phillips, 2002)
- providing opportunities to jump from steps or low platforms

7. Sliding and Playing on Swings

Slides and swings give toddlers opportunities to control and learn about their body in different spatial orientations and to practise different skills. Sliding allows toddlers to:

Photo 7.32

- climb to the top of the slide
- balance while sitting at the top of the slide

FIGURE 7.3   **Snow Song Created by Preschool Children**

> *(To the tune of "Frère Jacques," do the actions to the song.)*
>
> Snow is falling, snow is falling *(hand motions to make snow fall, bending to the ground)*
>
> Jump, jump, jump *(jump onto a snowflake taped to the floor)*
>
> Jump, jump, jump *(jump onto a snowflake taped to the floor)*
>
> Snow is all around us *(twirling around)*
>
> Snow is all around us *(twirling around)*
>
> Jump, jump, jump *(jump onto a snowflake taped to the floor)*
>
> Jump, jump, jump *(jump onto a snowflake taped to the floor)*

- balance as they move down the slide—sitting or lying on their back, landing at the bottom with control
- learn how to control speed of movement—how fast is comfortable, how fast is safe
- learn how to stop or slow down during and at the end of the sliding activity
- learn how to get off a slide safely
- gain self-confidence in their ability to control their actions

Playing on swings allows toddlers to:

- climb on and off a non-stable object
- balance while sitting on the swing as it is in various positions
- learn about how fast or high they are comfortable swinging
- learn how to slow down or stop
- learn how to get off a swing safely

Physical Activity Programs for Preschool Children

"Preschoolers' expanding motor abilities allow them to attend to what is going on around them rather than having to concentrate just on how they walk and hold things. Preschoolers can now easily take part in many physical activities, satisfying some of their natural curiosity about the world and learning from their experiences. Their physical skills give them more independence." (Kaplan, 2000: 278)

Brain development continues during the preschool years. In fact, by the time a child is three years old he or she has twice as many synapses or brain connections as an adult. As children mature, some of these connections are lost or pruned. This process is thought to strengthen existing connections. It is therefore critical to continue to provide opportunities for preschoolers to strengthen connections already established and continue to build new connections.

Preschool children continue to build on past motor experiences, further developing and refining these skills. In addition, their body proportions have changed. The head gradually becomes more proportioned to the rest of the body, thus making the pre-schooler less top heavy. "The preschooler gradually loses that baby like appearance. The amount of fat decreases during this period, with the added weight resulting from the growth and development of muscle tissues." (Kaplan, 2000: 278). As a result, preschoolers' movements have become smoother and more coordinated. Developmentally appropriate activities are outlined below under the appropriate developmental milestones for preschoolers.

1. Developmental Milestone: Running

A) ACTIVITIES TO CONTROL STOPPING AND STARTING Three-year-olds establish control over stopping and starting. Activities that help them develop this skill include:

- group games that encourage children to stop and go—stop and go to music (Table 7.2), stop and go to the beat of a drum, stop and go in accordance with voice prompts
- dramatic play activities that encourage stop and go activities—crossing guards, police officers, traffic signs
- obstacle courses featuring various shapes or objects that are firmly attached to the floor or ground and that require children to stop when they reach a certain point—stop in a red circle, jump into a circular shape or hoop and stop, slow down across yellow squares, stop at the end of a square
- simple variations of Simon Says—Use simple directions such as walk or run slowly, walk or run quicly, stop, and go; when children miss a direction, smile at them and say something like "Simon caught Karen," then continue the game.

B) ACTIVITIES TO CONTROL TURNS AND SPEED Four-year-olds learn to control turns and speed while running. Activities that help them develop this skill include:

- pathways on the ground or taped to the floor that have many curves or sharp corners to navigate—Ask children to pretend they are cars speeding along the road but to be careful not to leave the road or they will crash.
- obstacle courses that encourage children to run around objects such as chairs, boxes, or blocks—Children can pretend they are vehicles navigating rough terrain, animals running away from something, or chasing a bunny around the course.

X − obstacle in way

→ − direction of travel

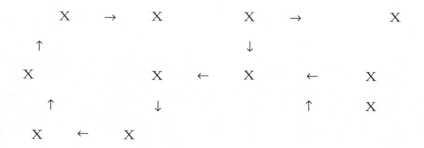

- running while kicking a ball in front of them
- follow the leader—in the yard or open indoor space, adult leads children around obstacles such as chairs, boxes, blocks, or tables; children can become leaders when they become more skilled at this task

C) ACTIVITIES TO SUPPORT RUNNING DURING PLAY Five-year-olds use running as part of their play. Activities that help them develop this skill include:

- running around a track along the outside of the room or playground—Measure distance of track to estimate how many laps make up a kilometre; have children count laps they run to build up kilometres for keeping fit; graph the results daily.
- games with simple rules—Run around a circle while clapping your hands, have children initiate how to run and move.
- obstacle courses that children help create—Encourage children to complete course by running backwards or sideways (Figure 7.4 shows examples of obstacle courses and instructions children have created).
- group games that involve retrieving objects—Place a number of blocks and toys in a large box at the end of the playground or in a large room; children sit or stand behind a starting point in groups of two or three; call out two or three

FIGURE 7.4

Obstacle Courses Developed by Children

Obstacle Course I

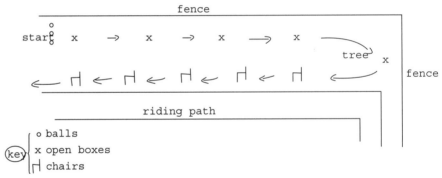

Rules: Children run between boxes or chairs.
        You cannot run until someone is at the next box
        or chair. you must stop to drop a ball in each
        box while standing up or to balance a ball
        on each chair. You cannot continue until the ball is in
        the box or on the chair.

Obstacle Course—inside or outside

        Run around the chairs while dribbling a ball.

        start   end

        when you get to the end, pick up the ball
        and run back to the start.

children's names to run and find a block or toy and bring it back to the starting point; blocks and toys can be used to create a balanced structure that can change as children bring more toys and blocks back to the starting point.

- individual activities with balls—kicking a ball into a net (running and kicking the ball, kicking a ball from standing then running to get the ball and try again) using hockey sticks to place a ball into the net, dribbling a ball while walking or running, running and throwing a ball into a basket or container on the ground

2. Developmental Milestone: Jumping and Hopping

A) THREE-YEAR-OLDS Most three-year-olds tend to jump using straight legs and do not bend their knees when they land. Hopping tends to use two feet.

- Play jumping games—jump like a(n)… (children fill in an animal or object of choice).
- Jump in time to music (see Table 7.2 on page 201).
- Imitate objects that children have observed, such as bouncing balls or mechanical toys that jump.
- Encourage jumping onto, into, and down from items—obstacle courses provide excellent opportunities to engage in these types of activities.
- Encourage jumping on climbing equipment—jump down from the end of a slide, jump from a low platform, jump down the ramp or steps.
- Encourage children to try to balance on one foot as they count to three.

B) FOUR-YEAR-OLDS Four-year-olds jump starting in a crouching position. They start to hop on one foot, but hopping is wobbly and is not sustained over time.

- Encourage individual children to see how far they can jump. Measure and mark the distance. See if children can improve their distance over time.
- Take pictures of children jumping using the crouch position at take off and landing with bended knees. Show children the pictures so they can see how different individuals jump. Ask children to try different jumping techniques and talk about them.
- Practise jumping in different areas—grass, sand, snow, water (puddles), pavement. Ask children to describe how each surface feels and which is more fun or more effective.
- Set up opportunities that encourage children to jump over low obstacles such as low blocks, the edge of a tire into its centre (photo 7.33), or a low bench.
- Encourage children to hop along a straight path taped to the floor or on the ground.
- Create a stepping stone path across a pretend river (river can be created with blue material securely taped down with paper stepping stones on top). Children can hop or jump from stone to stone.
- Replicate natural conditions indoors. Tape down puddles or snowflakes to jump or hop onto to music (see Table 7.2 on page 201) or have children create songs to hop and jump to (see Figure 7.3 on page 212)

Photo 7.33

C) FIVE-YEAR-OLDS Five year olds' jumping and hopping activities become smoother and more coordinated.

- Set up hopscotch games outside or inside (Figure 7.5)
- Develop a jumping pit outdoors. Use a piece of wood firmly attached to the ground as a starting point. Children jump into sand. Provide items such as small coloured flags to mark the distance jumped or hopped to. Children can practise improving the length of their jumps.
- Build an obstacle course such as the one shown in Figure 7.2 (see page 207). Encourage children to jump through the obstacle course.

FIGURE 7.5

Variations of Hopscotch

Game 1—Easiest Level

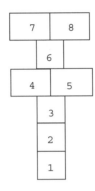

Game 2— More advanced

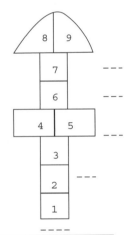

Key: --- throw lines

Instructions

1) Individual play
   Use marker such as a beanbag. Jump into first box, with two feet or one. Put marker down. Jump into each box in turn. On return, pick up marker. Repeat steps.

2) Group play (Up to three individuals)
   Pick a number out of a *container. This is starting point. Jump to appropriate spot, drop marker. On return, leave marker in spot. Step or jump over spot with marker in it. Repeat steps as long as children are interested.

*Adult should ensure that only even or odd numbers are in container to ensure success of activity.

Instructions

Similar strategies identified in easi variation.

Variations:

1) Throw marker tc appropriate spot. Child should throw marker until succe rather than missin a turn.

2) Create differen throw lines to enhance success

3. Developmental Milestone: Climbing

Three-year-olds climb using one foot at a time. Four-year-olds ascend and descend using alternating feet. Five-year-olds have increased climbing abilities such as climbing a rope or climbing a ladder with the bottom free.

Climbing activities are similar for all age groups. Children need to learn to use alternating feet and hands to climb. Most climbing apparatus provides opportunities for a variety of climbing activities that are suitable for all preschool age groups. Adults must be aware that climbing up is much easier than climbing down because children can see where they are going. Children may get stuck when climbing down. This can be a very frightening experience so children may need guidance to help them place their feet in the correct spots to climb down.

- Take children on field trips where they can climb natural elements such as trees or stumps (see photo 6.1 on page 162) or to playgrounds that offer different challenges such as monkey bars or poles (see Figure 6.4 on page 179).
- Provide opportunities for climbing in natural settings, such as encouraging children to use stepping stools or ladders (under supervision) to get items on shelves they cannot ordinarily reach.

4. Developmental Milestone: Riding

Three-year-olds ride pedalled riding toys but still find stopping and navigating corners difficult. Four-year-olds ride pedalled riding toys with ease and are able to stop and navigate corners effectively. Five-year-olds start to ride bicycles with training wheels and by the end of this period may start to ride without training wheels.

Activities for riding are similar for all age groups. The environment needs to be set up to encourage children to gain experiences with:

- speed—Children need straight sections to practise various speeds without worrying about navigating corners or stopping suddenly.
- stopping and starting—Provide riding paths that end on another path or sharp corners that encourage children to slow to a stop.
- steering—Obstacle courses encourage children to steer around obstacles.
- safety rules—Use known safety signs such as one way, yield, stop, or sharp corner.

5. Developmental Milestone: Skipping

Three-year-olds use a shuffling step while skipping. Four-year-olds use one-footed skips but their movement is stiff and undifferentiated. Five-year-olds use an alternating-foot pattern to skip but movement is halting.

Skipping is a natural activity that all children engage in. Provide opportunities to:

- skip to different types of music (see Table 7.2 on page 201)
- model skipping

- use skipping instead of running or walking in obstacle courses
- sing songs about skipping—for example, "Skip to My Lou"—while children skip
- point out and discuss when someone is skipping so that children can start to identify differences between various modes of walking, running, and skipping

Regular Fitness Activities for Preschool and School-Age Children

Preschool children not only have further developed and refined their motor skills, but their understanding of the world around them has also improved. These skills continue to become more refined and developed over the school-age years. As children begin to understand more about their body and how it functions, they need to be exposed to healthy living habits. Regular exercise is part of that healthy living. Any regular exercise program needs to include the following components:

- warm-up and stretching activities—prepare the body for more rigorous exercise, prepare individuals mentally and protect the body from muscle strain or other injuries such as cramps
- main workout—exercises that work the heart, lungs, and muscles and increase balance and coordination
- cool down and stretching activities—relax the body after exercising

1. Warm-up and Stretching Activities

When children engage in warm-up activities, it is important to discuss where the child should feel the stretch. All stretches should be held for 10 to 15 seconds. Warm-up activities should last three to four minutes. *Rainbow Fun* (Toronto Public Health, 1999) identifies the following warm-up exercises:

- sit and reach (photo 7.34)—The child sits on the ground, stretches one leg out, tucks the other leg in toward the inner thigh, and gently stretches toward the extended toes. Avoid locking the knees. Discuss that the stretch should be felt along the back of the extended leg. Repeat on the other side.
- stork stretch (photo 7.35)—The child finds something to hold on to for balance. One foot or ankle is grabbed and gently pulled up toward the buttock. The hip should be tilted forward slightly. Discuss that the stretch should be felt in the front of the thigh. Repeat with the other leg.
- butterfly stretch (photo 7.36)—The child sits and brings both feet toward the body with the bottoms of the feet together and the knees bent. The child grabs ankles with his or her hands and gently pushes down on knees with his or her elbows. Discuss that the stretch should be felt along the inner thighs.
- hug your legs (photo 7.37)—The child lies on his or her back. One leg is grabbed under the knee and brought to the chest. While in this position, the ankle is rotated first one way and then the other way. Repeat with the other leg. Discuss that the stretch should be felt in the ankle.

Photo 7.34

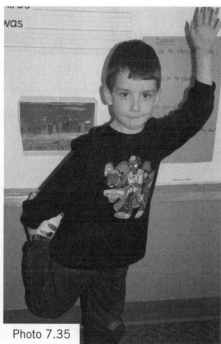

Photo 7.35

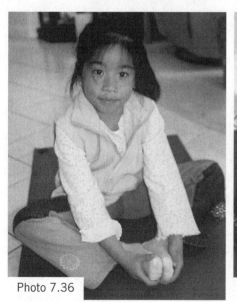

Photo 7.36

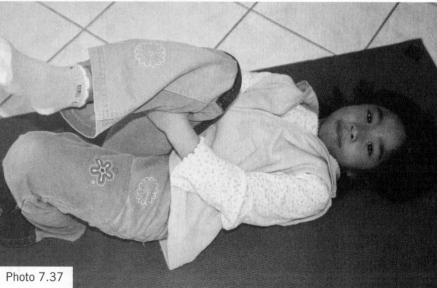

Photo 7.37

- reach up high—Children stand and raise their hands above their heads. Encourage children to stretch as high as they can reach. Discuss that the stretch should be felt on both sides of the waist.
- march on the spot—Children march on the spot, raising their legs high and swinging their arms. This can be varied to marching in circles or in different directions. Discuss that the stretch should be felt in the thighs and upper arms.

2. Main Workout

A) WORKOUT FOR LUNGS AND HEART Workouts for lungs and heart should be rigorous and last three to four minutes. Exercises could include running, riding, jumping, or climbing activities. Combine these types of activities with obstacle courses, follow-the-leader games, moving to music, and other games and directed activities (Table 7.4).

B) MUSCLE WORKOUTS Muscle workouts should involve different muscle groups such as arms, legs, or abdomen. Activities for muscle workouts are described in Table 7.5.

C) BALANCE AND COORDINATION ACTIVITIES All physical activities require a certain degree of balance and coordination. Encouraging better balance and greater coordination

TABLE 7.4   GAMES AND DIRECTED ACTIVITIES

Activity	Description
Red light, green light	- Children line up against a wall or behind a line. The object of the game is to move in a variety of ways across to another wall or line. When green light is called, children move. Movement should be encouraged in a number of ways—hopping, jumping, running in a circle. When red light is called, children must stop. When children reach the other side, the game can be repeated. - Music or playing a drum can also be used. When the music plays, children move. When the music stops, children stop.
Freeze into interesting shapes	- Children move in time to music, to verbal directions such as run in a circle, or to the beat of a musical instrument. When the music stops or the directions indicate stop, children freeze into interesting shapes. - Point out and discuss interesting body shapes that the children have created.
Use natural conditions such as wind or rain	- Children move slowly at first, marching or tiptoeing. - The adult gives directions that affect the children's movement—The wind is blowing. The wind is blowing harder. The wind is blowing the leaves in circles. The wind is bending the branches of the trees.
Natural conditions such as popping corn	- Children roll up in small balls. The adult tells the children that the heat is getting hotter and that the corn is expanding. When the adult calls out "pop!" the children jump up and try to form an interesting popcorn shape. Discuss the shapes formed.

TABLE 7.5 **ACTIVITIES FOR MUSCLE WORKOUTS**

Activity	Description
Inchworm	- Children bend their knees and reach down to touch the ground. - They walk their hands away from their bodies as far as they can go. - Then they move their feet to reach their hands. - Backs should remain straight.
Action activities	- We Are Going on a Lion Hunt—Children look for a lion, receiving instructions such as marching through high grass, moving the grass aside with their hands, climbing high hills, walking through water, squatting to look through the brush, or crawling through the grass so as not to be seen. When they find the lion, they squat and take a picture of it.
Sit-ups	- Children lie on the ground with their knees bent and their hands behind their heads. They sit up without pulling on their heads.
Pushing	- Children stand near a wall with feet flat on the ground, hands flat against the wall, and elbows bent. Children push away from wall until their arms are straight.

serves to strengthen all motor skills. Activities to improve balance and coordination are described in Table 7.6.

3. Cool Down and Stretching Activities

It is important to allow muscles and the body to relax gradually to prevent injury. Children will also have an opportunity to relax mentally and prepare for the next activity. Some cool down activities are listed in Table 7.7.

TABLE 7.6 **BALANCE AND COORDINATION ACTIVITIES**

Activity	Description
Jumping and hopping activities	- Children run and jump into a sand area. Measure the length of jumps and try to improve their skills. - Children bend their knees and jump forward. Next they hop forward on one foot. Repeat the jump and hop with other foot. - Hop across an area on one foot. Return by hopping on the other foot. Lines made with masking tape can be put in the classroom to encourage children to hop throughout the day. - Jump to music following a leader. - Play follow the leader. Leader visibly or verbally creates a pattern of movement including jumps, hops, walking, and changes in direction.

TABLE 7.6   CONTINUED

Activity	Description
Walking activities	- Walk on lines, both forward and backwards. - Walk on balance beams, both forward and backwards.
Riding activities	- Ride around obstacle courses. - Ride on different gradients such as uphill and downhill. - Ride forward and backwards.
Action songs	- Children respond through actions to words of songs such as "Itsy Bitsy Spider," "Head and Shoulders," and "Hokey Pokey."

TABLE 7.7   ACTIVITIES FOR COOL DOWN, STRETCHING, AND RELAXING

Activity	Description
Marching activities	- March on the spot or move in different directions. - Start briskly and gradually slow to a stop.
Gentle exercises such as swaying trees	- Children use arms and body to sway softly to blowing - winds and eventually slow down and stop.
Spinning tops	- Children are spinning tops and spin standing up or sitting down. When they run out of steam, they slowly stop and fall over. Children lie quietly on the floor or ground for a while.
Stretches	- The warm-up stretches discussed earlier can be used for cool down as well. - Children give themselves hugs—in a standing or sitting position, they cross their arms and wrap them around themselves. Hold for 10 seconds. - Arm stretches—stand with feet apart and bend one arm behind the head. Place other arm on elbow and gently press back. Repeat on other side.

TABLE 7.7 CONTINUED	
Activity	**Description**
Breathing	- Deep breathing—in a standing position, take a deep breath in through the nose. To the count of five, let it out slowly through the mouth. Repeat three times. - As a breath is taken in through the nose, raise arms high above the head. As the breath is released through the mouth, lower the arms back to sides of the body.

SUMMARY

Children should engage in regular physical activity from the time they are born. Regular motor activities reinforce and strengthen connections made in the brain. Stronger brain connections increase the efficiency of motor tasks. Children who are physically active experience a number of benefits. *Rainbow Fun* (Toronto Public Health, 1999: 3) identifies the following benefits of a regular physical activity program for young children:

- strengthens bones
- improves muscle strength and endurance
- improves flexibility
- works the heart and lungs
- helps develop coordination and balance
- helps maintain a healthy weight
- improves skills
- increases self-esteem
- provides an outlet for stress
- improves learning
- builds cooperative skills

KEY POINTS

Brain development through stimulation

- Active physical play
- Discussion of motor activity child is engaged in
- Practice of motor skills in a variety of settings
- Reinforcement and motivation to engage in motor activity
- Myelinization of motor pathways to increase speed and efficiency of motor activity

Physical activity programs for non-mobile infants

- Sensory motor stage—Child learns through movement by using the senses.

- Reflex actions—some disappear very early, others are refined with practice and maturity
- Infants' motor tasks—gain control over head, gain upper body strength
- Activities to gain awareness of body parts—noisemakers attached to arms or legs, frequent touching and talking about body parts, moving various body parts, gentle massage, grasping activities, moving to music
- Motivation to move—Position infant in clear areas to encourage unobstructed movement; provide materials within reach to encourage swatting, grasping, shaking, manipulating; move to music; play games that encourage movement, such as clapping and banging; water play such as splashing and swirling; help child by supporting them while sitting, pulling them to sitting or standing positions.
- Develop control over movement—manipulative toys (squeeze, pull, twist, reach, turn, shake), textured toys, toys with edges to encourage variety in grasping skills, activities to develop object permanence

Physical activity programs for mobile infants

- Pulling up to stand—crib sides, sturdy furniture, help child pull up to standing, provide incentives to stand, provide experiences with different type of surfaces to stand on
- Walking with support—walk while holding hands, sturdy toys that can be pushed while walking, sturdy surfaces
- Walking—stable starting point, transfer skill by walking on different surfaces
- Crawling—encourage crawling, provide safe areas for crawling, provide variety of surfaces to crawl on
- Climbing—close supervision, teach child to go down stairs backwards, play climbing games
- Play with balls—rolling, throwing, dropping, use alternatives such as beanbags or sock balls, exercise with large balls, carrying and dropping activities
- Sliding/swinging—provides experience with speed and different orientation of space

Physical activity programs for toddlers

- Walking/running—variety of open surfaces, directed walking or running activities, navigating simple obstacles, neighbourhood walks, ball activities,

bubble play, moving to music or beat of musical instruments
- Speed of movement—learn how to stop, provide various surfaces that require different skills, provide natural barriers, use natural activities such as stopping at a stop light, move to music, use rolling toys to chase, encourage use of riding toys
- Squatting and bending—toys on low, sturdy shelves; baskets/containers to fill and carry; large objects that need to be picked up with two hands; throwing, bouncing, and rolling activities; peekaboo in squatting position; following simple directions
- Riding—variety of riding toys, regular part of program, variety of weather conditions, opportunities to problem-solve, practise safety rules
- Climbing—problem solving; increase agility; increase balance; coordinate actions; climb ladders, ramps, steps, sturdy furniture, and benches
- Jumping—jumping on or into things, jumping through obstacle course, set up situations to encourage jumping, jump in time to music, jump from various heights
- Swinging/sliding—balance, control speed of movement, learning to stop, learning to get off safely, gaining confidence in actions

Physical activity programs for preschoolers
Three-year-olds:

- Stopping and starting—stop and go to music or directions, dramatic play, obstacle courses with stop and start symbols, simple games
- Jumping and hopping—simple games, jump like a frog, jump in time to music, jump into or onto items, imitate items or animals that jump, jump from various heights, balance on one foot

Four-year-olds:

- Control speed of movement—move along designated pathway, create obstacle course encouraging different speeds of movement, ball activities such as running and kicking, follow the leader
- Jumping—jumping to gain distance, observe pictures of children jumping, practise jumping on different surfaces, jump over low obstacles, jump or hop along a path, imaginary games such as jumping across stepping stones or imaginary puddles

Five-year-olds:

- Running—designated tracks, games with simple rules, obstacle courses created by children, individual ball activities, obstacle courses that encourage movement in different directions
- Jumping—games such as hopscotch, jumping pits, obstacle courses

Common activities

- Climbing—climbing natural elements in environment such as trees, stumps, ladders, and stepping stools; visit playgrounds that encourage different skills
- Riding—experience with speed, stopping, starting, and navigating; practise safety rules
- Skipping—modelling, skipping to music, skipping instead of walking or running activities, skipping to songs, observing skipping

Fitness activities for preschool and school-age children

- Warm–up/stretching—prepare body for exercise, sit and reach, stork stretch, butterfly stretch, hugging legs, reaching up high, marching on the spot
- Workout for lungs and hear—rigorous exercise such as running, riding, and jumping; climbing activities that use games; imitating weather conditions or natural conditions; following directions
- Muscle workouts—strengthen different muscles through imitation games such as inchworm, action games, or specific skill builders
- Balance and coordination activities—hopping and jumping, walking, riding, following directions
- Cool down/stretching—relax body and prepare for transition, marching, imitating nature or moving toys, stretching, breathing activities

EXERCISES

1. In a small group, discuss why you think physical activity has been neglected in our society. List some strategies that could be used to increase awareness of the need for physical activity in your community.

2. Divide into small groups of no more than six people. Each group needs six balls of different coloured yarn. Each of the groups represents a neuron that receives and sends messages. Sending a message requires you to throw the ball of yarn to another person while holding onto the end of the yarn. To receive a message, the yarn must be caught. If the yarn is dropped, the connection is lost. Continue with this activity for about five minutes. At the end of five minutes, look at how many times the yarn has been passed along the same path. In instances when you have connected numerous times, a strong neural connection has been made. If you have connected only one or two times, these connections should be cut (pruning). Reflect on the activity. How does this relate to your understanding of neural development? What have you learned from this activity?

3. You have been hired in an infant program. You notice that the infants have very little opportunity to engage in physical activity. Develop five strategies that will help the staff and families understand the importance of starting physical activity with infants.

4. Develop a physical activity program for toddlers for one week. You should ensure that the activities are carried out every day and are both indoors and outdoors. Activities should reflect both directed and free-play physical activities.

5. You are in a child-care centre that has poor outdoor facilities and no indoor facilities to engage in gross motor play. The playground is small and does not have any open spaces. You are within walking distance of a large park and there is a public school across the street. The school has a large primary play structure. You have contacted the school and received permission to use the outdoor space during certain times of the day. What types of physical activities would you develop in the three locations—park, school ground, and indoor environment—for a group of preschoolers?

6. You are in a setting with school-age chidren ages six to ten. When you suggest that you would like to develop a fitness program, the children groan and indicate that they would rather do other things—watch videos, play games, or play computer games. How might you motivate this age group to participate? Develop six strategies.

7. Observe a group of preschoolers in physical activity. Record your observations in the chart below.

8. Develop:
   a) a warm-up activity for a group of toddlers
   b) a main activity for a group of school-age children
   c) a cool down activity for a group of preschoolers

CHART 1

Date: _____

Setting: _____

Skills Observed	Documentation
Developing endurance	
Developing strength	
Developing coordination	
Developing agility	
Developing balance	

*Glossary

Beat (page 197) The steady pulse that underlines a musical creation.

Developmental teachable moment (page 205) An opportunity to expand learning taking place at a particular time that is based on knowledge of child development and observations of children using an activity a child is engaged in.

Endurance (page 206) The ability to sustain motor activity over time.

Eye–hand coordination (page 199) The ability to reach for an item and grasp it successfully; over time, ability is refined so child can learn to perform intricate tasks such as cutting on a line, printing, and sewing.

Myelinization (page 194) The development of a myelin sheath around axons; allows neurons to transmit electrical impulses more quickly.

Non-mobile infants (page 196) Infants not yet able to move from location to location by crawling or walking.

Object permanence (page 199) The understanding that an object still exists even if it not in sight.

Reflex actions (page 196) Involuntary actions.

Rhythm (page 197) Time-based concepts in music such as beat, length of sound, and tempo.

Sensory motor stage (page 196) Birth to two years of age; as infants mature they increasingly are able to use their sensory and motor abilities to organize their behaviours and activities

Spatial orientation (page 206) Where an individual or object is in relation to the rest of the space, such as in the middle, at the side, or on top.

Swarming behaviour (page 207) Typical toddler behaviour; when toddlers see or hear something of interest they promptly run to participate in the activity.

REFERENCES

Baby Reflections. (2000). *If you're happy and you know it sing along.* Arlington Heights, IL: Baby Reflections.

Baby Reflections. (2003). *Bach for baby's brain.* Don Mills, ON: Baby Reflections.

Begly, S. (1997). How to build a baby's brain. *Newsweek, 28,* 28–32.

Belfry, J. (2003). Canadian children face activity and fitness crisis. Child and Family Canada. http://www.cfc-efc.ca/docs/cccf/00010_en.htm, accessed 22 September 2003.

Countdown Kids. (2003). *Rock-a-bye baby.* St. Laurent, QC: Mommy and Me Enterprises.

Hancock, L. (1996). Why do schools flunk biology? *Newsweek, 127,* 58–59.

Health Canada. (2002). Canada's physical activity guide for children. http://www.hc-sc.gc.ca/hppb/paguide/guides/en/children/index.html, accessed 22 September 2003.

Kaplan, P. (2000). *A child's odyssey.* Third edition. Belmont, CA: Wadsworth/Thomson Learning.

McCain, M., & Mustard, F. (1999). *Early years study final report.* Toronto: Publications Ontario.

Nash, M. (1997). Fertile minds. *Time, 149,* 48–56.

Papalia, D., Wendkos Olds, S., Duskin, R., & Feldman, R. (2001). *Human development.* Toronto: McGraw Hill.

Partridge, K. (2003). Fat action. *Today's Parent, 20,* 90–130.

Phillips, C. (2002). *Dance baby dance.* Toronto: Fisher-Price.

Raffi, & Allender, D. (1987). *Shake my sillies out.* New York: Crown Publishers, Inc.

Schickedanz, J., Schickedanz, D., Forsyth, P., & Forsyth, G. (2001). *Understanding children and adolescents.* Fourth edition. Needham Heights, MA: Allyn & Bacon.

Sharon, L. &. B. (2002). *Mother goose & more.* Toronto: Fisher-Price.

Shore, R. (1997). *Rethinking the brain.* New York: Families and Work Institute.

St.Clair Entertainment. (2003). *Baby's first playtime.* St. Laurent, QC: St. Clair Entertainment.

Toronto Public Health. (1999). *Rainbow fun.* Toronto: Toronto Parks and Recreation; Halton Region Departments of Health, Social and Community Services.

Wingert, P., & Underwood, A. (1997). Hey—look out, world, here I come. *Newsweek, 28,* 12–15.

8

CHAPTER

Health and Safety Issues

Chapter Outline

"Teachers of young children make numerous decisions each day, not just as they interact with children, families, and personnel, but as they are called on to make policy decisions affecting program and practices. To be effective, teachers cannot base their decision making on their own personal bias and predilection, nor simplistic, naïve opinions. Rather, their decisions must be based on an understanding of the complexities involved in each new, potentially controversial polarizing issue." (Seefeldt & Galper, 1998: iii)

Chapter Outcomes

After reading this chapter, the reader will:

1. Identify the issues related to health and safety of children.

2. Discuss how each of the following factors affects the health, safety, and well-being of children and their families:
   • poverty
   • quality of the daycare experience
   • attitudes toward children and child care
   • substance abuse
   • depression
   • stress
   • special needs

3. Define abuse and discuss how it affects children's health, safety, and well-being.

4. Identify and discuss the symptoms of child abuse.

5. Discuss how you might help families and children living in poverty.

6. Identify strategies to help children cope with depression, stress, and substance abuse.

Introduction

Those who work in early childhood education face many health and safety issues regarding children and their families. Adults working with children need to understand these issues to:

- provide quality programs for children
- interact effectively with the families of children
- identify appropriate resources
- advocate for the well-being of professionals, children, and families

The following example of the Sekar family illustrates many of the issues that are most common in Canada.

Issue 1: Poverty

"Children are dependent on their families for income, care, food, shelter, health and safety and relationships. Consequently, while children's well-being and future prospects can be affected directly by developmental, enriching environments, they are also enhanced if their families are sustained economically and socially through employment and community support." (Friendly & Lero, 2002: 2) Despite a publicized resolution to reduce poverty made by the Canadian government in 1998, there has been a 43 percent increase in children living in poverty within Canada (Hertzman, 2002). Poverty affects children on a number of levels—nutrition, safety, growth and development, adult–child interactions, access to appropriate health care, child care, stimulating experiences, and social inclusion.

Consider the Sekars, a family of four living in Winnipeg, Manitoba. The Sekar children are ages two and four. (Although the Sekars are based on a real family, names, geographical location, and circumstances have been changed to protect the privacy of both the family and the daycare.) The Sekars' annual living expenses, totalling $27 584, are listed in Table 8.1. The poverty line (minimum salary required to meet all necessary expenses) in Manitoba is $35 471 (Canadian Council on Social Development, 2003). Saed, Rachel, and their two children, Michael and Cassia, are currently living below the poverty line. Both children receive full subsidies at the daycare they attend. Saed lost his full-time custodial job due to downsizing. Rachel previously worked part-time as a grocery clerk. Now both parents work full-time hours, but at several part-time jobs. The family's combined income is $18 250. Overall, they are looking at a shortfall of $9334 to meet their expenses.

To meet the shortfall, Saed and Rachel discuss selling their car but decide that they need it to get to their various jobs. Instead, they find a basement one-bedroom apartment that has a free washing machine and dryer. They save $2000 a year on rent and $416 on laundry. They also cut food costs by $2000 by eliminating many expensive fruits and vegetables from their diet and by substituting fruit drinks for fruit juices. They cut clothing costs drastically by shopping in second-hand stores. This saves them another $2000. Even with all of these cost-saving measures, they still have not achieved the necessary savings to pay their bills and so decide to sell their car.

1. Effects on the Children and Family

- *Nutrition.* The children and family eat fewer nutritional foods. They can no longer afford to purchase food based on nutritional value alone, but rather buy foods that are cheaper. Once they sell the car, it also becomes too difficult to purchase foods from a variety of sources to take advantage of sales. The added time needed to use public transportation further limits their time at home. The Sekars start to rely on the most convenient grocery store. As a result, more packaged foods and canned goods are purchased. Meals become very irregular. Sometimes breakfast

TABLE 8.1 **SEKAR FAMILY'S ANNUAL EXPENSES**

Category of Spending (Annual)	Michael	Cassia	Rachel	Saed	Total
Food	805	1077	1564	1564	5010
Rent—two-bedroom apartment					8073
Household operations—laundry, cleaning supplies, paper products					416 (laundry) 444 (cleaning supplies)
Personal care	103	103	411	269	886
Health care (family)					374
Dental care	82	82			164
Medical supplies					96
Clothing	463	512	1198	1125	3298
Transportation (family car)					8199
Communications—phone, mail					624
Child care					Full subsidy
Total expenditures					$27 584

is skipped altogether because it is too difficult to get everyone up and ready on time.

- *Health*. Due to the higher intake of sugar, fat, and carbohydrates, the family gains weight. Cassia develops two cavities. Both children spend more time away from home. Using public transportation adds one and a half hours to their day. Sometimes their day is longer if their parents go shopping. As a result, both children go to bed later and get up much earlier. Both cry more often. They are often cranky and tired when they arrive at the daycare. The family often has cold-like symptoms. Michael is diagnosed with allergies to mould. The apartment the Sekars live in is damp, and the carpet is mouldy around the doors and in the corners. The landlord refuses to replace it.

- *Time spent as a family*. The children now spend the maximum time allowed in daycare. They are dropped off at 7:30 a.m. and picked up at 5:30 p.m. They leave the house at 6:30 a.m. and often do not get home until 7:00 p.m. Both parents work long hours. Saed often works in the evening and does not get home until late at night, after the children are asleep. Rachel works weekends. The family has little opportunity to spend time together since one parent is usually working while the other takes care of the children. The children start to watch more TV while one parent sleeps or completes household chores.

- *Stress*. All family members experience increased stress levels. Saed worries about his ability to care for his family. He works long hours to try to earn enough money. He has to give up one of his jobs because he can no longer get to it by public transit. As a result, he increases his hours at another job, but this does not make up for the loss of the better-paying part-time position he gave up. He is also trying to find a permanent job and feels very guilty about the change in his family's living circumstances. Rachel always seems to feel tired. She no longer has the energy to do simple things such as reading to the children at bedtime or taking them to the park.

- *Family interactions*. The family stops talking to each other in meaningful ways. Arguments increase. The children often hear and see their parents argue, doors slam, their father leave, and their mother in tears. They learn to keep out of the way so that arguments do not involve them. The parents often shout at the children. There are few opportunities to act in nurturing ways toward each other. The children are often confined to the bedroom if they misbehave.

- *Safety*. The children now have to share a bedroom with their parents. Both parents and children lack privacy. This often results in arguments and expectations of behaviour that are not developmentally appropriate for young children, such as being quiet when a parent is sleeping, being left alone in the living room when the parents want privacy, and watching too much unsupervised TV to keep them occupied. Both children become quieter and more withdrawn. The apartment is dark and musty. Little daylight streams in through the high, small windows. At times it is hard to tell whether it is day or night. Everyone always feels cold and at least one person always has a cold. There is no park or outdoor area in which the children can play. In fact, both parents are worried about crime in the neighbourhood and thus venture outside only when necessary.

- *Stimulation.* The children have few toys or books. Most of their stimulation comes from the TV.
- *Recreational activities.* Neither time nor money permits any type of activity as a family. Saed starts to go drinking with his buddies after work and often comes home drunk. This further depletes the family's resources and increases arguments between the parents.
- *Social support.* Because the family moved and now has little time to socialize, they lost all of the supporting friends and neighbours they had in their previous location. They have no time to develop connections in the new neighbourhood. They no longer have opportunities to talk about their problems or call on neighbours for sporadic child-care services so they can do things such as grocery shopping.

In summary, economic circumstances dictate the Sekars' living conditions. "Families who live in poverty have less time to spend with their children. They work longer hours, are more likely to suffer from ill health, stress and depression, are more likely to have established patterns of dysfunctional family life, and are less likely to have appropriate social support." (Crowther, 2004: 235)

2. Effects on the Daycare

- *Behaviour of the children.* Both children often arrive in the morning crying and cranky. Both children are more withdrawn and tend to be more involved in solitary play. They often leave the area if another child comes to play. Cassia often shouts at children to leave while Michael simply clutches his toys and runs away. If children do not leave, Cassia throws a temper tantrum. Both children are easily upset by other children or adults, especially if voices express anger or disappointment. Cassia tends to play near an adult whenever possible. Michael often demands to sit on a caregiver's lap. Both children tend to use many sensory materials such as sand, water, and playdough. Cassia spends a lot of time in the dramatic area with dolls—reading to them, bathing them, feeding them, and taking them for walks.
- *Behaviour of the parents.* When the children are dropped off, the parents tend to leave them and rush off. This causes some resentment among daycare staff, as family members are supposed to ensure that their children are settled before they leave. Often the parents forget to sign the children in or out. They are often late to pick up their children. They never pay the late fee charged. The parents never seem to have time to discuss their children's day or progress.
- *Health.* Both children seem to have continual colds. Their noses are always running. They seem listless and it is difficult to wake them after sleep time. They are always hungry and request more than one serving at every meal. Neither child enjoys physical activity. During group active play, Cassia chooses to sit on a bench.

- *Cleanliness.* Both children look unkempt. Their clothes do not fit well, and their hair is often uncombed. The other children start to tease Cassia about her clothes.

In summary, the daycare staff finds it more difficult to deal with the behaviours of the children and the parents. As a result, the children are identified as having behavioural problems. The staff becomes frustrated in dealing with the children. They identify the parents as not caring for their children appropriately. As a result, further barriers to establishing an open dialogue between staff and parents are created.

Issue 2: Quality of the Daycare Experience

The daycare centre that Cassia and Michael attend meets all regulations for the operation of a daycare in Manitoba. The staff responsible for Cassia and Michael finds it very frustrating and difficult to deal with the problems presented by the children and the family. The following problems are identified:

- *Behaviour of the children.* The children are often cranky or crying when they are dropped off in the morning. The staff finds it difficult to settle the children into the morning routine. In fact, the children often do not settle down until after snack time. The staff finds that they have to monitor snacks very closely, because both children tend to take more than their share if not watched. Each morning starts with a 20-minute good-morning circle. It is challenging to get Michael to listen and Cassia will not sit near any of the other children. Mealtimes are problematic because both children request multiple servings and become agitated when they are only allowed two. The children make sleep time difficult because they are hard to settle and therefore disturb the other children. Both are cranky and whiny when they wake up. The staff also identifies that the children have to be watched closely because they are inclined to hog toys or become physically or verbally aggressive toward other children. The staff is concerned because neither child can follow the rules appropriately. Cassia refuses to participate in group activities and Michael does not listen when told to do something.
- *Behaviour of the parents.* Neither Rachel nor Saed seem to follow the guidelines established in the parent handbook. They simply drop off their children in the morning without undressing them or stopping to speak to the staff. They often forget to sign the children in or out. They do not spend time interacting with the staff. When they pick up the children, they seem agitated and rush to get them dressed to leave. They do not take time to inform staff that they are leaving. The parents also are consistently late. Staff often has to stay late without compensation to accommodate the parents.
- *Health.* The children always have colds and at times have a fever. The parents are reluctant to pick up their children when they are ill. The staff cannot understand why the family drops off the children when they are obviously ill.
- *Cleanliness.* The children look neglected. It does not look as if they receive proper personal care. The staff starts to resent the time spent each day to help the children wash their faces, comb their hair, and scrub their hands. Often the staff also

has to find alternate clean clothing for the children. This also means that these clothes need to be washed regularly, an extra chore for the staff.

Some quality underpinnings of the services offered by this daycare are missing. One standard of practice that leads to quality within a daycare setting is interaction with families—"establishing and maintaining an open, cooperative relationship with each child's family." (Doherty, 2003: 21) A subcategory of this standard indicates that the centre needs to "create an environment where families feel comfortable asking questions, sharing information, and expressing their needs and preferences." (Doherty-Derkowski, 1994: 21)

The staff has not taken the time to look closely at why Rachel and Saed do not follow the guidelines established in the parent handbook. The staff makes assumptions based on limited interactions with Rachel and Saed. Had they made overtures such as "I notice that you seem to be in a hurry in the morning when you drop off the children. How can we help?" the staff might have learned that:

- the children have been up since 5:30 a.m. to ensure that they get to the daycare and the parents get to work on time
- the parents have only 30 minutes to get to work via public transit after dropping off the children
- if the parents are late for work, they could lose their jobs
- the parents are often late because they are travelling during rush hour and cannot get to the daycare any earlier
- when the children are picked up, the parents are in a rush to catch the next bus to ensure getting home before 7:00 p.m.
- the parents cannot leave work early to ensure picking up children on time but also cannot afford to pay a late fee; this situation creates worry and stress for the parents
- the parents cannot afford to take a day off work to care for the children when they are sick; they could lose their jobs, and any wages lost would make it even more difficult to manage family expenses for the month

Another standard of practice that leads to quality services is to "use observations to access children's skills, abilities, interests and needs." (Doherty, 2003: 19) A subcategory of this quality standard indicates that centre staff needs to "use observations in an objective, non-judgmental way to assess children's skills, abilities and interests." (Doherty, 2003: 19) The staff has already decided that the children are challenging. Had they observed Michael and Cassia more closely, they might have become aware that:

- the children's behaviour is most inappropriate in the early morning hours
- the children request more than one serving at snack time
- the children's behaviour improves after snack time

Alternative strategies could have been used to avoid the children's behaviours early in the morning. When Michael and Cassia arrive, they are obviously hungry and tired. To alleviate the negative experiences the children have when they arrive in the morning the staff should have:

- provided a snack for the children when they arrived
- provided restful, nurturing activities of choice such as being read to or opportunities to use sensory activities such as water play or sand play

It is hard for children to be productive when they are hungry. It is equally hard for them to adjust to other children and adults when they are tired. Providing a peaceful transition to the program offers children emotional support to face the rest of the day. These types of strategies address another important standard, "protect and promote children's physical health and well-being." (Doherty-Derkowski, 1994: 7) Protecting children and promoting physical health and well-being include:

- providing nutritional snacks to meet children's nutritional needs
- helping children follow appropriate health practices such as washing hands and face and brushing hair
- providing restful activities during the day as needed

Another subcategory of the standard to provide a safe environment for children is to "provide experiences that are appropriate for each child's developmental level." (Doherty, 2003: 8) It is not developmentally appropriate for toddlers to have a circle time of 20 minutes. Toddlers learn best from activities that encourage them to make choices, be actively involved in what they are doing, and solve their own problems. When toddlers are forced to engage in developmentally inappropriate activities, they respond with inappropriate behaviour, as is evident with Michael.

Meeting children's physical health and well-being also requires that staff members "recognize symptoms that may indicate illness, allergy, injury or common childhood diseases." (Doherty, 2003: 7) Both children have periodic colds and sniffles. Interaction with the parents would have identified that part of the problem is an allergic reaction to mould. Appropriate medication could be brought in by the parents and given to Michael. Posting some alternative solutions for children who are ill might have helped the parents find the support they needed to care more effectively for their children when they are ill.

A third occupational standard relates to the quality of the interactions between children and staff—"establish and maintain a psychologically safe environment for each child and for the group of children." (Doherty, 2003: 8) A subcategory of this quality standard indicates that centre staff needs to "convey acceptance of and respect for children's open expression of their feelings, whether positive or negative, through facial expression, language, or appropriate physical action." (Doherty, 2003: 8)

Young children may not realize when they are hungry or tired; they simply understand that something is not right. Both children clearly indicate through their behaviour that they are tired and hungry—crying, cranky, taking extra helpings of snacks. The staff missed the opportunity to help the children deal with their feelings. Children need adults to provide a safe emotional environment in which they can express and understand their feelings. As soon as the children arrived, the adults could have:

- greeted the children by getting down to their level and interacting with them using a pleasant, welcoming facial expression and tone of voice (photo 8.1)

Photo 8.1

- acknowledged the children's feelings and provided a reason why the child felt the way he or she did. "You have already had a long morning. You must be hungry and tired" (photos 8.2 and 8.3).
- helped the children find a solution to their feelings. For example, a group of children is playing basketball and two boys get into an argument about interfering with attempts to throw the ball into the hoop. Soon they are arguing about the rules (photo 8.4). Pritti notices the interaction and asks the boys to explain what happened. She responds to the anger expressed: "I understand that you might feel angry. It is disappointing to miss your shot. It is not all right to hit or shout at each other. What could we do to solve this problem?" (photo 8.5). The children decide to take turns running and throwing the basketball into the hoop. Pritti walks away but watches the interactions from a distance. The children continue to play appropriately.
- helped the children find something relaxing to do; the adult might walk around with the children to find peaceful activities or may have a favourite activity ready when the children arrive (photo 8.6)

In a quality learning environment, the staff should support and promote the children's physical development—"encourage and support children to engage in a balance of fine and gross motor activities every day." (Doherty, 2003: 12) The children do have opportunities to practise fine motor skills in a variety of art activities and in manipulative activities with puzzles, beading, and small stacking toys. Both outdoor and indoor physical activity is sporadic. Children only go outside if the weather is not too cold and if it is not raining. Most gross motor activities are confined to music and movement, large group activities. Neither Michael nor Cassia participates well in

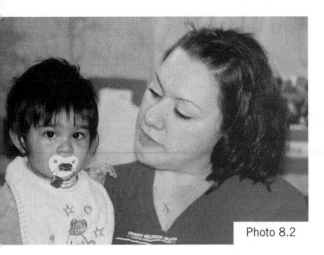

Photo 8.2

Photo 8.3

Photo 8.4

Photo 8.5

Photo 8.6

these activities. Michael tends to run until he is told to sit down because he has not listened and Cassia totally refuses to participate and is allowed to sit on a bench and watch. As a result, both children miss another opportunity to develop and enhance necessary gross motor skills.

In summary, the children's physical and emotional well-being is further jeopardized by the lack of some pertinent quality care in the centre they attend. Michael and Cassia are placed in situations that cause them additional stress.

- The adults in their daycare do not provide warm, nurturing, and responsive care. The children's behaviour clearly indicates that the interactions between the adults and children are inappropriate. Michael does not listen to the adults, and Cassia prefers to and is allowed to play alone.
- The environment does not adequately provide for emotional safety. The staff tries to force both children to do things that neither child is comfortable or ready to do, such as participating in circle time and in adult-directed activities during gross motor play.
- The children's physical health and well-being is not optimally provided for. The children have to wait to eat and are monitored so that they do not eat too much, even though both children are hungry.
- Interactions between adults and children do not adequately support communication and social development. Cassia is given little encouragement to interact with other children. The staff is relieved to see her playing quietly without a problem and thus misses the opportunity to encourage her to interact with other children. Much of the dialogue with Michael is concerned with his need to listen to instructions or learn to share his toys. Neither strategy is developmentally appropriate for toddlers.

Issue 3: Attitudes toward Child Care

According to Fergusson (2002), there are a number of social attitudes that directly influence the well-being of children.

1. There is a general lack of respect toward early childhood educators, who are often thought of as babysitters rather than professionals. Child-care workers are "not respected by other professionals or society at large for their professional expertise." (Fergusson, 2002: 1) This point is often dramatically illustrated during transition times. Children moving from a daycare system to the school system usually do so without contact between the two service providers. Much of what has been learned about the child during the preschool years is lost and the new teacher has to rediscover pertinent information about the child's development. This is not in the best interests of the child and may lead to frustration in both the child and family members. The child's progression is not a smooth journey from one system to another but often an abrupt stop and start.

2. Funding for child care does not meet the demand for service. "Regulated settings provide only ten to twenty percent of the child care for Canadian children, leaving the vast majority of children in an informal, unregulated and hence non-professional sector where wages are usually even lower and working conditions are poorer." (Fergusson, 2002: 1) Children in unregulated care may suffer due to lack of quality. For example, consider the experiences of two mothers with children in unregulated care.

   Example 1: "I was shocked when I picked up my 14-month-old child that there were a total of 10 children present. My child had been crying, her diaper was dirty, and she had developed diaper rash. When I confronted the child-care provider, she said that she had to make a living and the kids were safe from harm. I promptly removed my child from this service and was much more careful in choosing the next setting."

   Example 2: "When I picked up my four-year-old from the babysitter, he complained that he was hungry. I questioned her and she answered that he had chosen not to eat what had been provided. Since he hadn't finished his meal, he was also denied his dessert. He also didn't like the afternoon snack—celery. I asked her what she had served for lunch. She said macaroni and cheese. I pointed out to her that I had told her that my son does not like the texture or taste of macaroni and cheese. She answered that she couldn't cater to all the children and that the rest of the children loved this lunch. I could not believe that she would try to force my child to eat something he did not like and then punish him for not eating. I looked for new arrangements and, believe you me, I questioned the new child-care provider much more closely."

3. Canadians hold "the belief that the care of children is the private responsibility of their parents rather than an issue of public concern." (Fergusson, 2002: 2) According to a national survey (Focus on the Family Canada Association, 2003) 72 percent

of families believe that the best care a child can receive is from a parent who is not working and caring for the child at home. This attitude is certainly shared by political systems across Canada. Every jurisdiction has a lack of regulated child-care spaces. Only 10 percent of Canadian children under the age of 12 have access to regulated child care. (Hanvey, 2003). This means that most children are placed in a system of unregulated care. In such a system, there are no checks and balances on quality. It is left to the discretion of the caregiver how to care for the child.

Unfortunately, most caregivers have no formal training in early childhood education and as a result may not care for children in the most appropriate manner. For example, in February 2002 a private home care service was shut down in St. Albert, Alberta, and the owner was charged with caring for too many children. Not only was this home care centre overcrowded, but parental concerns about physical and behavioural changes in children resulted in hair and blood samples being sent to the FBI laboratory in Washington, D.C., to test for exposure to illegal drugs. The results are still pending. The reaction to this episode by Iris Evans, Alberta's Minister of Children's Services, caused a host of angry responses. Evans was quoted as saying, "I'm not trying to antagonize the parents . . . I'm simply saying that it's our belief that [parents] have to do . . . due diligence as the primary people responsible for the children and, if they are reacting negatively to things I've said, I'd like to know what they really dispute. If you do all your due diligence I would think that perhaps more [parents] would have discovered the problem." (Ross, 2002) Evans' stand on this issue clearly indicates her belief that parents are directly responsible for their children. This clearly ignores the role of the government in protecting children. Several parents stated this problem very clearly: "I take the responsibility for trusting a con artist and basically being deceived. But I also feel the government has to shoulder some of the burden for this guilt, because they allowed through this licensing act the person's ability to misrepresent themselves to government and to me and get away with it"; "We're very disappointed the minister chooses to blame the victims and hasn't offered any constructive or remedial action on the behalf of her child services authority." (Ross, 2002)

4. In Canada there is a perception that child care is a commodity to be purchased (Fergusson, 2002: 2). In sharp contrast to other services such as education and health care, families who work are expected to pay for the care of their child. In some jurisdictions, families may receive subsidized care. Additionally, the federal government provides tax deductions to families with children in care. However, "these barely affect the majority of middle income families, and are equally available to those using unregulated care (if tax receipts are provided), thus sustaining the informal sector." (Fergusson, 2002: 4) Again, the emphasis is on unregulated care that leaves vulnerable individuals—children—in a system of haphazard care.

- The Canadian child-care system promotes a complete "lack of respect accorded to the youngest children when we leave too many of them at risk in their care setting." (Fergusson, 2002: 2) If only 10 percent of Canadian children who need care are in regulated environments, most children needing care are in environments that provide no assurance that their physical and emotional health or development is adequately ensured.

- A popular belief is that children are best cared for in small, independent groups in home settings (Fergusson, 2002: 7). There are several drawbacks to this type of system that affect not only the individuals caring for children but also the children and families.
  - Child-care providers are often isolated from other professionals. This provides few opportunities to share information or observe new ideas or practices beneficial to young children and their families.
  - The smaller the staff, the less flexibility of working hours. Staff may get few breaks from the children or the workplace. This may lead to work stress and will affect how the staff deals with children, families, and any problems that may occur during a regular day. Individuals need to have regular breaks from the children to maintain their own mental equilibrium.

In summary, social beliefs and attitudes affect the ability of early childhood educators to work effectively with young children. These attitudes are the basis for many other negative factors (Fergusson, 2002: 8):

- *Poor pay.* Poor pay leads to frequent staff turnover and often to the hiring of unqualified staff. Children need stable, consistent environments and will experience increased stress if there are frequent staff changes. Children will also experience increased stress if staff members lack the training to provide developmentally appropriate programs for children.
- *Poor working conditions.* Individuals who work in child care spend the majority of their days with children and within child-sized environments. Breaks are few and the hours of work are long. This often leads to high staff turnover. As already discussed, this leads to increased stress for children and families.
- *Limited professional respect.* Qualified early childhood educators have the knowledge and training to know what is best for the children and families they serve. Few early childhood educators are involved in policy writing or in the political decision-making process. This perpetuates a system that places child-care providers in the category of babysitters with little recognition of their work. It also perpetuates a system of unregulated care for children—a system of dubious quality (Goelman, Doherty, Lero, LaGrange, & Tougas, 2000).

Issue 4: Child Abuse

1. What Is Child Abuse?

✳ **Child abuse**

"The term '**child abuse**' refers to violence, mistreatment or neglect that a child or adolescent may experience while in the care of someone they either trust or depend upon, such as a parent, sibling, other relative, caregiver or guardian. Abuse may occur, for example, within the child's home or that of someone known to the child." (Department of Justice Canada, 2003: 1) "According to the children and family act, child abuse by a person means that the child

- "has suffered physical harm, inflicted by the person or caused by the person's failure to supervise and protect the child adequately;
- "has been sexually abused by the person or by another person where the person, having the care of the child, knows or should know of the possibility of sexual abuse and fails to protect the child; or
- "has suffered serious emotional harm, demonstrated by severe anxiety, depression, withdrawal, or self-destructive or aggressive behaviour, caused by the intentional conduct of the person." (Canadians Against Child Abuse Society, 2003: 1)

There is no accurate information about the number of abused children in Canada. Information can only be gleaned from cases reported to police or child protection agencies. The Canadians Against Child Abuse Society reported 16 359 cases of physical abuse and 6474 cases of sexual abuse in 1996. This represented 47 percent of crime reported in Canada that year. In 1997 the increase since 1996 in physical abuse was 550 percent and in sexual abuse was 67 percent (Canadians Against Child Abuse Society, 2003: 1).

2. Symptoms of Child Abuse

Child abuse may be classified as physical, sexual, neglect, or emotional. A child that has been abused may be subjected to one or more forms of abuse.

- *Physical abuse.* **Physical abuse** involves using deliberate force to cause injury or the risk of injury to a child. Physical abuse includes hitting, biting, shaking, pushing, kicking, choking, burning, or assaulting a child with a weapon. It may also include such actions as holding a child under water, female genital mutilation, or using harmful restraints (Department of Justice Canada, 2003: 1). For symptoms of physical abuse, see Table 8.2.

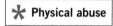

- *Sexual abuse and exploitation.* "**Sexual abuse** involves using a child for sexual purposes." (Department of Justice Canada, 2003: 1) Sexual abuse includes touching or fondling a child sexually, inviting a child to fondle or touch sexually, intercourse, rape, incest, sodomy, exhibitionism, or involving children in pornography or prostitution (Department of Justice Canada, 2003: 1–2). For symptoms of sexual abuse and exploitation, see Table 8.2.

- *Neglect.* **Neglect** involves repeated failure to provide for a child's physical, emotional, or psychological well-being. Physical neglect includes failure to provide children with adequate shelter, clothing, cleanliness, medical care, and food. Emotional neglect includes failure to provide children with love, safety, and a sense of self-worth (Department of Justice Canada, 2003: 2). For symptoms of neglect, see Table 8.2.

TABLE 8.2 **SYMPTOMS OF CHILD ABUSE**

Category of Abuse	Description of Symptoms
Physical abuse	General symptoms: - repeated unexplained injury or vagueness about cause of injury - bruises hidden by clothing, wearing clothes inappropriate for the season - child talking about or acting out harsh treatment with toys, particularly dolls or puppets - frequent unexplained lateness or absenteeism - unusual fear of adults; child may cringe when approached from a certain angle - frequent complaints about pain, especially recurrent abdominal pain - difficulty walking or sitting - recurrent urinary tract infections - fecal soiling or retention - lack of giving, seeking, or receiving affection - appearance consistently thin, drawn, and tired - child withdrawn and uncommunicative, or disruptive and outspoken - sudden, drastic changes in behaviour - evidence that child has received inappropriate food or drugs Bruises and welts: - on the face or other parts of the child's body - unusual patterns or shapes of bruising, such as bite marks, or marks made by an object such as a strap, belt, or belt buckle - clusters of bruises that may indicate repeated physical abuse - bruises in various stages of healing, which could indicate repeated physical abuse over time - any bruising on an infant's body Burns: - from liquid—burns in the shape of a sock or glove on feet/legs and hands/arms that indicate hands or feet have been submerged in a scalding liquid - from objects—cigarettes, ropes, hot surfaces such as the elements of a stove or an iron; these types of burns usually leave a distinct pattern on the body that reflects the object used, such as the circular pattern of stove elements - may occur anywhere on the body but may be hidden by clothes; check buttocks and genitals

TABLE 8.2 CONTINUED

Category of Abuse	Description of Symptoms
Physical abuse	Abrasions (cuts, scrapes, tears): - cuts on lips, eyes, or any other area of the face or body - cuts or scrapes in the genital area Head injuries: - frequent undiagnosed headaches or earaches - bleeding scalp or missing hair - black or swollen, bruised, bloody eye(s) - swollen jaw or mouth - missing teeth
Sexual abuse and exploitation	Physical signs: - difficulty walking or sitting - complaints of pain or itching around genitals or when urinating - soreness, redness, bruising, or chaffing around genital, anal, or mouth areas - vaginal discharge - stained, dirty, bloody underclothes Behavioural signs: - precocious behaviour—child may express knowledge of sexual behaviour through actions (sexual play with toys or peers) or language - refusal to change clothes or be assisted during toileting - unwilling to go to the washroom - fear of certain individuals expressed through reluctance to be alone with that person or to leave with that person - sudden changes in behaviour—becoming withdrawn, thumb-sucking, wetting themselves, loss of appetite, aggressive or disruptive behaviours - talk of sexual assault or portraying it during play (drawings, dramatic play)
Neglect	Physical: - clothing—soiled diapers, unwashed clothing, clothing not suitable for weather conditions - body—body odour, dirty hair, tangled hair, dirty nails, lack of dental hygiene, cavities in teeth Supervision: - left unattended - lack of supervision during play

TABLE 8.2 CONTINUED

Category of Abuse	Description of Symptoms
Neglect	Medical: - lack of dental care - lack of medical care - often ill—colds, flu, cough, childhood diseases Shelter: - homeless - unsafe housing—structural problems, wiring problems - inadequate heating - unsanitary conditions—lack of cleanliness, dampness Nutrition: - child always hungry - underweight, weight loss, smaller size than age indicators - lacklustre skin - diet not balanced for child's growing needs - child may suffer developmental lags
Emotional abuse	- may be quiet and withdrawn or have aggressive and disruptive behaviour patterns - may seem unhappy or solemn and rarely smile - may react without emotions to unpleasant circumstances - may have developmental lags, especially in social and cognitive development - may have low self-concept - family members may voice derogatory comments about the child in the child's presence - may be afraid of adults - may exhibit behaviours more suitable to older or younger children

 Emotional abuse

○ *Emotional abuse.* **Emotional abuse** involves harming a child's sense of self. It involves deliberate acts or lack of actions that place a child at risk of serious behavioural, cognitive, emotional, or mental health problems. Specific examples of emotional abuse include verbal threats, social isolation, intimidation, exploitation, making unreasonable demands, terrorizing children, or exposing children to family violence (Department of Justice Canada, 2003: 2). For symptoms of emotional abuse, see Table 8.2.

Many symptoms of child abuse may also be indicative of other problems. Children may suffer from medical conditions or developmental or behavioural disorders. Children may also be affected by other physical, environmental, or emotional problems. It is important not to jump to conclusions about a child's behaviour. Careful observation is needed to confirm a diagnosis of child abuse. For example, Melanie was a recent graduate of an early childhood education program. One of her children seemed to be neglected. His hair was always greasy and it did not look like it had been combed or washed. His head was covered with dandruff that was continually shedding. Melanie decided to approach the mother with this problem but was nervous about how to raise this subject. Melanie told the mother that she had noticed that her son's hair seemed to be quite greasy and full of dandruff. Before Melanie could continue, the mother told her that the child suffered from psoriasis and needed daily medication. Melanie was relieved and thankful that she had decided to talk to the mother first before reporting this instance to her supervisor.

3. Consequences of Abuse

Children who have been abused often suffer from a number of disabling conditions. These may include:

- *Poor attachment patterns.* Healthy development requires that children form healthy attachments to their primary caregivers. Research has shown a strong correlation between early attachment and later social and cognitive development. Children who have not formed a strong attachment pattern early in life are:

    - less likely to engage in **symbolic play** (play involving actions or materials that are representative of another action or material, such as using a hand as a digger or shrugging one's shoulder to indicate a lack of understanding)

    - less likely to engage in **parallel play** (playing beside other children, using similar materials but engaging in individual play) and group play

    - less likely to take control of their own experiences

    - more likely to throw tantrums

    - more likely to act aggressively toward peers

    - more likely to show emotional dependence toward primary adults

    - more likely to be inhibited to approach adults

    - more at risk to develop **attention deficit disorder** (a disorder in which children seem to be in continual motion, have a very short attention span, and are easily distracted)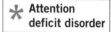

    - less socially competent than their peers

    - more likely to engage in aberrant behaviours

    - more likely to suffer from developmental delays (Schickedanz, Schickedanz, Forsyth, & Forsyth, 2001; Pimento & Kernested, 1996)

- *Failure to establish healthy habits for a lifetime.* Recent research has indicated that there is a strong link between conditions in early childhood and later health. "We know now that the risk for many chronic diseases is set, at least in part, in early life. This has become very clear for mental health problems such as depression in adult life. It is clear that the development during the very early years (including *in utero*) affects risks for high blood pressure and non-insulin dependent diabetes. There may also be an effect on vascular diseases such as coronary heart disease." (McCain & Mustard, 1999: 44)
- *Inadequate neural development.* Healthy brain growth and development requires stimulation of all the neural pathways (visual, auditory, tactile, olfactory, and taste) and essential care (appropriate shelter, nutrition, interactions, and experiences). A child who is abused may never develop the neural networks that lead to optimal growth and development (Nash, 1997; McCain & Mustard, 1999; Begly, 1997).

4. Issues about Child Abuse

There are many reasons why child abuse continues to exist in Canada. The Department of Justice Canada identifies the following reasons.

1. Instances of child abuse often remain hidden.
   - A child may be too young to realize that he or she is being abused and may not be able to communicate what has happened.
   - A child may choose not tell what has happened to him or her.
   - A child may be threatened, coerced, or manipulated by the abusive adult to prevent the child from talking about the abuse to anyone.
   - A child may feel that the abuse is his or her fault and may fear punishment if he or she tells anyone what is happening.
   - Older children may feel ashamed and therefore may wish to keep the abuse secret.

2. Even though child abuse must be reported by law, instances of suspected or witnessed child abuse may not be reported.
   - Individuals may not want to become involved. For example, John (a four-year-old) has a friend, Isaac, who lives next door. Isaac often has bruises on his arms and legs. John's parents suspect that Isaac is physically abused. They are afraid that if they report the abuse, John's parents might become nasty neighbours. As a result, they do not report the suspected abuse.
   - Some individuals may condone the use of physical punishment as behaviour management and therefore may not report it. A national survey by Focus on the Family Canada identified that 72 percent of Canadians "believe that spanking *should* remain a legal option for Canadian parents." (Focus on the Family Canada Association, 2003: 6) On January 30, 2004, the Supreme Court of Canada upheld the rights of parents to spank their children and

schoolteachers to physically discipline children ages 2 to 12 years with "reasonable force." The court set some guidelines to acceptable discipline, such as that it is unacceptable to hit a child with an object or to hit a child on the head.

- Some individuals may not believe that reporting abuse is in the child's best interest. For example, as a child Elizabeth was removed from her mother due to neglect and subsequently placed in a variety of foster homes. She feels that she would have been happier if she had remained with her mother. When confronted with a similar situation—she suspects that her daughter's friend Jennifer is being neglected—she does not report it. Instead she encourages Jennifer to visit regularly so that she can provide some of the necessary care herself.

- Some individuals may believe that reporting abuse will not solve the problem. For example, Barnabas lives in an isolated northern community. He suspects that one of his neighbours is neglecting his children. Barnabas feels that there are no services to offer to the children in that community. Therefore he does not report the neglect.

- Some individuals may be reluctant to report a family that is using their services for fear of reprisals.

- Some individuals may simply not understand that they have a responsibility to report child abuse or who to report it to. Individuals who are unsure of what to do about a situation often will not do anything. Often individuals do not realize that child abuse can be reported anonymously.

3. Some individuals may lack knowledge about the signs and symptoms of child abuse.

- The appearance of physical bruises may be attributed to other conditions. While learning new physical skills, young children can be clumsy and may fall a lot. Therefore, bruising may be attributed to "natural clumsiness." Older children may be involved in contact sports, and bruises may be attributed to these activities.

- Symptoms of neglect such as lack of cleanliness or hunger may be attributed to other causes. Often these conditions are attributed to poverty. Lack of medical care may be attributed to parental beliefs such as disallowing medical attention for religious reasons.

- Children who suffer emotional abuse may exhibit behaviours that have the appearance of "normal behaviour." For example, some of these children may be less social or may tend to avoid interactions with others. At certain ages, lack of sociability is developmentally normal. For example, toddlers do not share toys readily. They may resort to grabbing, hitting, or biting to get what they want. The behaviour of a child who is withdrawn may be attributed to shyness.

- Individuals simply may not believe that family members could possibly abuse their child. For example, Jeremy is a police officer. His three-year-old daughter appears to show signs of sexual abuse. The early childhood educator cannot believe that a police officer could possibly be an abuser. When she finally reports her suspicions, she is shocked to find out that Jeremy was indeed abusing his daughter.

In summary, child abuse is a debilitating condition for children. Often individuals may compound the effects of child abuse unwittingly. "There are also factors that may increase a child's vulnerability to being abused or compound the effects of abuse. For example, a child's caregiver may experience barriers that prevent them from acquiring the necessary skills, resources and supports to prevent abuse, or they may lack access to the services and supports they need to address it." (Department of Justice Canada, 2003) Adults need to become aware of what they can do to prevent child abuse. Prevention requires that adults working with children gain knowledge and awareness about:

- symptoms of child abuse
- the impact of child abuse on the victims
- legal reporting requirements
- who to report suspected child abuse to (police, child protection agencies)—"In all provinces, it has been law since 1968 to report ill treatment of children. Under Section 19 of the Child Welfare Act, everyone having information, whether confidential or privileged of the abandonment, desertion, physical ill-treatment or need for protection of a child was required to report the information to a Society (children's services agency) or the Director of Child Welfare." (Canadians Against Child Abuse Society, 2003)

5. What Can You Do?

- Help the child develop self-confidence. Ensure that the child engages in activities that are developmentally appropriate and that guarantee success. For example, when Ji-Koo starts daycare he is living in a foster home. His foster parents indicate that he seems reluctant to try anything new. Meena notices that Ji-Koo is watching several children complete puzzles. When the children leave the area, he walks over to the puzzles but does not touch them. Meena quickly walks over and asks if he would like to try to do a puzzle with her. Ji-Koo nods shyly. When Meena and Ji-Koo finish the puzzle, Meena says, "That was a hard puzzle. We did a good job." Ji-Koo shows a hint of a smile. A little later he asks Meena if they can do another puzzle together.
- Model appropriate behaviour guidance techniques and post positive guidance techniques.
- Support the child in the context of the family. For example, Sharon is a single mother with a two-year-old son, Sean. She finds it difficult to manage the long hours of her job and her young son. She often complains about Sean and belittles him in front of others, calling him a "stupid hyperactive kid." The daycare staff decides to interact with Sharon on a positive note and provide her with some information on support services. Before Sharon picks up Sean, the staff ensures that he has eaten, has been changed, and is looking forward to seeing his mother. After the first few times of this, Sharon seems to look forward to seeing

her son. Sean often waits at the window for her to arrive and runs to greet her. Sharon indicates that she cannot believe that Sean is really happy to see her. The staff also makes sure to point out a number of positive things Sean has done, such as being the first of the toddlers to climb up and down the new climber. Gradually, Sharon's language with Sean becomes more positive. She begins to notice the milestones he is achieving at home and shares them with the staff.

- Interact openly with family members. Meena hears Sharon berate her son, Sean. Sharon is calling him stupid because he is slow to take off his clothes. She walks over to Sharon and offers to help. Sharon gratefully accepts. She again starts to call Sean stupid, but Meena quickly intervenes and says, "This snowsuit is hard for you to get off. I notice the zipper gets stuck quiet easily. Why don't I start it and you can pull it down yourself?" To Sharon she quietly says that they are trying to nurture every child's self-esteem by offering positive interactions. Sharon does not respond, but Meena notices that she does not call Sean stupid any more when Meena is around.

- Provide resource listings to help families. Sharon picks up some information about respite playgroups offered in her community. A group of parents has created a cooperative Saturday morning playgroup program. Sharon can drop off Sean for a morning and do her shopping in peace. In return, she has to volunteer her time once a month. Through this service, she meets other families in a similar position to her own. She gradually develops a support network for herself and her son.

Issue 5: Medical

Many of the medical issues discussed in this section have been described in other parts of this chapter. It is important, however, to look at these issues again in the context of how they affect the well-being of the child.

1. Poverty

Although health care is universally accessible in Canada, families living in poverty may find it difficult to access appropriate medical care. Some factors affecting their care are as follows:

- Many families do not have access to benefits such as dental plans, drug plans, and appropriate sick leave. Many families cannot afford appropriate medications or dental care, nor can they afford to take time off work because of illness.
- Many parents are faced with loss of wages and possible dismissal from their jobs if they stay home with their sick children. Very few communities have sick-child care facilities because most people believe that the best place for a sick child is at home. These policies and attitudes do not address the issue of a parent who cannot afford the loss of salary or the loss of a job. Alternative child care is usually not available, and private care is not affordable.

- Advice given to poor families often comes from individuals who have no idea what it is like to try to balance an impossible budget. See the example of the Sekar family discussed earlier in this chapter. Another example follows: Tadesse has a rare medical condition. To control her medical problems, her doctor has prescribed medication that costs $250 per month. Tadesse has no drug plan. Her doctor has also told her that a different diet could greatly improve her health. The diet he prescribes is too expensive for the salary she earns.
- Families often live in substandard housing that may lead to increased likelihood of illness or accidents, such as damp living quarters, housing that is difficult to heat or cool, unsafe structures, poor ventilation, and dark and depressing environments.

2. Substance Abuse

"Substance abuse refers to the inappropriate use of drugs or mood-altering substances. It can result in personal, family, health, social, legal and financial problems." (Campbell & Devon Dodd, 1993: 2) Substance abuse includes abuse of both legal and illegal drugs such as alcohol, prescription drugs, over-the-counter drugs, medication, illicit drugs, and solvents. Substance abuse may result in physical or psychological dependence on the substance used and may affect both the individuals themselves and the family members of individuals.

Substance abusers:

- may become violent and use physical violence after using abuse substances
- may sexually exploit children after using abuse substances
- may use abuse substances to "diminish their feelings of guilt or shame or to assist in denial of their acts" (Campbell & Devon Dodd, 1993: 3)
- may use substance abuse to cope with their circumstances
- often neglect their children
- may use excessive medication to control the behaviour of others

Children of substance abusers:

- are often exposed to watching violence against one parent in the home
- are often physically or sexually abused
- may have developmental delays
- may exhibit behavioural disorders
- are more often diagnosed with attention deficit disorder
- may be inattentive and show lower cognitive functioning

In utero substance abuse may lead to:

- spontaneous abortions
- premature births
- fetal distress
- physical or mental retardation

- birth defects
- withdrawal symptoms at birth (Tomison, 1996)

A) WHAT CAN YOU DO?

- Become informed about support services. An individual trained in early childhood education cannot handle a substance abuse situation without help. " The need for a comprehensive, collaborative approach to substance abuse and child maltreatment has already been recognized." (Tomison, 1996: 20)
- Post support services that families can access. It is important to remember that other family members may also be victims of abusive situations (Campbell & Devon Dodd, 1993). Women, children, seniors, and individuals with disabilities are most frequently also victims. These individuals also need support services.
- Consult with specialists to learn how to deal with the child within the program.
- Attend workshops to learn more about symptoms and strategies to help children in substance abuse situations.

3. Depression

Depression is one of the most common illnesses in our society, affecting more than 1 in 10 people (Byrne & Pape, 2004: 7). "Depression is a form of mental illness that affects the whole body—it impacts the way one feels, thinks, and acts." (Child Care Resources, 2004: 1) Depression is usually associated with adults, but in recent times there has been a growing concern that an increasing number of children also suffer from it. "Children are currently experiencing pessimism, sadness and depression at an unprecedented rate," warns Abela. "Depression is not age defined or exclusive to adults. By the time they're 14 years old, up to nine percent of children have already experienced at least one episode of severe depression." (Abela, 2003: 1)

Unfortunately, children living with parents who are depressed are four times as likely to be depressed themselves (Abela, 2003). Abela found the following factors in depressed parents that lead to depression in children. The depressed parent:

- makes pessimistic remarks about himself or herself, the world, and the future
- has low self-esteem
- has poor coping strategies
- shows rigid and extreme personality traits such as self-criticism and dependency

A) SIGNS OF DEPRESSION IN CHILDREN As with any depressive state, the signs of depression are not just feeling blue or talking about having a bad day. Feelings of depression are evident over time; the individual is unable to snap out of the depressive state. The following signs may help predict a depressive state in children:

- changes in personality—more irritable, angrier, moody, whining
- changes in eating and sleeping habits—loss of appetite or increased appetite, difficulty falling asleep or too much sleeping
- loss of energy, chronically listless and tired

- loss of interest in activities and people around them—friends, play
- frequent complaints of headaches, stomach aches, aching arms and legs
- feeling sad, discouraged
- fearful, anxious, tense
- low self-esteem—child may indicate that he or she cannot do something or is "no good" at certain things
- lack of motivation or enthusiasm to do anything
- indecisiveness and forgetfulness
- difficulty concentrating on tasks

B) WHAT CAN YOU DO?

- Observe the child's behaviour carefully. If behaviour persists over time, refer the child to the appropriate professional.
- Inform yourself about depression through libraries, hotlines, the Internet, and other professionals.
- Inform yourself about services in your community and post information about these services so that others can access them.
- Develop a program for the child with the help of professionals such as a crisis intervention specialist, a learning resource consultant, or medical professionals.

4. Illness

Daycare environments pose some degree of an increased health risk for children. Children are exposed to other children who are sick. There is a greater risk of viral upper respiratory infection—nose, throat, mouth, and voice box—and illnesses such as the common cold, ear infections, and diarrhea. Early childhood educators can decrease the risk of spreading infections by following the sanitation procedures outlined in Chapter 3.

Issue 6: Stress

1. Family Stress

"Work is the leading cause of stress throughout the world. In one study, of office workers in 16 countries, including Canada, 54% of the respondents cited work as a current cause of stress in their lives and 29% cited money problems—which are also work-related since one's job is the main source of income for most people." (Brym, Lie, Nelson, Guppy, & McCormick, 2003: 307) Additional causes of stress include:

- demands of the job, such as increased number of hours of work in many jobs (Reade, 2003)
- difficulties balancing work and life (Reade, 2003)

- fewer resources available, such as how to cope with illness in the family and work
- financial worries (Reade, 2003)

When families feel stress, children pick up on this stress. Children under six are much less capable of coping with stress because of their stage of development.

- Young children's thinking centres on part of an event and therefore they lack the ability to see all aspects of a problem.
- Young children have limited experience with coping with problems and therefore have few stress management techniques from which to choose.
- Young children find it difficult to understand another person's viewpoint. It is therefore very difficult for a child to observe stress behaviours in the adults around them that they do not understand but can sense are disruptive.
- Young children have not yet established a pattern of dealing with their own physical responses to changes in stimuli such as stress behaviours. A child whose heartbeat has increased or is sweating because he or she is anxious about a situation has no strategies to calm himself or herself.

Children who are exposed to continual stress at home will react in individual ways depending on the degree of stress they are exposed to, the adult strategies used to help them cope with the stress, and their individual personalities. Signs of stress in children include the following (Jewett & Peterson, 2002):

- physical reactions such as sweating palms, crying, increased heartbeat
- changes in behaviour such as self-comforting actions (thumb-sucking, rocking), aggressive outbursts (yelling, hitting), nervous habits (biting fingernails, twirling hair), toileting accidents, and disturbed sleep patterns (sleeping too much, difficulty sleeping)
- complaints of pain such as stomach aches or headaches
- avoidance behaviours such as running away or excessive shyness, avoiding social interactions, and excessive solitary play
- obsessive behaviours such as excessive worrying, hypervigilance (running to the window repeatedly to check if a parent is arriving), "obsessive interest in objects, routines, food, and persistent concern about 'what comes next' and clinging" (Jewett & Peterson, 2002: 3)

2. What Can You Do?

Since young children find it difficult to understand their own feelings and the feelings of others, it is important that adults become aware of and respond to children's behaviours appropriately. Some strategies for helping children cope include the following (Carraway, 2004: 3–4).

- *Model calmness and self-control.* There are many stressful instances during an average day. Some children might find it difficult to part from their caregivers in the morning, while others may find it difficult to adhere to certain routines such as cleanup. During these times, early childhood educators can model calm ways of dealing with these situations. Children can see that there are different ways to handle stressful situations, and stress levels are lowered rather than increased.

- *Provide body contact.* During times of stress, body contact such as hugs, touching, or holding can provide stress release for some children. Other children may react better if an adult is in close proximity. Careful observation to discover which strategy works with which child is essential (photo 8.7).

- *Put predictability in the day.* Ensure that core routines are predictable and constant over each day. Predictable routines include washing hands before and after eating, cleanup after activity periods, or a snack when the child arrives. Some rituals can also be included, such as waving goodbye from the window when a caregiver leaves or rubbing backs at naptime.

- *Allow extra time.* Children may need extra time to complete a task. A child may experience increased stress levels if forced to complete a task in the same time period as others. Provide warnings of transition times and extra time to make the transition.

- *Partner with one another.* Share information with parents. Identify strategies that work both at the daycare and at home. This may give families coping strategies to use at home. Post common coping strategies to which families can refer.

Photo 8.7

Photo 8.8

- *Provide nutritious food and time to rest.* It is essential to provide children with restful activities such as naps and quiet time (reading, puzzles, sensory activities). Stress is depleting; children need to re-energize their systems with nutritious food. This also gives children another strategy in learning to cope with stress (photo 8.8).

- *Acknowledge feelings.* Talk about the child's feelings in ways he or she can understand and that allow the child to make sense of what he or she is feeling. Additional strategies include **bibliotherapy** (stories that deal with similar stressful circumstances), dramatic play opportunities such as puppetry or role-playing, art activities, music, movement, or other activities that allow children to express their feelings (photo 8.9).

  ✳ **Bibliotherapy**

- *Help children separate fantasy and reality.* Children may feel that they are responsible for the events in their lives. Children's beliefs about what they see and hear is **egocentric** (believing that everyone else feels, believes, and thinks as they do and being unaware of other perspectives). A child may have done something totally unrelated such as refusing to do what a parent asked. When the parent becomes upset and starts to cry, the child may feel that the parent is unhappy

  ✳ **Egocentric**

Photo 8.9

Photo 8.10

because of him or her. Reinforce that adult problems are the problems of the adult and are not caused by the child. Strategies similar to those listed under "Acknowledging feelings" may be used.

- *Decrease competition.* Active play should be encouraged, but eliminate any idea of competing to be best or first. Activities should be open ended and encourage a variety of ways to complete any task. Emphasis should be on the process rather than the outcome. Avoid such descriptive language as "pretty picture" or "excellent structure." Instead, talk about the colours, design, or techniques used in the picture; the type of materials; the alignment of the materials; or the height of the structure made.
- *Listen.* Find opportunities to interact one on one with the child. During these times, let the child lead the activity. Listen and respond, focusing on what the child is sharing (photo 8.10).

- *Treat the stress.* Enlist professional help to identify appropriate strategies to assist the child on a daily basis.

Issue 7: Special Needs

Inclusive care

In most jurisdictions in Canada, inclusive care is recommended or mandated. **Inclusive care** means that all children, regardless of abilities or disabilities, attend the child-care settings in their community and that each child receives the support he or she may need. Some issues that have been raised concerning the attendance of children with special needs include:

1. *Concerns about the safety of children.* If care is taken to adequately set up the environment for all children, including children with special needs, there should be no concerns about safety. Strategies to provide safety in inclusive programs are outlined in Table 8.3.

2. *Children with special needs may need more one-to-one attention.* Involve other children in helping where possible. Children love to help. For example, Jordan, a three-year-old, has to wear leg braces and use crutches to move around. He finds it difficult to bend down to get the toys he wants. Joni has explained to the children why Jordan has to wear the braces and how this makes things difficult for him. The children often ask him what toys he wants and where he wants to play. They then carry items for him to the area he has specified. Strategies such as these model empathy and increase all children's self-esteem.

TABLE 8.3 STRATEGIES TO PROVIDE SAFETY IN INCLUSIVE PROGRAMS

Adaptation	Safety Measures
- Mobile units such as wheelchairs - Mobile assistive devices such as canes or walkers	- The creation of larger traffic flow areas encourage more safe passage for individuals with physical disabilities. Strategies include creating clear, uncluttered passageways between activity areas within playrooms; large paved or hard surface walkways outside; doorways that are wide enough and have handicapped access buttons; and ramps to all access points including climbing equipment. - Safety rules need to be established within programs to prevent accidents such as being run into by a wheelchair. - Safe storage of mobile equipment when not in use is essential (canes or walkers out of the traffic area and off the floor, wheelchairs in locked position).
- Placing toys at various levels	- Children who are developmentally delayed may engage in potentially dangerous behaviour such as placing small objects in their mouths (choking hazard). Rather than removing these toys altogether, they could be placed in higher locations so that only older children can reach them or in areas out of reach that require children to ask for them. Close supervision can then be provided.
- Close supervision	- Observe children closely from a distance. Listen for escalation of noise or raised voices. Be prepared to move quickly to prevent problems. - For example, Dillon shouts at Joel, "Mine!" Joni hears Dillon shout and immediately looks in that direction. She sees Dillon raise a block in his hand and quickly walks over and asks him where he wants to put it. Dillon adds the block to his structure rather than hitting Joel with it.
- Environment safe from tripping or falling	- Ensure that all surfaces are clean and that spills of water, sand, or paint are immediately cleaned up. - Cover raised surfaces such as ridges between carpeted and tiled floors. - Clear toys from floor to prevent tripping.
- Adaptive equipment	- Ensure that adaptive equipment such as standing frames is sturdy and secure. - Provide furniture that is sturdy enough to pull oneself up with or walk along.

SUMMARY

There are many issues that negatively affect the health and well-being of children. These issues are easily mitigated by caring professionals who provide responsive care to children and families by:

- becoming informed about the families they serve
- providing a healthy and safe environment that meets all of the children's needs

- forming partnerships with other professionals to more adequately meet the needs of the children and families in their care
- providing a respectful environment that encourages open dialogue and discussion

KEY POINTS

Issue 1: Poverty
- Nutrition—inability to buy nutritious foods, substitution of less healthy foods
- Health—higher intake of sugar fats and carbohydrates leads to weight gain, less exercise, less money for appropriate living accommodations, higher possibility of illness, less money to spend on appropriate children's clothing
- Time—long work and daycare days lead to less time spent with family members in quality interactions
- Stress—greater stress to make a living and balance daily life, more family strife, fewer social support networks
- Safety—children engage in more unsupervised activities
- Stimulation—less money to purchase appropriate toys and engage in recreational activities

Issue 2: Quality of the daycare experience
- Increase in challenging behaviours of children
- Seeming lack of personal care in children's appearance
- Increased illness of children
- Seeming lack of interest of parents—late, disregard for routines of daycare

- Decrease in family/staff interactions
- Children's physical and emotional health jeopardized

Issue 3: Attitudes toward child care
- Social attitudes—lack of respect for daycare staff, inadequate funding, belief that families should take care of children, belief that child care is a commodity to be purchased, lack of respect of children, belief that children are cared for best at home

Issue 4: Child abuse
- Physical—symptoms include pain, bruising, burns, abrasions, unexplained injuries, and fear
- Sexual—symptoms include difficulty walking or sitting, pain, bruising, soreness of genital area, fear, precocious behaviour, and refusal to comply with toileting routines
- Neglect—symptoms include lack of personal hygiene, medical/dental care, supervision, appropriate clothing, shelter, and nutrition
- Emotional—symptoms include quiet, withdrawn or disruptive, aggressive behaviours and unhappy, fearful, precocious behaviours
- Consequences of abuse—poor attachment patterns, fewer age-appropriate play activities, more inappropriate behaviour patterns, less socially competent,

more emotionally dependent, more likely to suffer from developmental delays

- Issues about child abuse—hidden instances, lack of reporting, apathy, social acceptance of physical punishment as a form of discipline, fear, lack of knowledge about reporting
- What can you do?—help child develop self-confidence, model appropriate behaviours, support child in context of family, interact with family members, provide resources to families

Issue 5: Medical

- Poverty—lack of money to provide dental/medical care, inability to care for sick children, substandard housing
- Substance abuse—alcohol, drugs, medication, solvents; gain information about support services; make information about support services available to families; consult with specialists
- Signs of depression—changes in personality, changes in sleeping or eating habits, loss of energy, sadness, fear, low self-esteem, lack of motivation, indecisiveness or forgetfulness, lack of concentration
- Illness—preventing spread of disease in daycare

Issue 6: Stress

- Causes—job demands, balance between home and work life, fewer resources, financial worries
- Children have fewer mechanisms to cope with stress
- Signs of stress in children—physical reactions, changes in behaviour, pain, avoidance behaviours, obsessive behaviours
- What can you do?—model calmness and self-control, provide physical contact, provide predictability, allow extra time, communicate with families, provide rest and nutritious food, talk about feelings, help children distinguish between fantasy and reality, de-emphasize competition, listen, consult experts

Issue 7: Special needs

- Provide safety—accessible traffic flow, safe storage, sturdy equipment and furniture, toys at various levels, supervision, lack of obstructions on floors and pathways, adaptive equipment
- Involve all children in helping each other.

EXERCISES

1. Discuss how poverty affects the well-being of children and their families. Identify the factors that influence quality of life for families living in poverty.
2. Discuss how the quality of a daycare experience might affect children's health, safety, and well-being.
3. For each point listed in the discussion of attitudes toward child care (see page 240), give specific examples from your experiences to agree with or negate each point.
4. Identify the symptoms of:
   a) physical abuse
   b) sexual abuse
   c) neglect
   d) emotional abuse
5. You notice that one of the children ducks every time you approach her from a certain angle. You suspect that this child may have suffered physical abuse.
   a) What steps do you need to take to confirm or deny that this child might be suffering physical child abuse?
   b) If you confirm that this might indeed be a case of physical abuse, what steps should you then take?

6. Why is it important to recognize the symptoms of child abuse?

7. How might children who live with or interact with individuals who are substance abusers be affected?

8. A parent comes into the child-care centre. She has obviously been physically abused. When you question her, she starts to cry and indicates that her husband only hits her when he is drunk. How might you guide her in obtaining help and support her child in the program?

9. Using the list of signs of depression in children (see page 253), give some specific examples of how you might expect children to react to stress.

10. A four-year-old has been registered in the child-care centre. This child is in a wheelchair that he can propel by himself. He is also non-verbal, but uses effective sign language to communicate.

 a) What physical adaptations must be made to the indoor and outdoor environments to accommodate this child?

 b) What adaptations must be made in the program to ensure this child's full participation?

11. What strategies might you use to help children:

 a) experiencing stress

 b) living with a parent who is depressed

✳ Glossary

Attention deficit disorder (page 248) A disorder in which children seem to be in continual motion, have a very short attention span, and are easily distracted.

Bibliotherapy (page 257) Using stories that deal with circumstances similar to those the child is experiencing.

Child abuse (page 242) "Violence, mistreatment or neglect that a child or adolescent may experience while in the care of someone they either trust or depend upon, such as a parent, sibling, other relative, caregiver or guardian." (Department of Justice Canada, 2003: 1)

Egocentric (page 257) Children's belief that everyone else feels, believes, and thinks as they do and lack of awareness of other individuals' perspectives.

Emotional abuse (page 246) Involves harming children's sense of self.

Inclusive care (page 258) Care that ensures that all children, regardless of abilities or disabilities, attend the child-care settings in their community and that each child receives the supports he or she may need.

Neglect (page 243) Involves repeated failure to provide for a child's physical, emotional, or psychological well-being.

Parallel play (page 247) Children play beside each other, using similar materials, but engage in individual play.

Physical abuse (page 243) Involves using deliberate force to cause injury or risk of injury to a child.

Sexual abuse (page 243) "Involves using a child for sexual purposes." (Department of Justice Canada, 2003: 1)

Symbolic play (page 247) Play involving actions or materials that are representative of another action or material, such as using a hand as a digger or shrugging one's shoulder to indicate a lack of understanding.

REFERENCES

Abela, J. (2003). *Preventing depression in children alleviates adult condition.* http://www.mcgill.ca/releases/2003/April/depression/, accessed 1 March 2004.

Begly, S. (1997). How to build a baby's brain. *Newsweek, 28,* 28–32.

Brym, R., Lie, J., Nelson, A., Guppy, N., & McCormick, C. (2003). *Sociology: Your compass for a new world.* Scarborough, ON: Thomson Nelson.

Byrne, C., & Pape, B. (2004). *All together now: How families are affected by depression and manic depression.* Ministry of Health. http://www.hc-sc.gc.ca/english/ , accessed 1 March 2004.

Campbell, C., & Devon Dodd, J. (1993). *Family violence and substance abuse.* Health Canada. http://www.hc-sc.gc.ca/hppb/familyviolence/, accessible 1 February 2004.

Canadian Council on Social Development. (2003). *Canadian welfare income as a percentage of the poverty line by family type and province, 2001.* council@ccdd.ca, received 4 December 2003.

Canadians Against Child Abuse Society. (2003). *Canadians against child abuse society.* http://www.cacas.ca/, accessed 2 January 2004.

Carraway, L. (2004). *Helping young children cope with stress.* http://snohomish.wsu.edu/childcare/stress/stress.htm, accessed 1 April 2004.

Child Care Resources. (2004). *Child care—Childhood depression.* http://www.childcare.org, accessed 1 March 2004.

Crowther, I. (2004). *Introduction to early childhood education: A Canadian perspective.* Scarborough, ON: Thomson Nelson.

Department of Justice Canada. (2003). *Child abuse: A fact sheet from the Department of Justice Canada.* http://canada.justice.gc.ca/en/ps/fm/childafs.html, accessed 16 March 2004.

Doherty, G. (2003). *Occupational standards for child care practitioners.* Ottawa: Canadian Childcare Federation.

Doherty-Derkowski, G. (1994). *Quality matters: Excellence in early childhood programs.* Toronto: Addison-Wesley.

Fergusson, E. (2002). *Babysitters or professionals? The role of social attitudes in the recruitment & retention of child care workers.* Child

Care Connections. http://www.childcarecanada.org/, accessed 17 December 2003.

Focus on the Family Canada Association. (2003). *Canadian attitudes on the family.* http://www.focusonthefamily.ca, accessed 16 March 2004.

Friendly, M., & Lero, D. (2002). *Social inclusion through early childhood education and care.* Toronto: Laidlaw Foundation.

Goelman, H., Doherty, G., Lero, D., LaGrange, A., & Tougas, J. (2000). *You bet I care! Caring and learning environments: Quality in child care centres across Canada.* Guelph, ON: Centre for Families, Work and Well-Being, University of Guelph.

Hanvey, L. (2003). *The progress of Canada's children.* Ottawa: Canadian Council on Social Development.

Hertzman, C. (2002). *Leave no child behind! Social exclusion and child development.* Toronto: Laidlaw Foundation.

Jewett, J., & Peterson, K. (2002). Stress and young children. *ERIC Digest* [On-line]. http://www.ericfacility.net/databases/ERIC_Digests/ed471911.html, accessed 1 April 2004.

McCain, M., & Mustard, F. (1999). *Early years study final report.* Toronto: Publications Ontario.

Nash, M. (1997). Fertile minds. *Time, 149,* 48–56.

Pimento, B., & Kernested, D. (1996). *Healthy foundations in child care.* Scarborough, ON: Nelson Canada.

Reade, J. (2003). *Focus on the healthy workplace in Canada and around the world.* http://labour.hrdc-drhc.gc.ca/worklife/fhw-en.cfm, accessed 1 March 2004.

Ross, L. (2002). Parents irked at Evan's day-care advice. *Edmonton Journal Final.* Ref Type: Internet Communication.

Schickedanz, J., Schickedanz, D., Forsyth, P., & Forsyth, G. (2001). *Understanding children and adolescents.* Fourth edition. Needham Heights, MA: Allyn & Bacon.

Seefeldt, C., & Galper, A. (1998). *Continuing issues in early childhood education.* Toronto: Prentice-Hall International.

Tomison, A. (1996). *Child maltreatment and substance abuse.* National Child Protection Clearinghouse. http://www.aifs.org.au/nch/discussion2.html, accessed 3 January 2004.

9

CHAPTER

Effective Networking

Chapter Outline

"Health education should be interpreted in the broadest sense—teaching children about well-being. Your health education program should focus not only on physical health and safety, but also on topics such as emotional health, growing and changing, and the environment. You should promote personal health, the health of those around them, and their world. Ideally, your health education plan should draw upon the resources of teachers, parents, nutritionists, mental health specialists, special needs staff and others, including community agencies and resources." (Shapiro Kendrick, Kaufman, & Messenger, 1995: 11–12)

Chapter Outcomes

After reading this chapter, the reader will:

1. Define the concept of networking and discuss the value of networking in early childhood settings.

2. Identify and discuss the importance of networking with families.

3. Describe the roles of each of the following in networking with early childhood educators:
   • health care professionals
   • mental health professionals
   • licensing professionals

4. Identify and describe the value of networking with community members.

5. Describe how to build a network.

6. Explain the importance of networking to advocate on behalf of children and families.

Networking in Early Childhood Settings

Networking

Networking usually occurs between individuals who have common interests. Individuals network to share ideas, expertise, and resources; exchange information; and look for ways to improve quality experiences for a group of individuals. Networking in early childhood education is common. Families network to support each other, such as in single parent groups, or support each other around common issues, such as the special needs of their children. Early childhood educators network with families, other professionals, politicians, and community members to improve quality for the families they serve. For example, many communities have established common early childhood educator interest groups—infant, toddler, preschool, or supervisors groups. Through networking, early childhood educators are able to:

- decrease the sense of isolation—Many individuals work in small group settings located in various communities with minimal contact with other centres or professionals. Through networking, individuals are able to decrease their sense of isolation by talking about common problems and forming support groups around common issues, such as creating a developmentally appropriate program to increase the physical activity of preschoolers.

- work collaboratively toward a common goal—It is always easier to reach a goal when more individuals are sharing the load. For example, a new playground structure was needed at the Loyalist College Daycare facility. Funding for the equipment was available, but there was not enough funding to cover the installation cost. The staff, families, and faculty members of the college's early childhood education program volunteered their time on a weekend to put the structures in place.

- share expertise—Early childhood educators gain a lot of knowledge through experience and training, and are in an excellent position to share some of this knowledge. For example, at the Sunshine Kinderschool, families expressed concern about when and how toddlers should be toilet trained. The staff promptly created a bulletin board that covered various aspects of toilet training, such as quick bullets about ages and stages of toilet training, some bullets about do's and don'ts, and some suggested references (Internet, articles, and books). The articles, copies of the Internet resources, and books were placed on a table in the parents' corner. The bulletin board also had a section on safety. Information from the Children's Safety Association of Canada (2004) was regularly posted in this section.

- share information—Information sharing can be done in several ways (Table 9.1). It is important to use a variety of mechanisms to support each family's specific needs. For example, some family members can spend time in the centre reading information or asking questions. Others may need to take information home because of a busy work schedule.

TABLE 9.1   **INFORMATION SHARING**

Type of Information	Description
Print-based references	- Books, magazines—placed in family corner; could be signed out or used while in centre - Articles—could be posted; placed in binders and signed out or used while in the centre
Written communication	- Forms (Table 9.2), dated pages, individual notebooks—placed in a convenient area accessible to family members and staff. This information can help both families and staff meet children's emotional needs. Information about health and safety is included in Chapter 3.
Verbal communication	- Family members are encouraged to participate at all levels—discussing their children, being involved in the program, being involved in planning, being involved at a board level. The centre strives to establish a respectful, active listening atmosphere to encourage communication.
Periodic newsletters	- Newsletters share information about the program, such as common issues, changes in policies, interesting events, asking for help with various aspects of the program, and reflections on future events.
Information displays such as parent boards	- Post weekly activities, menus, schedule. - Invite feedback from families. - Post information about upcoming events. - Post resources related to health or safety issues (photo 9.1).
Meetings	- Informal—sharing information about a child's night/day when child is picked up or dropped off - Formal—scheduling meetings to discuss child's progress or if there are some problems - Group meetings—discuss common issues or concerns - Guest speakers—pediatrician, public health nurse

Photo 9.1

TABLE 9.2 **INFORMATION SHARING FORM**

Child's name.............................

Recorder.................................

Category	Description	Date
New likes		
New dislikes		
New milestones		
Unusual occurrence		
Other		

Networking with Families

Although child-care providers are responsible for the health and safety of the children in their care, they must realize that the primary responsibility for care rests with the parents or guardians and their families. Children are part of the family for a lifetime and in child care for only a limited time. Families have the primary responsibility to make decisions about their children's health, safety, and well-being.

It is critical that child-care providers build a solid network with their families that respects and nurtures all individuals within that network—children, families, staff, and other professionals. Child-care providers are in contact with a number of individuals and are therefore in an ideal position to:

- provide vital links to resources that increase understanding and knowledge of health care and safety issues and information about required immunization; safe materials such as cribs and car seats; pool safety; treatment of common childhood illnesses such as measles and colds; and creating environments and interactions with children to build and increase children's self-esteem
- share information about children's emotional health and well-being—For example, when Anderson arrives in the morning, he is teary and reluctant to leave his mother. His mother indicates that she has encouraged him to think happy thoughts while she is gone. All children have photos of family members posted. Cindy quickly retrieves a photo of Anderson and his family and sits down with him to look at it (photo 9.2). Anderson points to each of his family members. Cindy comments on how happy they look and asks Anderson to talk about who they are and why they are having so much fun. Cindy follows the strategy that Anderson's mother has started. As a result, Anderson is able to settle down and have a successful day. The photograph and a description of the positive behaviour guidance used by Cindy are posted on the parent board. This not only serves to model positive interaction strategies but also shows how effective these positive interactions can be. Additionally, the centre can provide charts (see Table 9.2) that family members are encouraged to fill in when they drop off their children. This gives staff members valuable information about the children that allows them to tailor more closely a program and interactions that are respectful of each child's experiences. During the day, staff members can also add to these charts. This gives family members a chance to read about what has happened during the day and ask for clarification or make comments as needed.

Photo 9.2

- post information about physical well-being—Information about children's nutrition could be shared by posting weekly menus or anecdotal information about children's activities. This technique becomes particularly useful if family members add suggestions about their children. For example, some of the toddlers are involved in toilet training. Strategies for toilet training are posted on the bulletin board. A section of the bulletin board is left blank and labelled "Additional Ideas." Family members add ideas that have been successful for them, add lists of resources, and also post additional articles. To ensure that children are getting an appropriate balance of indoor and outdoor activities, the staff creates a bulletin board of outdoor activities and the value of these activities (Figure 9.1). Some family members have previously been concerned about taking children outside in the rain. When they see the photographs and descriptions of their children engaging in meaningful activity outside, a better dialogue is created between staff and family members. Family members begin to understand the importance of outdoor activity. As a result, children arrive at the centre dressed more appropriately for the weather.

FIGURE 9.1

Example of Outdoor Play Documentation

Value of the Activity

Children learn:

• to dress appropriately for various weather conditions

• to observe the effects of weather conditions on their bodies—hot, cold, wet

• what happens to various surfaces when they are wet—slippery, muddy

• how to walk/run/ride on surfaces that are slippery

• to enjoy sensory activities—splashing in puddles, walking in the rain

• about nature—observing the effects of raindrops falling on different surfaces

• to use materials in different ways—creating mud mixtures, collecting rainwater in different containers to compare and measure

• hold workshops—Workshops on common health, safety, and well-being issues can be hosted by the daycare. Other professionals, such as public health nurses, dentists, or medical doctors, could be asked to present pertinent information to families and staff. This provides opportunities for staff and families to learn together and implement strategies that are appropriate in both home and child-care environments. For example, when the staff realized that some families were reluctant to send their children outside in rainy conditions because they thought the children might catch a cold, they consulted with a public health nurse. They then decided to hold an information evening, the topic of which was "Surviving the Rainy Day Blues." This workshop included information on:

  ○ rainy day blues

  ○ foods to chase away the blues

- ○ myths about how common colds are spread
- ○ solutions to rainy day blues (indoor and outdoor activities)

The workshop was a resounding success. Not only was the facilitator able to use the documentation panels developed by the staff (see Figure 9.1), she was also able to reinforce the value of outdoor activity in different weather conditions. She was able to reassure families that their children were not likely to suffer any ill effects from this activity.

- link to resources in the community—Child-care centres need to know about the resources for children within the community. Information about these resources can be made available to families through the creation of an annotated directory. This directory serves a dual purpose: It is an essential resource to staff and can be displayed as a family resource. Directories should include:

  - ○ the name of the agency
  - ○ the type of service provided by the agency
  - ○ contact information—name, telephone number, and e-mail address

- document children's learning about health and safety issues—An effective strategy for sharing information about children's learning and reinforcing safe and sanitary practices is to create a display about children's learning (Figure 9.2). This method can help reinforce the concepts that are being learned:

  - ○ Children can review what they have learned.
  - ○ The information is shared between all participants—families, children, other professionals, community members, and staff.
  - ○ Staff can review and adjust learning based on children's and family's interest and input.

As discussed in Chapter 3, there are a number of issues associated with children's health and safety that concern practitioners and parents equally. To facilitate an optimal environment for nurturing the healthy growth and development of children, the efforts of both home and child care should be coordinated. Some strategies to help in this process include the following:

1. Establish joint awareness of sanitary practices. Sanitary practices are essential to stop the spread of disease (see Chapter 1). These practices should be presented in the parent handbook and discussed when the child is registered in the program. This gives both parties a greater understanding of what practices will be used and why. Appropriate routines such as handwashing should be posted in all washrooms and also could be sent home in a newsletter for use at home (Figure 9.3).
2. Establish a comfortable family area that encourages individuals to sit and browse through materials and resources as suggested in Table 9.1.
3. Establish an open, respectful atmosphere to encourage dialogue around issues or concerns families might have. This involves **active listening** (listening to the content of the message without personal bias and clarifying the intent of the message when the meaning is unclear or to ensure that the meaning is clear). For example, when Delilah drops off her daughter, Kamaya, she indicates that she

✳ Active listening

FIGURE 9.2

**Examples of Documentation of
Children's Learning about Nutrition and Healthy Practices**

Cooking—Mario

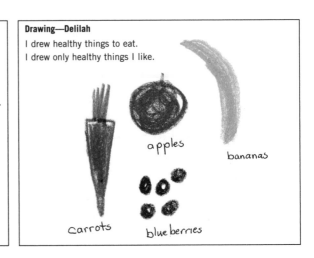

I learned how to make my own salad.
I only put in things good for your body.
I put in baby carrots, celery, and cauliflower.
I added some plain yogourt to it.
It was delicious.

Drawing—Delilah

I drew healthy things to eat.
I drew only healthy things I like.

apples

bananas

carrots

blueberries

Dictated Stories—Braelyn

This triceratops was really, really naughty. He decided to eat some ice cream. Ice cream is especially bad for you. It causes decay in your teeth. So, I scolded the triceratops and told him that he was bad.

I then took him to the sink and made him brush his teeth.

He told me that he would always brush his teeth after eating bad things, but that he wouldn't stop eating ice cream. I told him it was okay once in the while, but I was watching him.

Hand Washing—Josh

Wash hands.
Eat!
Wash hands.

Music

The children made up the following song to the tune of "Row, Row, Row Your Boat."

Wash, wash, wash your hands,

Wash before you eat,

Scrub your nails and dry your hands,

Now it's safe to eat.

FIGURE 9.3

Sanitary Routines for Parent Handbook

To limit the spread of disease and other contaminants as much as possible, the following sanitary measures will be used.

a) Appropriate handwashing before all meal preparation, before eating, and after eating. Children are monitored during washroom routines to ensure that hands are washed after toileting. Please check the signs posted over the sinks. If you would like a copy of this procedure, please speak to the staff.

b) Personal hygiene routines are used to encourage self-help skills and develop greater self-awareness. Routines include brushing teeth, washing hands and face, and combing and brushing hair. Children are expected to bring their own toothbrushes, toothpaste, combs, and brushes.

c) All toys and equipment will be disinfected regularly.

d) The facilities are cleaned daily.

e) Face cloths and blankets are washed at least once a week or as needed.

has a problem with certain aspects of the daycare program. Paul, the early childhood educator, responds, "Do you have time to tell me what aspect of the program you have a problem with?" Delilah responds that her daughter really enjoys the program but that as a parent she cannot understand why the centre insists on taking children out in the rain. Delilah indicates that she is afraid her daughter will become chilled and catch a cold. Paul asks her if she has had time to look at the display board about outdoor play (see Figure 9.1 on page 270). They both walk over to it and discuss the values of outdoor play identified. Paul also gives Delilah some information to read about how children catch a cold. When Delilah returns the next day, she thanks Paul for the information and also brings appropriate outdoor clothing for Kamaya to wear. She indicates that she is still hesitant but thinks that the value of outdoor play is sufficient to convince her to support the activity.

4. Ensure that any advice given is sound and falls into the early childhood educator's role. Avoid a counselling role. This is best left to appropriate experts—social workers, doctors, nurses, or audiologists. Be prepared to refer family members to other services, and make information about other services readily available. For example, Jocelyn, the mother of a preschool child, asks for advice on what to do with one of her older children who is in grade two. She indicates that this child is "hyperactive" and asks Tracey, a staff member, if she thinks she should follow the teacher's suggestion and put her child on Ritalin. Tracey rightly suggests that Jocelyn consult with a specialist such as her family doctor and or the school psychologist.

5. Establish clear guidelines for emergency situations such as illness of a child or closure of the centre (Figure 9.4). These should be given to families in writing and discussed at registration. Some of these procedures could be reinforced by periodic

FIGURE 9.4

Sample Health Policy for Parent Handbook

Children's optimum growth, development, and learning are dependent on many factors. An important one is their state of health. The following policies are intended to minimize the health risks inherent in caring for children in a group setting while maintaining flexibility to respond to individual situations. The primary purpose of this health policy is to protect, maintain, and improve the health of each child in care, and that of the program staff.

1. **Registration Form**

   The centre's Confidential Registration and Record Form must be completed.

2. **Medical Examination**

   A medical examination must be completed before the child enters the program. This examination will inform the centre of:

   - any chronic health condition such as allergies
   - any restrictions necessary to the child's routine/diet
   - any regular medication/treatment required
   - method of administration of medical/treatment

3. **Emergency Contacts**

   The family must provide an emergency contact—name, address, and telephone.

   - The contact person must be available immediately at work or home during the hours the child is at the centre.
   - The emergency contact information must be updated as required.
   - The emergency contact must be informed by parents that he or she is the contact person.

4. **Maintenance of Records**

   Records are kept on file in the office of the executive director.

5. **Illness**

   If a child shows any one of the following symptoms, the child should not be brought to the centre:

   - elevated temperature
   - vomiting
   - diarrhea
   - consistent complaints of pain such as stomach ache, earache, or sore throat
   - injuries requiring medical attention

If the child exhibits any one of these symptoms while at the centre, the family will be notified to come and pick up the child. It is important to both the child and other children in the program that the ill child is picked up as quickly as possible.

Children may return to the centre when all symptoms have disappeared and/or a doctor indicates that it is safe to return. In the case of a contagious illness, the child may return only once the contagious period is over.

6. **Serious Accident or Illness**

   In the event that a child receives a serious injury or become seriously ill, the following steps will be taken:

   - Notify family member.
   - Transport to emergency department by ambulance.

   Please note that the Emergency Form must be signed by primary family members to give permission for emergency care.

7. **Medication may be given only if the following methodology has been followed.**

   - Permission to Give Medication Form has been filled in and signed.
   - Medication is in its original container that identifies the dosage, doctor's name, and type of medication.

All medication will be kept in a locked cabinet in the playroom out of children's reach.

workshops as needed or by periodic reminders in a newsletter. For example, during "cold season," post or send flyers home that provide helpful suggestions and reminders about what to do if a child is ill. These reminders could include information about when the child should be kept home, activities the child might be able to engage in while convalescing, and "feeding a cold."

6. Participate in joint workshop experiences. This gives a clear indication that there is joint interest in developing a common knowledge about effective practices with children. For example, when new playground guidelines were created in Ontario, many centres found that they had to revamp and change their playground equipment. To avoid confusion and a lot of questions, many child-care centres held meetings. The licensing agent was invited to discuss the changes and why these changes had been made.

Networking with Other Professionals

There are many professionals within the community who share in the goal of raising a generation of healthy children. These professionals can be divided into the following categories: health care professionals, mental health professionals, educational professionals, and other professionals in the community.

When networking with any professionals, it is extremely important to recognize that there are laws throughout Canada about sharing information. In 2000, the House of Commons passed the Personal Information Protection and Electronic Documents Act. The Act applies to all organizations that collect, use, or disclose personal information in the course of their activities (Geist, 2004). These organizations are not permitted to share individual information about children without the permission of the parent or guardian. If such information is to be shared, family members must sign a release form to grant permission to share information with the health care professional. Individuals who share information without permission are liable and may face punitive actions. For example, a student in an early childhood education program was at a bar with friends. The individual talked about a child with special needs who was in a field practicum program she was participating in. She disclosed confidential information about the child's disability and prognosis and did not realize that the child's parents were sitting at a table nearby and overheard the conversation. The parents complained to the student's college about the incidence and she was asked to leave the program.

1. Health Care Professionals

Professionals in this group include individuals who look after the physical health and well-being of children. This group of professionals might include physicians or pediatricians, nurses, dentists, audiologists, ophthalmologists, physiotherapists, and other medical health experts. A health care professional could act in an advisory or consulting role to the daycare facility.

When deciding on an appropriate health care professional to act in an advisory or consulting capacity for a child-care setting, the following criteria should be considered:

The health care professional be well established in the community and should have (Shapiro Kendrick, Kaufman, & Messenger, 1995):

- pediatric experience and regular contact with children
- knowledge of infectious diseases in group settings
- awareness of developmental and medical needs of young children
- awareness of community medical resources

It may be difficult to find a qualified individual to act as a health care consultant for the daycare setting. The following resource list serves as a starting point to help locate an individual:

- family members of children enrolled in the program
- community health centres, health clinics, hospitals
- public health nurses
- doctors, pediatricians, nurse practitioners, family doctors
- retired health care professionals

To use the services of a health care professional most efficiently, regular contact with that individual should be encouraged. Information might be shared about the program and the children and families in that program. It is not permitted to share individual information about children without the permission of the family. If such information is to be shared, family members must sign a release form to grant permission to share information with the health care professional. The more aware a professional is about the program and the children in that program, the more effective the relationship becomes. The health care professional should be flexible enough to address needs as they arise. Periodic visits could be encouraged to review, as needed:

- sanitary practices
- medical record keeping
- safety procedures
- procedures for handling children who are ill or need medication

Networking with a health care professional is beneficial in a variety of ways. A health care professional can:

- assist in the development of health and safety policies for the centre
- provide advice about common childhood illnesses, outbreaks of specific contagious diseases, and what to do when a child becomes ill
- provide resources to the centre on health- and safety-related issues
- advocate about health and safety issues to staff and families
- consult on various issues such as how to handle differing medical opinions of other professionals or family members, or when children should be allowed to return to the centre after being ill with a contagious disease

- provide specific training as needed; for example, training to provide emergency treatment such as administering an **epipen** (emergency medication provided via a needle for a severe allergic reaction)
- provide information about other medical resources
- assist in developing a health and safety program for children and families

Some child-care settings, such as the Early Year Centres in Ontario (Ontario Early Years, 2003), have collaborated with local health care agencies to provide regular services to families of young children. These services include weekly scheduled visits by a public health nurse to:

- provide information and advice on breast-feeding
- conduct drop-in clinics

Families may obtain advice and information from a public health nurse about (photo 9.3):

- breast-feeding and related issues such as the mother's health and well-being
- the newborn's health—checking general health and growth of the infant
- other family-related health concerns
- specific illnesses
- referral needs

2. Mental Health Professionals

Professionals in this group include individuals who look after the social and emotional health and well-being of children and their families. This group of professionals

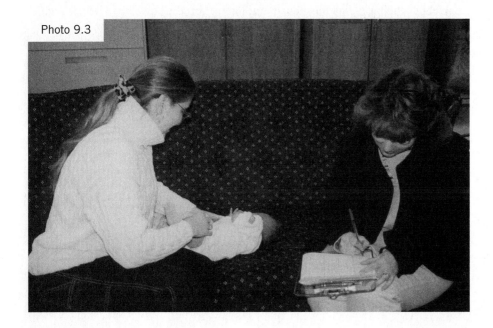

Photo 9.3

might include social workers, individuals from child protection agencies, mental health workers, resource consultants, and psychologists. As previously stated, these individuals could also act in a supportive advisory role to the centre.

When deciding on an appropriate mental health professional to act in an advisory or consulting capacity for a child-care setting, the following criteria should be considered. The mental health professional should be well established in the community and have (Shapiro Kendrick, Kaufman, & Messenger, 1995):

- pediatric experience and regular contact with children
- experience with children's interactions and behaviours in group settings
- knowledge of the social and emotional development of young children
- awareness of community resources

It may be difficult to find a qualified individual to act as a mental health professional for the daycare setting. The following resource list serves as a starting point to help locate an individual:

- family members of children enrolled in the program
- mental health clinics within the community or in hospitals
- outreach mental health programs
- community mental health centres
- government departments of social services
- child protection agencies
- child psychologists and psychiatrists
- retired mental health professionals.

To use the services of a mental health professional most effectively, regular contact with that individual should be encouraged. It helps the professional to know more about the program's procedures and interaction patterns if he or she is to offer effective advice. As stated previously in this chapter, before any specific information is shared about children and their families, written permission must be obtained from a parent or guardian. The mental health professional should be flexible enough to address needs as they arise. Periodic visits could be encouraged to observe:

- interactions between children and between children and adults
- children's activities and routines
- general set-up of the learning environment

Networking with a mental health professional is beneficial in several ways. A mental health professional can:

- assist in setting up an appropriate social environment for young children
- provide advice about specific behaviour patterns of children
- provide resources to the centre on:
  - positive child guidance practices
  - creating a positive social environment
  - developing increased social and emotional competence in children

- consult about issues such as suspected abuse and child guidance techniques
- provide specific training as needed; for example, training to help identify symptoms of child abuse
- provide information about other community resources

3. Licensing Professionals

Professionals in this group include individuals who consult and look after the overall quality of the program. Most often, these individuals inspect the centre once a year to ensure that general licensing requirements have been met. However, these individuals may be contacted to obtain information about how to meet the licensing criteria more effectively. There are a number of requirements that relate directly to the health and well-being of young children:

- overall general safety—Chapter 6 listed many of the safety requirements related to licensing criteria
- sanitary environment—often checked by someone from public health as well as being a licensing criteria (see sanitary practices in Chapter 3)
- fire safety regulations—usually inspected by the fire marshal within each community (see Chapter 1)
- nutritional requirements—also part of the licensing criteria (see Chapter 5)

It usually is not difficult to find these qualified individuals. These individuals routinely visit the child-care environment at least once a year to ensure that the licensing criteria for that centre have been met. Since these individuals are highly knowledgeable about child-care regulations, they are ideal for consultation. Networking with a licensing professional is beneficial in several ways. A licensing professional can:

- assist in setting up a safe, healthy, and appropriate environment for young children
- provide advice on specific regulations such as fire, health, or daycare requirements
- provide resources and suggestions to implement a safe and healthy environment
- consult on various issues such as regulations, changes in regulations, or how to modify the environment to meet regulations
- provide specific training as needed; for example, training for emergency evacuation
- provide information about other community resources

Networking with Community Members

There are many resources within each community that can be tapped to create effective networks. These community networks can be classified in health-related categories—safety, nutrition, fitness, and education.

1. Safety

The obvious community link for safety issues is the police department. Most police departments have active programs that support community efforts. Creating a network with the police department provides opportunities for child-care programs to become aware of the types of services offered and to collaborate on tailoring safety programs for the centre's needs. Some of these programs include:

- *Road safety.* A variety of resources could be available:
  - loaned equipment such as battery-operated vehicles, traffic signs and lights, uniforms, and safety mascots
  - pamphlets on road safety, road safety videos, or safety posters
  - visits at a police station or by police officers at the centre—In many instances, a real drama play opportunity can be set up. First police officers could go outside with children to practise road safety. Follow-up activities about road safety could be set up in both indoor and outdoor environments. This can be particularly useful in areas where children are using riding toys (photo 9.4). Children learn that traffic flow around the circular riding path is one way. They also learn to stop and let individuals join the flow of traffic.

Photo 9.4

- *Personal safety.* Personal safety includes how to react to strangers, what to do when one is lost, or how to access help when one feels threatened. A variety of resources could be available:
  - posters, pamphlets, colouring books, or videos
  - visits at a police station or by police officers at the centre—Use this opportunity for role play. Children can engage in role-play situations that will help them learn how to deal with personal safety issues. Follow-up activities include reading books on this topic and setting up role-play situations within the learning environment.

- *Bike safety.* Most communities have a bike rodeo safety week in the spring. This situation can be adapted to preschoolers using their riding toys.

- *Safety around pets and other animals.* Teaching children about safety in approaching and handling animals could be done with the help of an animal trainer or veterinarian. It would be especially effective if that individual was accompanied with a pet to demonstrate appropriate practices.
  Some communities have petting zoos. Most often these areas have animal trainers who monitor the interactions of children and the animals. Chechnya learns when it is safe to pet a kangaroo and also how to pet it (photo 9.5). Appropriate handling includes:
  - when to approach an animal
  - how to approach an animal
  - how to touch an animal appropriately

Photo 9.5

2. Nutrition

Early childhood educators learn about appropriate nutrition within the curriculum of an early childhood training program. Often the types of foods recommended can be expensive. Working with a limited budget can stress individuals' ingenuity and creativity. Often mealtimes become mundane and of questionable nutritional value. A nutritional expert can provide the following advantages:

- help with nutritious meal planning
- advice on maximizing nutritious food purchasing dollars
- advice on nutritional cooking
- advice on developmentally appropriate foods
- advice on preparing food that is aesthetically pleasing

It may be difficult to find a qualified individual to act as a nutritional professional for the daycare setting. The following resource list serves as a starting point to help locate an individual:

- family members of children enrolled in the program
- hospitals, extended care centres, nursing homes, seniors' facilities
- universities, colleges, secondary schools
- Web-based guidance and help (Agriculture and Agri-Food Canada, 2004; Dieticians of Canada, 2004)
- retired nutritionists.

Networking with a nutritional professional is beneficial in several ways. A nutritional professional can:

- assist in setting up an appropriate mealtime social environment for young children
- provide advice about specific eating patterns of children
- provide resources to the centre on alternative food selections and nutritious meals and snacks
- consult on various issues—safety issues around food consumption, food allergies
- provide specific training as needed; for example, training to help prepare more aesthetically pleasing food
- identify other food-related resources in the community

3. Fitness

The lack of fitness among Canadian children has been well documented (Belfry, 2003; Partridge, 2003). To help children develop good fitness habits for life, early childhood educators must become informed about how to instill good fitness practices into the daily programs of children. Individuals well versed in various aspects of fitness could help:

- establish a developmentally appropriate fitness program
- increase awareness of the benefits of overall fitness for children

When deciding on an appropriate fitness professional to act in an advisory or consulting capacity for a child-care setting, it is critical to look for an individual who is well established in the community and has the following characteristics:

- knowledge of overall development and specifically physical development of young children
- awareness of physical needs of young children
- awareness of fitness resources for children in the community

Cooperative play

These characteristics are very important because in many communities fitness for young children is developmentally inappropriate. For example, many physical activities involve organized sports. Young children are not yet developmentally ready to engage in team sports since they are unable to understand of the complexities of many organized sporting activities. For example, children gradually learn to become involved in **cooperative play** (play involving planning together, role designation, and working toward a common goal collaboratively) late in the preschool years. Most games, such as baseball, involve aspects of cooperative activity—who will play what position, strategies used to accomplish the goal (how to hit the ball, where to it, how hard to throw the ball, where to throw it), and how results will be achieved (rules of baseball). Additionally, young children are still learning to coordinate their movements. Fitness activities should revolve around the child's developing skills rather than outside criteria set by the rules of a game.

It may be difficult to find a qualified individual to act as a fitness consultant for the daycare setting. The following resource list serves as a starting point to help locate an individual:

- family members of children enrolled in the program
- community fitness clubs, community recreation facilities, YMCA, YWCA
- Heart and Stroke Foundation
- community colleges and universities
- boards of education
- retired fitness professionals

To use the services of a fitness professional most efficiently, the fitness consultant needs to have information about the ages of the children in the program and the equipment and environments available for fitness activities. The individual should be flexible enough to address needs as they arise. Networking with a fitness professional is beneficial in several ways. A fitness professional can:

- assist in the development of a physical activity program for the centre—The preschool program at Capilano College wanted to expand children's ability to balance. By brainstorming ideas, the staff and college faculty were able to coordinate to add items that enhance existing balance activities to the children's outdoor play spaces. They added natural logs of various widths and tires placed end to end to the outdoor play spaces (photo 9.6).

Photo 9.6

- provide advice about motivating physical activities or providing individualized fitness plans as needed—Justin's parents are quite concerned about his weight problem. They finally consult a physician. Justin is placed on a diet and the family takes him to the YMCA for gymnastic and swim programs. The parents share this information with Justin's daycare staff and ask that the staff also encourage Justin to participate in physical activity. The staff finds it hard to motivate Justin. One of the children in the program has a parent, Janet, who is a fitness instructor at a local gym. She also runs a weekly physical activity program for young children and their families. The staff asks her advice on how to motivate children who are reluctant to participate in physical activity. Janet suggests that the staff observe when and how Justin is active and then build a program around his interests. The staff follows this advice and discovers that Justin is most active during music and movement times. They decide to incorporate music and movement activities outside. Janet helps them plan some of these activities. Justin starts to participate in these activities with the other children.
- provide resources and consult with the centre on physical fitness issues—cardiovascular, weight loss, endurance, strength, coordination
- advocate about the value of physical activity to staff and families—Justin's parents decide to help other families cope with children who are overweight and lack opportunities to participate. Together with the centre's staff, they create a list of various resources in the community that engage young children in physical activities.
- provide specific training as needed; for example, training to incorporate appropriate stretching exercises—The daycare staff finds that they do not understand some of the music and movement activities Janet has recommended. She offers to come in and show the staff how to do these activities.
- provide information about other physical activity resources

4. Education

Many program areas can be expanded to include expertise from the community—drama; music; physical activities; reading and writing; creative arts; and sand, water, and block play (Table 9.3). The more integrated activities become, the more likely it is that children will start to transfer knowledge and skills from one situation to another. For example, learning about crossing the street safely should be transferred to other similar situations, such as the following:

- becoming aware of other potentially hazardous situations, such as pedestrians watching for individuals on riding toys and riders watching for pedestrians
- becoming aware of what others are doing around us—watching out for individuals running or playing with balls
- becoming aware of potentially dangerous areas such as slippery surfaces and areas behind swings

TABLE 9.3 EDUCATIONAL RESOURCES

Program Area	Description	Resource
Drama	- Role-play community helpers such as doctors, nurses, firefighters, police officers. - Prepare own snacks.	- Doctors, nurses, firefighters, police officers - Nutritionists, college or university faculty, home economics teachers
Music	- Develop music that supports health and safety issues such as songs about nutrition, safety, feeling sick, and visiting a doctor, hospital, or dentist. - Ask a musician to play a variety of songs and tape them to use in physical activity programs.	- Musicians, music teachers, libraries
Reading and writing	- Choose books that deal with appropriate topics on food, health, and safety. - Set up books in various areas around the centre to attract attention and reinforce skills. - Develop a writing area where children can dictate stories about safety. The stories could be illustrated by the children and bound in a book to share with others.	- Libraries, librarians
Sand and block play	- Observe traffic and construction sites to identify safety measures. Children in the Loyalist College Curriculum Lab observed traffic patterns around the college. They created a road with marked lines along which they could drive their toy cars (photo 9.7). Over time this activity expanded to include traffic signs (yield, stop, one way, no entry), traffic lights, and traffic bumps.	- Traffic sites, construction sites
Water	- Learn about water safety in wading pools, swimming pools, and along rivers and lakes.	- Lifeguards, park rangers
Creative arts	- Post pictures of various health and safety issues in the creative arts area to encourage drawing/painting and creating three-dimensional structures.	- Magazines, photographs, newspapers

Building a Network

It takes time to build a network of individuals and resources within each community. It is an ongoing process, as communities are forever changing. Services close and new ones open; families move into and out of communities. The following steps will help build networks:

- Get to know the families of the children enrolled in the child-care centre. They are the centre's biggest resource and can collaborate to help build a network of resources.
- Establish a protocol that requires participation of staff and families. This might include charts that can be filled in by all staff and family members (Table 9.4).
- Contact individuals in the community to see what kind of help and how much time they may be able to commit to the program. Prepare an interview sheet to record responses (Table 9.5). Identify volunteers who can help with this process.
- Post information.

Photo 9.7

TABLE 9.4   COMMUNITY RESOURCES

Service	Type of Service Offered	Contact Name	Contact Information

TABLE 9.5   INTERVIEW RESOURCE INDIVIDUALS

Questions	Responses
I am calling on behalf of............. I wonder if you would be interested in supporting our organization in some capacity. We are looking for experts to help us develop [policies, programs, materials, problem-solving skills] to ensure the physical well-being of our children.	
What type of service could you supply?	
How much time could you commit?	
Can you think of any other resources we should be looking for?	

Advocacy

Many issues that families face are difficult to overcome without assistance. Many issues deal with policies that governments create around the well-being of families and their children, as identified in Chapter 8. One way to create change within any democracy is to advocate for those who cannot advocate for themselves. Early childhood educators are in an ideal position to advocate for children within the many communities across Canada. "Today's practitioners are increasingly being faced with the need to become involved in public-interest issues that impinge directly on their primary obligations to the children in their care." (Jensen & Hannibal, 2000: 4)

Another aspect of networking is to form networks for advocacy. Advocacy networks are extremely effective because a network brings individuals together from a variety of professions, with a variety of expertise, but who all share a common interest in the well-being of young children. Networks would include individuals from all of the groups identified in this chapter. Advocacy groups could focus on:

- identifying and eliminating the causes of poverty
- ensuring that all families have equal access to medical and dental care, sick leave, and drug plans
- ensuring that all families have appropriate housing
- increasing awareness and opportunity for family fitness, including early physical activity
- advocating for enhanced quality of early childhood education programs

SUMMARY

Through networking, early childhood educators are able to link with an increased number of resources, experts, families, and community members. These links serve to increase:

- awareness of the needs of children and their families
- resources available to all individuals within the network
- opportunities to collaborate and advocate for children and families
- opportunities to work together toward a common goal (Figure 9.5)

FIGURE 9.5
Community Networking

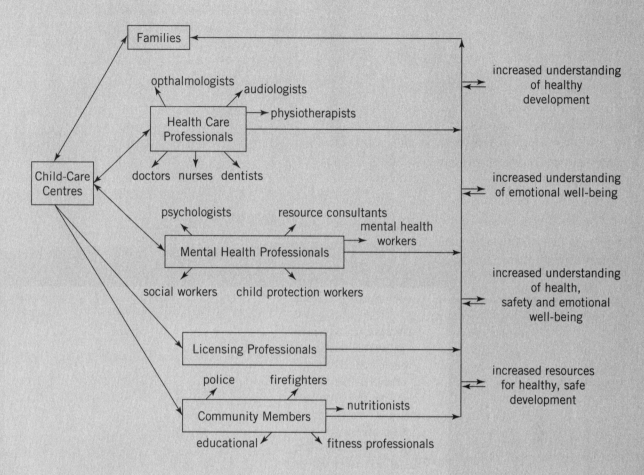

KEY POINTS

Networking
- A group of individuals who work together toward a common goal
- Advantages—decreased sense of isolation, opportunities to collaborate and share expertise and information

Networking with families
- Resource sharing, increased understanding

Methods of networking with families
- Posting information
- Providing resource areas
- Documenting children's learning
- Holding workshops
- Linking resources in the community
- Establishing clear guidelines with opportunities for discussion
- Establishing a respectful atmosphere

Networking with health care professionals

- Advise and consult on health and safety issues.
- Assist in development of health and safety policies and programs.
- Provide resources and specialized training, assist in advocacy.

Networking with mental health professionals

- Advise and consult to set up an appropriate social environment for children and manage behaviour.
- Provide resources and specialized training.

Networking with licensing professionals

- Advise and consult on overall general safety.
- Help create a sanitary environment.
- Interpret specific legislative requirements.
- Provide specialized training as needed.

Networking with community members

- Police officers—road and personal safety
- Animal trainers or veterinarians—safety in approaching and handling animals

- Nutritionists—preparing aesthetically pleasing, developmentally appropriate, nutritious meals
- Fitness professionals—assist in creating developmentally appropriate physical activity programs
- Education—linking all parts of a program to reflect learning in safety, well-being, and healthy development

Building a network

- Get to know families and resources within community.
- Identify volunteers who can collaborate.
- Develop a resource registry.

Advocacy network

- Fight poverty.
- Provide equal access to medical and dental care.
- Increase awareness and opportunity to engage in physical activity.
- Advocate for high-quality child care.

EXERCISES

1. Define "networking." In small groups, discuss what information you would need to develop a network in your community. Identify key individuals or organizations that could become part of a network. Chart this information.

2. You are working in a daycare in a small community. You wish to include families to help you plan health and safety awareness with your group of children. You have identified the following expertise in your family group—a dentist, a police officer, a public health nurse, and a kindergarten teacher. What strategies might you use to involve families in helping you set up a network to assist with this plan?

3. One of the children in your preschool group has been hospitalized with severe asthma. The children have become very interested in all aspects of care for someone who is ill. How might you use this situation to involve the professionals caring for the sick child to help set up an interest unit?

4. Emotional health and well-being is critical to establishing a positive learning environment. Explore the resources available in your community to help with setting up a positive learning environment. Use the following charts to guide you.

CHART 1

Aspects of Emotional Health	Type of Resource	Contact Information
Children who often appear sad and withdrawn		
Children with hard-to-control behaviour		
Suspected child abuse		
A family member who seems very negative toward the child		

5. Describe the process used in your community for:
   a) licensing a child–care center
   b) fire inspections
   c) health inspections

How might you network with these professionals to help you in the process?

6. Develop an inventory of your community of individuals who could become part of a network.

7. Using Table 9.4 and in a small group, interview three community members who might be able to help create a network with early childhood educators. Compare your results. Add resources to your list that you were missing.

8. Discuss why advocacy networks are more effective. Who might you include in such a network in your area?

CHART 2

Activity	Type of Resources	Contact Information
Cooking with children		
Drama		
Physical activity		
Reading and writing activities		
Outdoor play		
Music and movement		

✱Glossary

Active listening (page 271) Listening to the content of a message without personal bias and clarifying the intent of the message when the meaning is unclear or to ensure that the meaning is clear.

Cooperative play (page 282) Play involving planning together and working toward a common goal collaboratively.

Epipen (page 277) Emergency medication provided via a needle for a severe allergic reaction.

Networking (page 266) Occurs between individuals who have common interests in order to share ideas, expertise, resources, and information and to find ways to improve quality experiences for a group of individuals.

REFERENCES

Agriculture and Agri-Food Canada. (2004). *Agriculture and Agri-Food Canada Online* http://www.agr.gc.ca/, accessed 2 December 2004.

Belfry, J. (2003). *Canadian children face activity and fitness crisis.* Child and Family Canada. http://www.cfc-efc.ca/docs/cccf/00010_en.htm, 22 September 2003.

Children's Safety Association of Canada. (2004). *Children's safety.* http://www.safekid.org/, accessed 27 September 2003.

Dieticians of Canada. (2004). *Promoting health through food and nutrition.* http://www.dietitians.ca, accessed 5 October 2003.

Geist, M. (2004). *Federal privacy legislation.* http://www.privacyinfo.ca/legi_fedr.php?v=6, accessed 28 September 2003.

Jensen, M., & Hannibal, M. (2000). *Issues, advocacy and leadership in early education.* Needham Heights, MA: Allyn & Bacon.

Ontario Early Years. (2003). *What is an Ontario Early Years' Centre?* http://www.ontarioearlyyears.ca, accessed 7 April 2003.

Partridge, K. (2003). Fat action. *Today's Parent, 20,* 90–130.

Shapiro Kendrick, A., Kaufman R., & Messenger, K. (1995). *Healthy young children: A manual for programs.* Washington, DC: National Association for the Education of Young Children.

10 Health and Wellness of Caregivers

CHAPTER

"Early childhood educators really help to make the intelligent, compassionate, healthy, adaptive future human race. This is an accurate description of the impact your daily commitment can have on children and their future outcomes. What can you learn for your 'self' that will allow you to be available, fresh, interested, involved, and ready to take on this awesome task? Caregivers must learn to take good care of themselves, to not neglect their 'self' in a day of routines, and learn to identify and use the self-health techniques." (Watson, Watson, Cam Wilson, & Crowther, 2000: 43)

Chapter Outcomes

After reading this chapter, the reader will:

1. Identify why personal health and wellness is an important consideration when working with young children.

2. Define and identify strategies to improve the various components of physical wellness—diet, sleep, exercise, harmful habits, regular checkups, and safe practices.

3. Define and discuss strategies to improve:
   • emotional wellness
   • intellectual wellness
   • spiritual wellness
   • interpersonal and social wellness
   • environmental wellness

4. Discuss how the various aspects of wellness are interconnected.

5. Describe and discuss barriers to creating healthy living styles.

6. Discuss strategies to improve overall personal wellness.

The Importance of Caregiver Health and Wellness

Excellence in early childhood settings has often been linked to caregiver characteristics (Doherty, 2003; Goelman, Doherty, Lero, LaGrange, & Tougas, 2000), including:

- patience
- energy, coordination, and physical strength
- emotional stability, emotional warmth, sensitivity, and active involvement with children and their families
- self-understanding, a sense of humour, and a positive attitude
- good physical health (Wardle, 2003: 194)

The demands on an early childhood educator are highly rewarding, but also can lead to higher levels of stress as the daily routines are numerous and at times hectic. These daily routines include:

- caring for the well-being and safety of all children in care—physical and emotional well-being of all children as well as encouraging cognitive, social, and communicative growth
- ensuring that the environment is set up to challenge children's interactions with each other and the materials and equipment in the environment
- monitoring children's progress
- observing and recording pertinent information to assist in developing appropriate experiences for children and sharing information about children's experiences, development, and progress with family members
- interacting with children and their families
- maintaining a healthy schedule over each day that fosters optimal growth and development of all children
- interacting and coordinating activities with other staff members

Caregiver health and wellness are critical factors in helping a caregiver be able to meet the needs of children and families and the demands of daily routines. When the caregiver is not feeling well, has not had enough rest, is physically exhausted, or is generally "down," that caregiver will find it difficult to maintain the energy necessary to meet the demands of a daily schedule. The following example shows how easily the caregiver's balance can be disrupted by how he or she is feeling.

Janine has a slight headache when she wakes up in the morning. When Janine arrives at the toddler program, she finds that one of the children, Andrew, is fussy. He demands continual attention. He wants to sit on Janine's lap or be carried. When she puts him down, he cries. He refuses to sit or interact with Janine's teammate. After an hour of trying to cope with Andrew and the normal demands of the other toddlers, Janine has a pounding headache. She feels she can no longer bear to hear Andrew cry. She comes close to snapping at a simple request from one of the children. Finally Janine asks her supervisor to take over for her. Janine takes a tablet for her headache and quietly sits in the staff room until it subsides. When she returns to the room, she feels ready to cope again.

Janine knew she had reached her limit. She took appropriate steps to ensure that she could once again face the daily schedule with the same calm, patient, and enthusiastic manner she always shows the children and family members.

Optimal Wellness of Caregivers

Wellness refers to the "optimal health and vitality, encompassing physical, emotional, intellectual, interpersonal and social, and environmental well being" of an individual (Fahey, Insel, & Roth, 1999: 2). There are six dimensions of wellness: physical, emotional, intellectual, spiritual, interpersonal and social, and environmental (Figure 10.1). The optimal wellness of any individual depends on all of these dimensions as well as their interrelationship. Wellness or lack of wellness in one dimension may influence other dimensions. For example, poor self-esteem could lead to worrying about one's ability to do a job effectively. This could lead to a lack of sleep, which affects physical well-being. Wellness in any one of the dimensions can be improved, and improvement in one area often leads to overall improved wellness.

1. Physical Wellness

Physical wellness includes all of the factors that lead to overall physical good health. Many of these factors relate to individual choices we make.

A) BALANCED DIET A healthy diet should include the essential nutrients. **Essential nutrients** are nutrients that must be obtained directly from food, as they are not produced by the body. Six essential nutrients are needed to satisfy human physiological needs:

✳ **Essential nutrients**

- *Carbohydrates.* Carbohydrates are essential because they supply energy to the circulatory and nervous systems and to brain cells. Carbohydrates are found in grains, fruits, vegetables, and milk.
- *Fats.* Fats are essential because they provide insulation, energy, support, and protection for the organs of the body. Fats are broken into two categories—saturated and unsaturated. Saturated fats are found in animal products, coconut oils, and artificially saturated vegetable oils. Unsaturated fats are found in grain products, fish, nuts, and vegetables.
- *Minerals.* Minerals are important because they regulate body functions such as the growth and maintenance of tissues. Minerals are also important because they help release energy. Minerals can be found in almost all food groups.
- *Proteins.* Proteins are important to maintain healthy bones, muscles, blood, tissues, enzymes, and membranes. Proteins are also a source of energy. Food sources include milk products, fish, poultry, legumes (peas, beans, soybeans, alfalfa, and peanuts) eggs, and nuts.
- *Vitamins.* Vitamins are important because they help initiate or speed up cell functions. Vitamins can be found in all food groups (for different food groups, refer to Chapter 5).

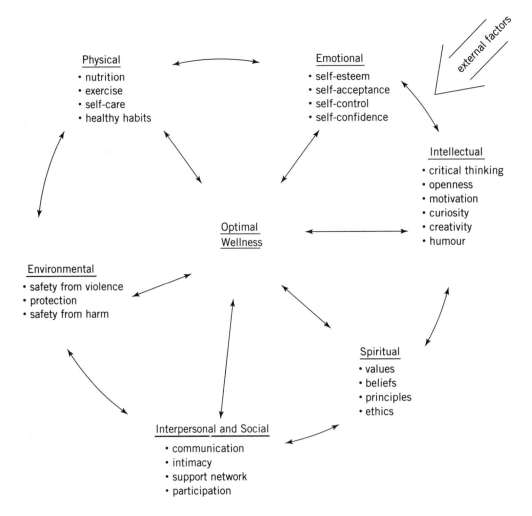

FIGURE 10.1

Optimal Wellness of Caregivers

- *Water.* Water makes up most of the body's weight (50 to 70 percent). Water is critical for cell function, transport of nutrients, elimination of waste, and body temperature regulation. There is water to varying degrees in all food groups. However, most of the body's water comes from drinking water and other liquids (Fahey, Insel, & Roth, 1999; Health Canada, 2003).

According to Health Canada, it is important to enjoy and include foods from all food groups every day (Table 10.1). "Eating many different kinds of foods, prepared in different ways is what variety is all about. Variety promotes:

- An adequate intake of essential nutrients;
- The use of foods and cuisines enjoyed by different ethnic and cultural groups; and
- The positive and pleasurable aspects of eating by exploring a wide range of foods varying in colour, flavour and textures." (Office of Nutrition Policy and Promotion, 2002: 2)

TABLE 10.1   DAILY NUTRITIONAL RECOMMENDATIONS

Type of Food	Quantity
Carbohydrates	- Essential required daily intake—50 to 100 grams - Average daily intake—250 grams - Recommended intake—55 percent of total daily calories
Fat	- Essential required daily intake—1 tablespoon or 15 grams - Average daily intake—5 tablespoons or 75 grams or 33 percent of daily **calorie** intake - Recommended intake—30 percent of total daily calories with less than 10 percent from saturated fats
Minerals	- Individuals eating a balanced diet consisting of all the food groups will usually meet their daily mineral requirements. Mineral supplements or foods rich in certain minerals may be recommended by a physician in cases of mineral deficiency.
Vitamins	- Individuals eating a balanced diet consisting of all the food groups will usually meet their daily vitamin requirements. Vitamin supplements may be recommended by a physician in cases of vitamin deficiency.
Water	- Foods and fluids account for 80 to 90 percent of the daily water intake needed. To make up the additional amount needed, 2 litres of water should be consumed daily.

✳ Calorie

Source: Fahey, Insel, & Roth (1999).

B) APPROPRIATE SLEEP Most adults need between seven and eight hours of sleep a night. However, sleep patterns are individual; some adults may require only 5 hours of sleep while others may require 10. Additionally, getting a good night's sleep is not always under an individual's control. Factors such as stress, illness, or demands of family life may make it difficult to get adequate sleep. Irrespective of why it occurs, inadequate sleep may have a number of side effects. These range in seriousness depending on how much sleep has been missed. Some symptoms of sleep deprivation include (Meridian Health, 2003):

- decreased creativity
- lack of motivation
- irritability
- lack of patience
- decreased effectiveness and efficiency
- lack of clear thinking
- poor performance on eye–hand coordination tasks
- overall poor job performance

The possible side effects of lack of sleep relate directly to the ability to work with children, as many characteristics of quality interactions with children could be impaired. A number of strategies can be implemented to help gain a more restful night's sleep:

- Establish a regular sleep schedule.
- Engage in regular exercise to promote better sleep patterns. Avoid exercising too close to bedtime as this might have the opposite effect.
- Establish relaxing bedtime rituals such as reading, listening to soothing music, or having a bath.
- Create an environment that helps sleeping. Each individual is different, but strategies such as curtains to block out unwanted light, comfortable temperature (often lower at night), appropriate ventilation, and comfortable pillows and bedding may help set the tone for sleeping.
- Limit the amount of time spent "trying to get to sleep." Instead, get out of bed and try some relaxation techniques, then try to get to sleep again.
- If sleep problems persist, consult a physician.
- Before going to sleep, avoid:

  ◦ beverages containing **caffeine** (a stimulant that can cause an alerting effect) such as coffee, tea, colas, or chocolate. Caffeine's effect on the body may remain for an average of three to five hours.
  ◦ smoking, as nicotine is a stimulant
  ◦ alcohol, as it may disrupt sleep and cause you to wake up periodically during the night
  ◦ food or drink before going to bed. It may make you feel uncomfortable and cause difficulty falling asleep.
  ◦ spicy foods, as these may cause heartburn (Fahey, Insel, & Roth, 1999)

C) REGULAR EXERCISE "Any list of the benefits of physical activity is impressive. A physically active lifestyle helps you generate more energy, control your weight, manage stress, and boost your immune system. It provides psychological and emotional benefits, contributing to your sense of competence and well-being. It offers protection against heart disease, diabetes, high blood pressure, osteoporosis, cancer, and even premature death. Exercise increases your physical capacity so that you are better able to meet the challenges of daily life with energy and vigor." (Fahey, Insel, & Roth, 1999: 20)

"Physical activity can be defined as the capacity of the heart, blood vessels, lungs, and muscles to function at optimum efficiency." (Graham, Holt/Hale, & Parker, 1998: 34) The effectiveness of physical activity is dependent on the amount of energy used. The more vigorous the exercise, the less time at it is needed. For example, walking at an accelerated pace for 30 minutes would give similar results to running for 15 minutes.

Adults should engage in three types of physical activities—endurance, flexibility, and strength—to keep their bodies healthy (Physical Activity Unit, 2004). Types

TABLE 10.2   PHYSICAL FITNESS ACTIVITIES

Activity	Description	Time
General guidelines	- Complete any activities listed below from at least two categories (endurance, flexibility, or strength). - See Chapter 7 for examples of stretching exercises	Complete one hour of activity per day
Endurance activities	**Endurance activities** strengthen the heart, lungs, and circulatory system (also known as **cardiovascular endurance**). "The ability of the body to perform prolonged, large-muscle, dynamic exercise at moderate-to-high levels of intensity." (Fahey, Insel, & Roth, 1999: 23) Types of activities: - Chores—gardening, cleaning the yard with the help of the children - Sports—cycling, skating, swimming laps, golfing (without a golf cart), tennis - Other activities—dancing, walking (take the children for a walk, walk to the store, walk during the lunch break, propel a wheelchair)	Four to seven days a week One activity for 20 minutes or two activities of 10 minutes each
Flexibility activities	**Flexibility activities** increase the range of movements. These exercises serve to relax the muscles and loosen the joints. Flexibility activities include gentle stretching exercises such as reaching, bending, or turning. These movements could become a regular stretching exercise (photo 10.1) or simply part of a regular routine. Types of activities: - With the children—stretching exercises (photo 10.2), music and movement activities, cleaning the outdoor play area - Chores—mopping floors, gardening, yardwork, vacuuming - Stretching exercises—Tai Chi, yoga - Sports—golf, bowling, curling	Four to seven days a week Five minutes of slow, light activity such as walking Engage in stretching exercises—hold each stretch for 10 to 30 seconds Twenty minutes per day or two 10-minute periods

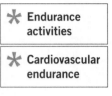

* **Endurance activities**

* **Cardiovascular endurance**

* **Flexibility activities**

TABLE 10.2 CONTINUED

Activity	Description	Time
Strength training	"**Strength activities** help your muscles and bones stay strong, improve your posture and help to prevent diseases like osteoporosis. Strength activities are those that make you work your muscles against some kind of resistance, like when you push or pull hard to open a door." (Physical Activity Unit, 2004: 3) Safe strength training: - If considering weight training, consult an expert to help set up an appropriate individualized program. - Start with five minutes of light endurance activities. - Use proper back and joint practices, such as bending with your knees and your back straight, to lift weights. - Use light weights with 10 to 15 repetitions, 2 to 4 times, and breathe regularly. - Follow up strength activities with gentle stretching exercises. - Try to do a variety of exercises to strengthen the muscles in arms, legs, and midsection of the body. Types of activities: - Chores—heavy yardwork such as building flowerbeds or laying flagstones; raking and bagging leaves/grass; lifting and carrying groceries, infants, or toddlers; wearing backpacks to carry water or snacks and books on field trips - Exercises—triceps curls (photo 10.3), curl-ups (photo 10.4), weight/strength training routines in a gym	Twenty minutes or two 10-minute sessions Rest one day between strength-building exercises

Source: Physical Activity Unit (2004); Fahey, Insel, & Roth (1999).

Photo 10.1

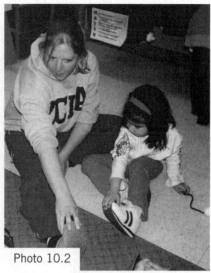

Photo 10.2

Photo 10.3

Photo 10.4

of activities and suggestions for activities are listed in Table 10.2. Many of these activities can be built into daily routines. By building these activities into a daily routine, a number of benefits can be realized:

- Individuals can choose from a variety of physical activities that are more enjoyable to them—you are much more likely to engage in physical activities you enjoy, such as golf or gardening.
- Physical activities can serve a dual purpose, thereby reducing time needed to exercise—chosen activities could be regular chores that need to be done but also fit into an exercise regime, such as propelling a wheelchair (strength and endurance), yardwork (strength, endurance, and flexibility), or vacuuming (flexibility).
- Caregivers can create a physical activity schedule that is individualized, builds on individual interests, and fits the personal lifestyle of the individual.
- Physical activity schedules can be flexible—individuals should be active for one hour a day; however, these activities could be broken up into 10-minute portions throughout the day to avoid boredom (Physical Activity Unit, 2004).

D) AVOIDANCE OF HARMFUL HABITS Individuals engage in many habits that can potentially become addictive. "**Addictive behaviours** are habits that have gotten out of control, with a resulting impact on a person's health." (Fahey, Insel, & Roth, 1999: 312) Some of these habits might include drinking alcohol, smoking cigarettes, or drug use. However, not all individuals become addicted. "There is no single cause for addiction. Characteristics of an individual person, of the environment in which the person lives, and of the substances or behavior he or she abuses combine in an addictive behaviour." (Fahey, Insel, & Roth, 1999: 313) Individuals engage in potentially addictive behaviours for many reasons, including a desire to:

✳ Addictive behaviours

- experience a pleasant emotional state such as the "buzz" gained from drinking too much alcohol or taking drugs
- fit in with a peer group by engaging in similar behaviours, such as going to bar with friends for a drink
- dull pain by taking drugs to relieve continual headaches without consulting a doctor
- relieve stressful situations such as balancing the demands of a job and family life
- use habits such as drinking or smoking to cope with stress or unpleasant circumstances, such as smoking a cigarette to calm oneself down

Often it is not a question of addiction. Even small doses of addictive substances can be harmful to an individual's health and lifestyle and may make it more difficult to cope with daily routines. For example, Terry, an early childhood educator, has developed a habit of smoking half a pack of cigarettes a day. She finds that she needs to go outside several times a day to smoke a cigarette. Her fellow staff members are soon able to predict these times. Terry becomes more irritable and starts to snap at people at the least provocation. She is not aware of her behaviour and is shocked when her supervisor talks to her about needing to make a change. Terry decides to quit smoking.

Terry does not think that her smoking has become addictive. She thinks that she will be able to quit quite easily and is surprised at how difficult it is. She makes several attempts before she is successful.

In summary, anyone wanting to work with young children seriously needs to consider the harmful effects of potentially addictive habits. The effects of these habits not only may be detrimental to the individual's health but also may have unpleasant effects on the children and co-workers around them.

- Possible effects on others
  - increased irritability
  - lack of patience
  - increased aggressiveness and hostility in some individuals
  - unpleasant odours such as smoke or alcohol on the breath

- Possible effects on the individual
  - unpleasant physical reactions such as sweating, flushing, headaches, hallucinations, nausea, hangovers, coughs, breathlessness, and eye irritations
  - impaired judgment
  - weakened sensory perception
  - reduced inhibitions

E) REGULAR CHECKUPS Early childhood educators work in close confinement with many individuals—children, families, other staff members, and other professionals. In environments that bring together many individuals, there is an increased chance of the spread of disease. Adults not only need to become familiar with the symptoms of many childhood diseases (Chapter 3) but also need to learn to recognize symptoms of potential ill health in themselves. Early recognition of illness will help the early childhood educator find appropriate treatment more quickly.

Adults should have annual, regularly scheduled doctor's appointments to ensure that they are in good health. Additional consultations with a doctor can be used to identify possible preventative measures—for example, flu shots or a regime of vitamin or mineral supplements—that could lower the risk of infection.

Regular dental appointments are also advised. Pain from dental problems such as an abscessed tooth can become very debilitating. Regular checkups usually help prevent major problems from occurring.

F) SAFE PRACTICES Many safe practices have already been discussed in other chapters of this book. Practising safe and healthy practices serves to:

- model appropriate practices to children and their families
- ensure congruency between messages given to children and families and actions—for example, if care providers ask children to eat healthy foods but eat less healthy foods themselves, the message will become much less effective
- ensure that optimal care is taken to provide a safe, sanitary, and healthy learning environment
- protect children from potential dangers such as injury from broken equipment or risk of infection from contaminated surfaces
- provide a quality program in all areas—social, emotional, physical, and cognitive

In summary, physical well-being is critical for caregivers of young children. Individuals in good physical health with a healthy lifestyle that includes appropriate sleep, regular exercise, good nutrition, and regular medical checkups will be more likely to act in a manner conducive to working with young children—enthusiastic, vibrant, nurturing, and energetic. These individuals will more likely have the energy and patience necessary to:

- plan and implement appropriate learning activities and environments
- deal effectively with problems as they arise
- understand and deal with children's behaviours
- show empathy as needed to children and their families
- communicate in positive ways
- participate actively with children

2. Emotional Wellness

"Optimism, trust, self-esteem, self acceptance, self confidence, self-control, satisfying relationships, and an ability to share feelings are just some of the qualities and aspects of emotional wellness. Maintaining emotional wellness requires monitoring and explaining your thoughts and feelings, identifying obstacles to emotional well-being, and finding solutions to emotional problems, with the help of a therapist if needed." (Fahey, Insel, & Roth, 1999: 2)

To work effectively with young children and their families, early childhood educators need skills that relate to their emotional well-being.

- *Optimism*. Kaya has worked with young children for more than six years. She was an honour student during her early childhood studies. She finds some of her experiences in child care frustrating. At times she feels that the children's environments lack the quality experiences the children deserve. She continues to work in the field because she is convinced that she can make a difference. She continually strives to find ways to improve the quality of care for children and the staff she works with—fundraising, conducting workshops, writing newsletters, advocating for improved working conditions. She continues to be optimistic about her ability to effect change.
- *Trust*. Kaya has gained trust in her abilities to provide quality experiences for the children and families under her care and to effectively supervise staff. She also trusts in her children's ability to create their own learning opportunities. She helps them do so by setting up an environment that encourages self-motivated exploration (photo 10.5).
- *Self-esteem*. Kaya has high self-esteem regarding her abilities as a teacher of young children. She demonstrates her self-esteem in her interactions with families and staff, which are always courteous, respectful, and honest. One of the children in her program is quick to anger. When Iman is angry, she becomes verbally abusive to other children and staff. Kaya tells Iman, "I do not like the words you are using." She is indicating to Iman that only her behaviour is unacceptable. She also talks to Iman and asks her what might help her control her anger. Iman

Photo 10.5

Photo 10.6

thinks a large pillow might work. This strategy proves successful. When angry, Iman goes to her pillow, puts her face in it, and talks to it. The sounds she makes are muffled and not distinguishable.

- *Self-acceptance.* Kaya accepts herself as she is. She knows that there are some areas in which she needs to increase her expertise. She actively pursues workshops and other in-service training to increase her knowledge and expertise as needed.
- *Self-confidence.* Kaya is confident in her abilities to meet the many challenges each day might bring. Her self-confidence is demonstrated in her calm acceptance of the children's behaviour and her quick interventions when needed. For example, one afternoon the children are getting very restless. It has been a cold, wet, and very windy day and the children have not been outdoors. Kaya calmly sits in a corner and starts to read one of the children's favourite books. She does not need to call the children to her. Her enthusiastic reading of the story naturally gathers the children around her (photo 10.6). Soon the atmosphere in the room is once again calm and quiet.

Caregivers can use a number of strategies to increase their emotional well-being. Individuals will have to try several of these strategies to find the ones that will be most effective for them (Table 10.3).

TABLE 10.3 **STRATEGIES TO IMPROVE EMOTIONAL WELLNESS**

✳ **Reflection**

Strategy	Description
Reflection—a process by which an individual examines and analyzes a personal behaviour	Janine has just finished implementing a physical activity with her children. She reflects on the experience by answering the following questions in writing: - What went well? - What changes need to be made? - What did the children gain from the experience? - How can I enhance the experience? - When doubting oneself, reflect on a pleasant memory. Use that memory to help regain a more positive frame of mind. Then try to reflect again to gain a more positive self-analysis.
Humour—"Hearty laughter stimulates beneficial, even life-preserving, chemicals in the body. The short-term effects are dramatic: tension is dispersed, apprehension is banished, our ability to think positively is increased, and contentment is restored." (George, 1998: 110)	- Share a joke—this brings individuals together to share a relaxing moment. - Laugh with the children—tell them funny stories, encourage them to tell funny stories. - Think of funny situations that make you laugh when needed. - Try to see the humour in situations and learn to laugh at yourself.
Self-observation—Observing one's own behaviours provides insights into both strengths and needs of caregivers.	- Develop a strength and needs list for yourself. - Develop strategies to improve your strengths and needs. - Revise the list as needed. - Develop a checklist to identify what is needed during activities—need or what improvements.
Express feelings in healthy ways.	- Learn to avoid using words such as stupid, senseless, or insane. - Stop and think about what you are going to say. This gives you an opportunity to reflect on more positive self-expression. - Share how you feel. This makes it easier for everyone to cope and provides possible support for you. If individuals know how you feel, they will be more empathetic and helpful.

TABLE 10.3   **CONTINUED**

Strategy	Description
Increase expertise—often individuals feel negative about themselves when they are in situations that are new to them or that they have no knowledge about. The easiest way to regain self-confidence is to increase one's knowledge about that area.	Increase expertise by: - taking additional courses, attending workshops - reading—journals, magazines, books, Internet - consulting an expert—university, college, community professional - brainstorming sessions at staff meetings
Communicate with others.	- If something someone said or did bothers you, go directly to the source of the problem. Using active listening strategies, talk directly to the individual involved. - Find a mentor or another individual to talk to, bounce ideas around with, listen to your perspective, or offer advice. - Communicate in a positive, respectful manner with everyone. - Share your feelings openly and honestly.
Learn to recognize individual strengths and needs.	- Develop a list of strength and needs—continue to expand it. - Offer to do things you are confident about. - Ask for help when unsure about what to do. - Recognize and acknowledge the things you do well. - Offer to help or initiate activities you do well.

3. Intellectual Wellness

Intellectual wellness is made up of many factors that influence how individuals feel about themselves and how they act. Components of intellectual wellness include (Fahey, Insel, & Roth, 1999):

- *Open-mindedness.* To be open-minded, an individual must be receptive to new ideas and also willing to act on them. For example, Yvonne has always served the preschool children their lunch. She feels that children make too much of a mess and take too long to serve themselves. When a new staff member starts working at the daycare, she suggests that the staff put out more than one platter, small pitchers for pouring, and large serving spoons. Yvonne immediately responds that she is willing to try letting children serve themselves. She is pleased when the strategy works.

- *Thinking critically and asking questions.* Jerome works in a daycare in a large, urban, downtown centre that has very poor outdoor facilities. The area is totally paved, surrounded on two sides by walls of a building, and fenced on the other two sides. The fences both face a busy intersection. The area was a parking lot previously. The daycare cannot get permission to remove any of the pavement. Instead, Jerome, the staff, and the families of the children create large wooden planters to place along the fence. They plant larger cedars in each of the planters. This provides a buffer between the road and the playground. They also create additional planters with large, quick-growing trees in them to create shade and place these strategically around the space. A large, raised sandbox with a canopy is placed in one corner. Instead of climbing equipment, a number of small, sturdy structures are placed around the playground—platforms of various levels, bridges connecting platforms, and a variety of ways (stairs, ladders, ramps) to reach the platforms. To protect children from falls, all platforms, ramps, and stairs are protected by railings. A slide ends in a raised sandbox. Jerome and the staff demonstrate their critical thinking skills in their creation of the outdoor environment. They think of innovative solutions and, over time, create an aesthetically pleasing outdoor environment (Figure 10.2).

FIGURE 10.2

Outdoor Play Space

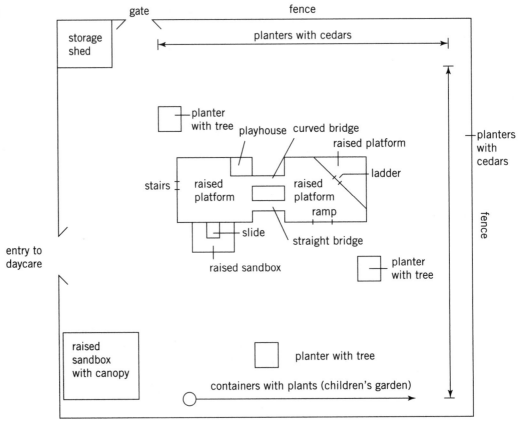

- *Creativity.* The above example, about the outdoor play space, also demonstrates creative thinking—the ability to find solutions to problems that are unique, individual, and innovative.
- *Lifelong learning.* Individuals who are lifelong learners are able to detect problems and solve them (Figure 10.2); they realize when they need more information and know where to find it (courses, reading, workshops, conferences); and they are motivated to gain new skills. When Jerome and his staff encountered the problems with the daycare's outdoor environment, they looked at outdoor space designs in problem areas and asked a variety of experts for advice.

Intellectual wellness continually evolves as we grow and develop over our lifetime. Every new contact and experience brings new learning. Continued learning is a powerful tool to keep us motivated, refreshed, and interested. Some strategies to help develop lifelong learning skills are as follows:

- Gain interests outside of work—read about other subjects of interest.
- Attend workshops, conferences, and in-service training opportunities.
- Embrace opportunities to gain new skills, such as learning a new hobby or learning more about a different age group of children than you are currently involved with.
- Get involved in community forums or advocacy groups.
- Brainstorm with other individuals such as staff members or family members to find new solutions to problems.
- Talk to other professionals in the community to gain insight into different resources available.

4. Spiritual Wellness

"To enjoy spiritual health is to possess a set of guiding beliefs, principles or values that give meaning and purpose to life especially during difficult times. Spiritual wellness involves the capacity for love, compassion, forgiveness, altruism, joy, and fulfillment." (Fahey, Insel, & Roth, 1999)

Most individuals already have a set of beliefs, principles, and values when they enter an early childhood education training program. These beliefs and values are revisited and reshaped many times during an individual's life. As an individual matures, gains more knowledge and experiences, and interacts with other individuals, his or her beliefs, values, and principles become refined or redefined. For example, at one time "spare the rod and spoil the child" was a common belief. Today, most people believe quite the opposite. This belief has changed as society has become more knowledgeable about how the brain develops and matures, what kinds of influences are best for the developing child, and what kinds of guidance techniques best support holistic development.

Canada is rich in cultural, linguistic, and ethnic diversity. This diversity is reflected in how we behave toward each other, the values and beliefs we bring to interactions, and the kinds of programs and services we provide for children and their families. "Living harmoniously in a culturally diverse society requires us to take the perspective of the other individual instead of looking at the world solely though our own cultural eyes." (Klein & Chen, 2001: 10) Learning to look and listen with open eyes and ears requires improving one's spiritual wellness.

As we move through life, we are continually exposed to a number of different beliefs, values, and philosophical systems. When working with children in an increasingly culturally diverse world, it is important to learn how to value different perspectives. In the process, our own systems evolve and are continually redefined. Some strategies to help in this process include the following:

- Become more knowledgeable about other beliefs, valuess, or principles (Therrien & Laugrand, 2001). "To build a rich multicultural program, educate children effectively, and build good relationships with families we need to continually learn about and respond to cultural, ethnic, and linguistic differences." (Copple, 2003: 1)

- Talk to families of children about their beliefs and values.
- Discuss differences in beliefs and values openly with families, other staff members, and community members.
- Participate in developing a mission statement for the workplace environment.
- Review:
  - codes of ethics developed by early childhood education associations across Canada
  - mission statements of various child-care organizations
  - children's rights (Covell, 2001)

5. Interpersonal and Social Wellness

Interpersonal and social wellness refers to engaging in satisfactory relationships both within and outside of workplace settings. Interpersonal and social wellness depends on:

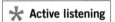
Active listening

- good communication skills such as **active listening** (listening without bias or personal agenda to a message) and responding to the intent of the message received— Maria has been doing the bulk of the cleaning at the end of the day for the last week. When her co-worker again says she has to leave, Maria asks her if there is a reason. Her co-worker indicates that she has to pick up her child from school because her husband is out of town for the week. She apologizes for not informing Maria of her problem earlier and tells Maria how appreciative she is of all the extra work she is doing.
- establishing good support networks both within the early childhood field and at home—Networks include groups of similar professionals such as an infant/toddler or preschool support group, neighbourhood reading groups, and parent support groups for children with special needs; or, networking can be as simple as getting together with a group of friends for an evening of fun.
- participating in events in the daycare setting such as annual picnics and also in community events such as fundraisers
- becoming aware of social and political issues in Canada and the world—Awareness of national and international events is important since some may affect the well-being

of all individuals. World events such as wars, terrorism, and health epidemics affect all members of society. Knowledge helps explain and soften the impact where needed.

With every new individual we meet, every new job situation, and every new social activity, interpersonal and social skills evolve and change. Individuals adapt their personal styles to the situations they are in. For example, one tends to communicate differently at a funeral than at a party with friends. The following are some suggested strategies to help adapt to the ever-changing social context of all individuals:

- Stay informed—read newspapers and magazines, listen to the news on radio, watch the news on TV.
- Establish networks for personal growth and development—friendships, attending social events such as dances or going out to dinner.
- Establish support networks at work—staff meetings, family meetings, or program planning meetings.
- Join professional organizations such as early childhood provincial, territorial, or national organizations, and participate in writing articles for their publications or become a member of their board.
- Participate in workshops or conferences by attending or presenting topics of interest.
- Practise good communication skills such as rephrasing messages to ensure that they have been understood correctly, or participate in writing regular newsletters about children's activities in the program.

6. Environmental Wellness

Health and safety are increasingly under the influence of environmental factors. These factors include:

- safety of the food supply:
  - Mad cow disease has been discovered in Alberta.
  - Trans fat found in deep-fried foods such as potato chips, french fries, chicken, and fish has been linked to increased LDL (bad cholesterol) and lower HDL (good cholesterol) levels, which in turn are linked to cardiovascular problems such as heart attacks.
  - Pesticides in food supplies affect overall health, with possible links to diseases such as cancer.
- pollution:
  - Air quality is often poor in major cities; pollution warnings force many individuals to stay inside on days when the pollution index is high or to move to other parts of the country where the danger is not as great.
  - Many lakes and rivers are closed during swimming season because of bacterial contamination.

- ○ Contaminated drinking water causes illness and death, as observed in Walkerton, Ontario, and North Battleford, Saskatchewan.
  - ○ Threats from ultraviolet radiation mean that:
    - careful protection against the sun is needed when going outside
    - there is increased fear of diseases such as skin cancer
- fear of contracting disease:
  - ○ mosquito bites leading to infection by the West Nile virus
  - ○ being stung by killer bees
  - ○ exposure to someone who may have a disease like SARS
- violence in society:
  - ○ wars—Iraq, Haiti, and Afghanistan
  - ○ terrorism—suicide bombers, attacks on September 11, 2001
  - ○ random acts such as children gunning down other children in schools or armed robberies
- increased violent weather such as severe winter storms or drought-filled summers

Unfortunately, many of these factors are out of the control of most individuals in society. However, steps can be taken to mitigate these circumstances:

- Become informed about the political parties at local and national levels—it is important that individuals know about political candidates' platforms so that they can make an informed choice when voting.
- Advocate against issues that are not in agreement with the beliefs of the people—in Canada and other parts of the world, there were massive peace demonstrations before the war in Iraq started. Through these demonstrations, Canadians sent a clear message to the federal government that they did not wish to go to war. Canada did not participate in the war.
- Protect yourself from the elements—this is an area where individuals have more control. It is possible to dress appropriately for cold or hot weather. It is possible to wear clothing as needed to protect against the sun or insects. Recommended products such as insect repellant are available to protect against insect bites.
- Protect yourself from unsafe food supplies—since most legislation in Canada about food and water supplies is in the hands of the federal government, it is important to become informed about issues and advocate for stronger controls. Individuals can also exercise greater care in their food choices. Read labels on food products and avoid items such as foods that contain trans fatty acids. It is possible to purchase organic foods, free-range meat, and bottled water.
- Remain positive—we can influence what our government does, protect ourselves against environmental conditions, advocate for increased legislation such as the Kyoto Protocol, and eat properly by taking more care in what we buy. We need to reassure others that there are things we can do and focus on the positive gains we are making.

In summary, environmental wellness is a growing concern at all levels of participation in Canada—families, educational institutions, governments, and the general public. *The Progress of Canada's Children* (Hanvey, 2003) identifies these environmental wellness issues clearly:

- need for physical activity
- safety of children in their communities
- climatic changes and children's health
- air quality and children
- effects of pesticides on children's health

Increased knowledge about issues that concern all of us also brings opportunities to do something about these environmental issues. It is up to all of us to become informed and to continue to advocate for stronger controls and improved conditions for all members of society.

Interconnectivity of Wellness

The six wellness areas discussed above—physical, emotional, intellectual, spiritual, interpersonal and social, and environmental—are interconnected (see Figure 10.1 on page 296). Changes made to one area of wellness will influence another area. Consider the following example. Throughout her school career, Jordaine has been an A student. She rarely participates in any sporting or social events. She considers herself to be a loner and not particularly interested in sports. At Christmas, her family invites her to go to a ski resort with them. Jourdaine takes some lessons and finds that she really enjoys cross-country skiing. When she returns home, she joins a cross-country ski group. When the season ends, some of the individuals in the group form a walking group. They encourage Jordaine to join, which she does.

Through these actions, Jordaine not only increases her physical fitness (physical wellness) but also becomes more social (interpersonal and social wellness). Her self-confidence in social groups increases (emotional wellness). She becomes more aware of the environment and eventually joins her group in advocating for the retention of dedicated parklands in Canada (environmental wellness).

Barriers to Healthy Living

Most individuals acknowledge that creating a healthy lifestyle is beneficial. Many Canadians have attempted to initiate a diet and exercise plan at least once in their lives. Many of these programs fail for a number of reasons:

- *Fads.* Fad diets are a big barrier to sustained weight loss. Most people want a "quick fix" and there are many programs available that offer just that. Unfortunately, programs that offer quick fixes usually fail. "Most of the fad diets fail on two counts:
  - Scientific inaccuracies and misinformation. As a result they are often nutritionally inadequate.

- ○ Failure to address long-term habit need changes. Persons are often 'set up' for failure to maintain a healthy individual weight once it is achieved. The basic behavioural problem involved in life-long food and exercise habit change, actually a new life-style, is unrecognized." (Rodwell Williams, 2004: 282)
- *Time.* Most successful programs involve long-term life changes in diet and exercise. Many individuals fail because it is difficult to find time in an already busy schedule of work, travel to work, and family life. It takes less effort to pop a frozen dinner in the oven or microwave or pick up fast food than to plan and prepare a more healthy meal.
- *Motivation.* Since any life change takes time and energy, it is hard to maintain the motivation to change one's lifestyle when the benefits are not obvious. For example, Tracey decides to join Curves, a women's fitness club. She also decides to change to a more healthy diet. After the first month of this regime, she has lost centimetres and 2 kilograms. Encouraged by her success, she continues for another month. This time there is no change in either centimetres or weight. Tracey becomes very discouraged and quits the program. She needs positive results to keep her focused.
- *Finances.* Joining exercise programs and maintaining a healthier diet cost money. Many individuals feel that they cannot afford a healthier lifestyle and therefore may not even try.
- *Idealism.* Our society is bombarded with advertisements about the perfect figure, the perfect weight, and the perfect looks. Many individuals decide to diet or exercise to attain this "perfect goal." The slim or muscular figures of movie stars and portrayed by toys such as Barbie and Ken have little to do with actual physical body types. It may be totally unrealistic to try to attain that "perfect look."
- *Past habits.* Lifestyle habits are developed as individuals grow up in families. Most habits are automatic because one has always acted this way. Therefore, young adults may continue to live the way they did when they were at home.
- *Lack of knowledge.* Individuals may feel that they have always lived a certain way and are fine and so is everyone else in their family. For example, the following rationalization may be offered: "My father smokes a pack of cigarettes a day, drinks his beer every night and is very overweight. It doesn't seem to have harmed him." These individuals feel that this justifies them living a similar lifestyle.

Strategies to Improve Overall Wellness

1. Make a Decision

The hardest part of trying to change one's behaviour is making the decision to change. This entails taking a critical look at oneself to identify:

- that a change is needed
- what changes need to be made
- what realistically can be changed

The most common problem is deciding to change everything at once, such as avoiding fast foods, exercising each day, having coffee only in the morning, packing a healthy lunch, and getting at least seven hours of sleep every night. These are too many changes to cope with at one time. It is much more effective to start with one change that can then lead to other changes over time.

2. Develop a Plan of Action

Any action plan should include realistic goals, types of activities to reach goals, timelines, rewards, and anticipation of problems. These components of an action plan can be remembered more easily as "SMART":

- **S**pecific—something that is tangible and easy to understand, such as arm curls
- **M**easurable—something that can be counted or timed, such as five arm curls
- **A**chievable—something that is within the ability of the individual to accomplish, such as using 2.25-kilogram weights to do the arm curls
- **R**ealistic—something that will keep you motivated to achieve, such as trying to lose 2.5 centimetres overall from the upper arms
- **T**ime frame—something that you will be able to accomplish in a given time frame, such as being able to do five arm curls by the end of the month

Sometimes it is helpful to consult a physician, dietitian, or fitness expert in setting goals. For example, Olanda decides that she needs to make some life changes. She feels that she is overweight, is not active enough, relies too heavily on fast foods, and does not sleep well at night. She consults her doctor and together they decide on some long-term goals to lose 9 kilograms, become more active, and as a result sleep better (Table 10.4).

3. Establish Motivation

Ongoing motivation is part of any action plan. In Olanda's case, this is built in through support groups and by establishing rewards when individual goals have been met.

- Visiting the dietitian each week gave Olanda opportunities to discuss her progress with the new diet and changes that might be needed to build in alternatives. Her dietitian gave Olanda advice about the kinds of foods she could eat when she dined out. Since this is a favourite activity of Olanda and her husband, it provides extra motivation to stay on the diet.
- Olanda's husband supports her plans for a new diet by participating in it. Both individuals can help each other maintain the diet and plan and prepare food.
- Olanda's colleagues at work are also helpful. They suggest effective recipes and do not try to tempt her with foods not on her diet.
- Building in a reward system at each successful step provides something to work toward. Olanda decides that at the end of the first month she and her husband will go out to a movie regardless of their weight loss. In fact, she loses 3 kilograms that first month and her husband brings home a bouquet of roses to celebrate her success.

TABLE 10.4   SAMPLE STRATEGIES TO CHANGE BEHAVIOUR

Goals	Strategies to Reach Goals	Timeline	Results
Goal 1 Establish a healthy diet.	Obtain a referral to a dietitian to help establish a healthy diet. Check in with dietitian every week to chart progress.	Four weeks	Lose 9 kilograms
Goal 2 Establish a support network.	Involve family members— Olanda's husband decides to participate in new diet. Inform colleagues at work to gain their support.	Ongoing	Celebrate success.
Goal 3 Establish a regular exercise program.	Walk every day—both Olanda and her husband like to walk. Olanda joins a staff member who walks regularly at lunch time.	One month after diet program	Start with 20-minute walk per day for first week; increase to 40 minutes within four weeks.

4. Implement the Plan

Olanda implements the plan gradually over time. Part of this process involves tracking her success. The types of observations recorded include:

- filling in a checklist with appropriate food choices daily
- initial and monthly measurements of thighs, hips, waist, chest, and upper arms
- initial and monthly weigh-ins
- tracking daily exercise and time

SUMMARY

A caregiver's overall health and wellness is of primary importance when working with children and their families. Caregivers who are well and healthy overall are more likely to be able to:

- demonstrate positive interaction patterns
- sustain positive activities with children and families

- remain energetic, enthusiastic, and vibrant
- maintain the pace of everyday living
- continue to work in the field of early childhood education

KEY POINTS

Quality characteristics of early childhood educators
- Patience
- Energy
- Coordination
- Strength
- Emotional stability
- Sensitivity
- Understanding
- Good physical health

Optimal wellness
- Physical wellness
  - Balanced diet of carbohydrates, fats, minerals, proteins, vitamins, and water
  - Lack of sleep leads to possible negative side effects—decreased creativity, motivation, patience, clear thinking, job performance, efficiency, and effectiveness; increased irritability
  - Strategies to improve sleep—avoid substances that interfere with sleep or ability to fall asleep, increase relaxation techniques that foster sleeping
  - Exercise—part of daily routines, total of one hour per day incorporating all three types of activities (endurance, strength, flexibility)
  - Endurance activities—four to seven days per week; choose from a variety of chores, sport activities, or walking activities
  - Flexibility activities—four to seven days per week, stretching exercises or chores and sports that incorporate stretching activities
  - Strength training—variety of activities to strengthen muscles of legs, arms, and mid-body through appropriate chores and exercises
  - Safe practices—model, ensure congruency between messages, optimal safety in the learning environment, protection from danger, optimal quality in learning environments
- Harmful habits—alcohol, drugs, and smoking may lead to addictive behaviours that can in turn lead to negative effects such as unpleasant physical reactions, impairment of overall functioning, increased irritability, aggressiveness, and hostility
- Regular checkups—medical and dental to monitor general health
- Emotional wellness—optimism, trust, self-esteem, self-acceptance, self-confidence
- Strategies to improve emotional wellness—reflection, humour, self-observation, expressing feelings, increasing expertise, communication, self-recognition
- Intellectual wellness—open-mindedness, critical thinking, problem solving, creativity, lifelong learning
- Strategies to improve intellectual wellness—outside interests, research, attending in-service activities, getting involved in community functions, brainstorming, talking to other experts
- Spiritual wellness—personal beliefs, principles, values
- Strategies to improve spiritual wellness—increase knowledge, research, gain familiarity with and discuss varying viewpoints, establish support networks, participate in community events, practise appropriate communication skills
- Environmental wellness—safety of food supply, pollution, radiation, disease, violence, weather conditions
- Strategies to improve environmental wellness—become informed on issues, become involved in advocacy, protect self from environmental conditions, remain optimistic

Interconnectivity of wellness
- Changes in one area influence other areas

Barriers to healthy living
- Fads
- Time
- Motivation
- Finances
- Idealism
- Past habits
- Lack of knowledge

Strategies to improve overall wellness
- Decision making
- Planning
- Implementing

EXERCISES

1. Identify the various roles you hold—career, family member, community member. How might each of these roles conflict with your desire to lead a healthier life?

2. Using the chart below, identify aspects of your lifestyle you would need to change to become physically healthier overall.

CHART 1

Aspects of Physical Wellness	Description of Changes
Diet	
Sleep	
Exercise	

3. Identify the aspects of emotional wellness. On a scale of 1 to 3 (1 being low, 2 medium, and 3 high) describe how you rate on all of these aspects. Discuss what strategies you might use to improve your areas of emotional wellness.

4. Discuss and identify the characteristics of a lifelong learner. How many of these characteristics do you possess? What strategies might you use when confronted with a new and challenging situation you know relatively little about? (For example, a child with special needs that you know nothing about enters the program. You are instructed to develop a program you have limited knowledge about for your preschool group.)

5. Identify your stand on guiding the behaviours of preschool children. Indicate how you arrived at these viewpoints. How were your values, beliefs, and principles influenced by your family, education, and community members?

6. Look over the list of environmental influences. Which ones affect you most? Why? What strategies could you use to mitigate your concerns?

7. You have a child in your program who is physically unfit. The child is overweight and does not participate in gross motor activities; when you speak to the parents, you are faced with strong resistance to help change this pattern. What strategies might you use to help facilitate a healthier program for this child?

✱ Glossary

Active listening (page 310) Listening without bias or personal agenda to a message.

Addictive behaviours (page 302) Habits that are out of control, with a resulting impact on a person's health (Fahey, Insel, & Roth, 1999: 312).

Caffeine (page 298) A stimulant found in substances such as coffee, tea, or colas that can cause an alerting effect.

Calorie (page 297) "The energy required to do the work of the body is measured as the amount of heat produced by the body's work. The energy value of the food is expressed as the number of kilocalories a specified portion of the food will yield when oxidized by the body." (Rodwell Williams, 2004: 63)

Cardiovascular endurance (page 299) "The ability of the body to perform prolonged, large-muscle, dynamic exercise at moderate-to-high levels of intensity." (Fahey, Insel, & Roth, 1999: 23)

Endurance activities (page 299) Activities that strengthen the heart, lungs, and circulatory system (also known as cardiovascular endurance).

Essential nutrients (page 295) Substances that must be obtained from food because the body does not manufacture them in sufficient quantities.

Flexibility activities (page 299) Activities that increase range of movements, exercises that serve to relax muscles and loosen the joints, and exercises that include gentle stretching such as reaching, bending, or turning.

Reflection (page 306) A process by which an individual examines a personal behaviour and analyzes it.

Strength activities (page 300) Activities that help your muscles and bones stay strong, improve your posture, and help prevent diseases such as osteoporosis.

REFERENCES

Copple, C. E. (2003). *A world of difference: Readings on teaching young children in a diverse society.* Washington, DC: National Association for the Education of Young Children.

Covell, K. H. B. (2001). *The challenge of children's rights for Canada.* Waterloo, ON: Wilfrid Laurier University Press.

Doherty, G. (2003). *Occupational standards for child care practitioners.* Ottawa: Canadian Childcare Federation.

Fahey, T., Insel, P., & Roth, W. (1999). *Fit and well: Core concepts and labs in physical fitness and wellness.* Mountain View, CA: Mayfield Publishing Company.

George, M. (1998). *Learn to relax.* San Francisco: Chronicle Books.

Goelman, H., Doherty, G., Lero, D., LaGrange, A., & Tougas, J. (2000). *You bet I care! Caring and learning environments: Quality in child care centres across Canada.* Guelph, ON: Centre for Families, Work and Well-Being, University of Guelph.

Graham, G., Holt/Hale, S., & Parker, M. (1998). *Children moving: A reflective approach to teaching physical education.* Mountain View, CA: Mayfield Publishing Company.

Hanvey, L. (2003). *The progress of Canada's children.* Ottawa: Canadian Council on Social Development.

Health Canada. (2003). *Review of Canada's food guide to healthy eating and related dietary guidance.* http://www.hc-sc.gc.ca/hpfb-dgpsa/onpp-bppn/food_guide_e.html, accessed 28 February 2004.

Klein, M., & Chen, D. (2001). *Working with children from culturally diverse backgrounds.* Albany, NY: Delmar.

Meridian Health. (2003). Many women lack sleep. http://www.meridianhealth.com/index.cfm/MediaRelations/News/BreakingNews/oct1603.cfm, accessed 28 February 2004.

Office of Nutrition Policy and Promotion. (2002). *Canada's food guide to healthy eating: Focus on preschoolers—Background for educators and communicators.* Health Canada. http://www.hc-sc.gc.ca/hpfb-dgpsa/onpp-bppn/food_guide_preschoolers_e.html, accessed 5 February 2004.

Physical Activity Unit. (2004). *Physical activity: What is it?* Health Canada. http://www.hc-sc.gc.ca/hppb/paguide/intro.html, accessed 29 February 2004.

Rodwell Williams, S. (2004). *Basic nutrition and diet therapy.* St. Louis, MO: Mosby-Year Book, Inc.

Therrien, M. E., & Laugrand, F. E. (2001). *Interviewing Inuit elders: Perspectives on traditional health.* Iqaluit, NU: Nunavut Arctic College.

Wardle, F. (2003). *Introduction to early childhood education.* Toronto: Pearson Education, Inc.

Watson, L., Watson, M., Cam Wilson, L., & Crowther, I. (2000). *Infants and toddlers.* First Canadian edition. Scarborough, ON: Nelson Thomson Learning.

Glossary

active listening listening to the content of a message without personal bias and clarifying the intent of the message when the meaning is unclear or to ensure that the meaning is clear. (pp. 271, 310)

addictive behaviours habits that are out of control, with a resulting impact on a person's health (Fahey, Insel, & Roth, 1999: 312). (p. 302)

allergens allergy-producing substances that cause a reaction when they come in contact with a foreign body. (p. 76)

anaphylactic shock an allergic response of the body that involves more than one organ and may be life threatening. (p. 76)

antibodies substances produced by the body in response to a bacterial or viral attack to destroy the disease-carrying viruses or bacteria. (p. 81)

attention deficit disorder a disorder in which children seem to be in continual motion, have a very short attention span, and are easily distracted. (p. 248)

beat the steady pulse that underlines a musical creation. (p. 197)

bibliotherapy using stories that deal with circumstances similar to those the child is experiencing. (p. 257)

caffeine a stimulant found in substances such as coffee, tea, or colas that can cause an alerting effect. (p. 298)

calorie "the energy required to do the work of the body is measured as the amount of heat produced by the body's work. The energy value of the food is expressed as the number of kilocalories a specified portion of the food will yield when oxidized by the body." (Rodwell Williams, 2004: 63) (p. 297)

cardiovascular endurance "the ability of the body to perform prolonged, large-muscle, dynamic exercise at moderate-to-high levels of intensity." (Fahey, Insel, & Roth, 1999: 23) (p. 299)

cephalocaudal development of bones and muscles proceeds from head to toes; infants learn to control their neck muscles first, then their trunk to roll over, and finally their leg muscles to learn to sit and walk. (p. 167)

child abuse "violence, mistreatment or neglect that a child or adolescent may experience while in the care of someone they either trust or depend upon, such as a parent, sibling, other relative, caregiver or guardian." (Department of Justice Canada, 2003: 1) (p. 242)

cooperative play play involving planning together and working toward a common goal collaboratively. (p. 282)

critical period "it refers to a limited time span during which the child is biologically prepared to acquire certain adaptive behaviours but needs the support of an appropriate stimulating environment." (Berk, 2002: 24) (p. 12)

cruising infant pulls herself or himself to standing and moves around furniture while holding onto surface. (p. 32)

developmentally appropriate activities, materials, experiences, interactions, and learning environments based on the abilities and developmental level of the child. (p. 100)

developmental teachable moment an opportunity to expand learning taking place at a particular time that is based on knowledge of child development and observations of children using an activity a child is engaged in. (p. 205)

dexterity ability to use fingers nimbly and efficiently. (p. 38)

egocentric thinking children's belief that everyone else feels, believes, and thinks as they do and lack of awareness of other individuals' perspectives. (p. 257)

egocentric stage of development child sees world from his or her perspective and cannot understand someone else's viewpoint. (p. 41)

emergent skills skills that are starting to develop but need practice in a variety of settings before a child becomes more proficient at them. (p. 39)

emotional abuse involves harming children's sense of self. (p. 246)

endurance the ability to sustain motor activity over time. (p. 206)

endurance activities activities that strengthen the heart, lungs, and circulatory system (also known as cardiovascular endurance). (p. 299)

environment includes the factors that influence growth and development—physical, social, economic, cultural. (p. 5)

epipen emergency medication provided via a needle for a severe allergic reaction. (p. 277)

Erikson's psychosocial stages of development

- Stage 1: Trust versus Mistrust—Infants gain a sense of whether the world is a safe place through positive interactions with caregivers, the environment, and materials.

- Stage 2: Autonomy versus Shame—As toddlers develop increased motor skills and mental capacities, they strive to gain autonomy.

- Stage 3: Initiative versus Guilt—As preschool children develop competence in motor, social, language, and cognitive skills, they start to initiate learning through experimentation, observation, imitation, and participation with peers and adults.

- Stage 4: Industry versus Inferiority—School-age children work more independently and cooperatively. They begin to value and take pleasure in productive work. (p. 102)

essential nutrients substances that must be obtained from food because the body does not manufacture them in sufficient quantities. (p. 295)

eye–hand coordination the ability to reach for an item and grasp it successfully; over time, ability is refined so child can learn to perform intricate tasks such as cutting on a line, printing, and sewing. (pp. 173, 199)

family day homes care of children provided in a home by an individual with or without children of his or her own. (p. 121)

flexibility activities activities that increase range of movements, exercises that serve to relax muscles and loosen the joints, and exercises that include gentle stretching such as reaching, bending, or turning. (p. 299)

full spectrum fluorescent lighting light fixtures that include the full spectrum of wavelengths of natural light. Full spectrum fluorescent lighting most closely matches sunlight. (p. 23)

health well-being of an individual; combination of wellness in all domains—social, emotional, physical, cognitive. (p. 4)

heredity characteristics transmitted from parents to a child at conception. (p. 5)

immunization a process that helps build defences against disease caused by viruses and bacteria. Individuals receive an injection that builds antibodies within the body to fight disease. (p. 81)

imitative play play that involves watching others and copying actions immediately or at a later time. (p. 106)

inclusive care care that ensures that all children, regardless of abilities or disabilities, attend the child-care settings in their community and that each child receives the supports he or she may need. (p. 258)

locomotor tasks tasks that involve moving from place to place, such as running, walking, skipping, or climbing. (p. 165)

manipulate explore objects by touching them, moving them, looking at them, and for young children, putting them in the mouth. (p. 33)

myelinization the development of a myelin sheath around axons; allows neurons to transmit electrical impulses more quickly. (p. 194)

neglect involves repeated failure to provide for a child's physical, emotional, or psychological well-being. (p. 243)

networking occurs between individuals who have common interests in order to share ideas, expertise, resources, and information and to find ways to improve quality experiences for a group of individuals. (p. 266)

non-locomotor tasks anchored movements such as balancing, twisting, rocking, or swinging arms. (p. 164)

non-mobile infants infants not yet able to move from location to location by crawling or walking. (p. 196)

object permanence the understanding that an object still exists even if it not in sight. (p. 199)

palmar grasp using the whole hand as a unit to pick up items. (p. 104)

parallel play children play beside each other, using similar materials, but engage in individual play. (p. 247)

pathogen a virus, bacteria, or parasite (fleas, lice, ticks) that causes a particular disease such as measles or meningitis. (p. 62)

phoneme a unit of sound that distinguishes one word from another—i.e., both *cat* and *phone* have three phonemes. (p. 12)

physical abuse involves using deliberate force to cause injury or risk of injury to a child. (p. 243)

preventive actions put in place to stop the possibility of accidents and illnesses occurring. (p. 16)

reflection a process by which an individual examines a personal behaviour and analyzes it. (p. 306)

reflex actions involuntary actions. (p. 196)

Reye's syndrome flu-like symptoms or upper respiratory problems. In severe cases, it can lead to death. (p. 73)

rhythm time-based concepts in music such as beat, length of sound, and tempo. (p. 197)

sensory motor stage birth to two years of age; as infants mature they increasingly are able to use their sensory and motor abilities to organize their behaviours and activities. (p. 196)

sexual abuse "involves using a child for sexual purposes." (Department of Justice Canada, 2003: 1) (p. 243)

spatial orientation where an individual or object is in relation to the rest of the space, such as in the middle, at the side, or on top. (p. 206)

strength activities activities that help your muscles and bones stay strong, improve your posture, and help prevent diseases such as osteoporosis. (p. 300)

susceptible host an individual (human or animal) who becomes infected by a pathogen and exhibits symptoms of a particular illness such as measles or meningitis. (p. 62)

swarming behaviour typical toddler behaviour; when toddlers see or hear something of interest they promptly run to participate in the activity. (p. 207)

symbolic play play involving actions or materials that are representative of another action or material, such as using a hand as a digger or shrugging one's shoulder to indicate a lack of understanding. (pp. 106, 247)

universal precautions procedures to protect individuals from accidental exposure to harmful infectious organisms. (p. 64)

vaccine tiny amounts of disease-causing viruses and bacteria injected to build antibodies within the body to fight off the disease. (p. 81)

Index

"AS IS" LICENSE AGREEMENT AND LIMITED WARRANTY